NYSTCE English Language Arts

003

Teacher Certification Exam

Sharon A. Wynne, M.S.

XAMonline, INC.

Boston

To obtain permission(s) to use the material from this work for any purpose including workshops or seminars, please submit a written request to:

XAMonline, Inc.
21 Orient Avenue
Melrose, MA 02176
Toll Free 1-800-509-4128
Email: info@xamonline.com
Web www.xamonline.com
Fax: 1-617-583-5552

Library of Congress Cataloging-in-Publication Data
Wynne, Sharon A.

NYSTCE English Language Arts 003: Teacher Certification / Sharon A. Wynne.
ISBN 978-1-60787-479-9

1. English Language Arts   2. Study Guides   3. NYSTCE
4. Teachers' Certification & Licensure.   5. Careers

Disclaimer:

The opinions expressed in this publication are the sole works of XAMonline and were created independently from the National Education Association, Educational Testing Service, or any State Department of Education, National Evaluation Systems or other testing affiliates. Between the time of publication and printing, state specific standards as well as testing formats and website information may change that is not included in part or in whole within this product. Sample test questions are developed by XAMonline and reflect similar content as on real tests; however, they are not former tests. XAMonline assembles content that aligns with state standards but makes no claims nor guarantees teacher candidates a passing score. Numerical scores are determined by testing companies such as NES or ETS and then are compared with individual state standards. A passing score varies from state to state.

Printed in the United States of America   œ-1
NYSTCE English Language Arts 003
ISBN: 978-1-60787-479-9

Table of Contents

COMPETENCY 1   **READING LITERATURE**

Skill 1.1   Analyzes and understands the explicit meaning of literary texts 1

Skill 1.2   Is able to make logical inferences about the meaning of literary texts 5

Skill 1.3   Is able to cite evidence from a text to support an argument about the meaning of a literary text 7

Skill 1.4   Recognizes the theme(s) of a literary text 8

Skill 1.5   Analyzes the connection between different elements of a literary text 9

Skill 1.6   Analyzes and interprets the meaning of language in a text (figurative, symbolic, context-specific, etc. 11

Skill 1.7   Recognizes the impact that language and word choice can have on a text 16

Skill 1.8   Analyzes the way in which authors' choices affect meaning and structure 17

Skill 1.9   Recognizes how techniques such as satire, irony, sarcasm, etc. can shape and contribute to an author's message 19

Skill 1.10   Is familiar with important works of American literature from the 18th, 19th, and 20th centuries; recognizes how different texts from the same period may deal with a similar topic 20

Skill 1.11   Is knowledgeable about different literary genres and a wide variety of work from various time periods, cultures, and countries (including the United States 31

Skill 1.12   Recognizes and interprets different points of view from literary works from countries other than the United States 45

Skill 1.13   Understands and recognizes how an author may draw on or be inspired by other works by other authors 47

Skill 1.14   Sees the connection between modern literary work and works from other eras, religions, and cultures 50

COMPETENCY 2   READING INFORMATIONAL TEXTS

Skill 2.1   Analyzes the meaning of informational texts using evidence and examples 52

Skill 2.2   Makes inferences based on evidence from the text 53

Skill 2.3   Recognizes the central idea of informational texts 54

Skill 2.4   Analyzes how an author develops an idea or event in an informational text 56

Skill 2.5   Is able to summarize an informational text 57

Skill 2.6   Discerns the meaning of key words and phrases in informational texts including figurative, connotative and technical meanings 58

Skill 2.7   Examines how a writer uses key terms 58

Skill 2.8   Analyzes the effectiveness of the structure an author uses to explain or support an argument 59

Skill 2.9   Can determine the author's point of view and purpose 59

Skill 2.10   Recognizes how author's craft can contribute to the persuasiveness of an informational text 61

Skill 2.11   Analyzes different sources of information in different formats (visual, quantitative, etc.) to solve a problem or answer a question 61

Skill 2.12   Assesses whether information is sufficient and relevant in determining whether an argument is valid 63

Skill 2.13   Analyzes important U.S. historical and literary documents to determine theme, purpose and text features 65

Skill 2.14   Analyzes texts related to diverse cultures and viewpoints 65

COMPETENCY 3   WRITING ARGUMENTS

Skill 3.1   Is able to introduce a claim, demonstrate its significance, and make it stand out from alternate claims 66

Skill 3.2   Can sequence claims, reasons and evidence 67

Skill 3.3   Develops claims and counterclaims thoroughly; provides evidence and points out the strengths and weaknesses of both 68

Skill 3.4   Anticipates the concerns, knowledge level, and perspective of an audience 69

Skill 3.5   Creates a clear relationship between claims/counterclaims, reasons, and evidence 70

Skill 3.6   Develops a conclusion that clearly relates to an argument..................... 70

Skill 3.7   Develops an argument through planning, writing, revision, and rewriting 71

COMPETENCY 4   WRITING INFORMATIVE AND EXPLANATORY TEXTS

Skill 4.1   Writes a clear introduction that establishes what is to follow 73

Skill 4.2   Organizes ideas, concepts, and information so that different elements build on each other 74

Skill 4.3   Develops a topic by selecting relevant facts, details, definitions, quotations and other examples 76

Skill 4.4   Uses varied transitions and syntax to clearly link ideas in different sections of a text.. 77

Skill 4.5   Uses precise, domain-specific language to help explain or inform about a topic.. 78

Skill 4.6   Writes conclusions that support the information presented...................... 79

Skill 4.7   Improves writing by planning, revising, editing, and rewriting 80

Skill 4.8   Selects evidence from literature or literary nonfiction to support analysis and interpretation 80

Skill 4.9   Employs techniques from different literary genres (e.g., allegory, irony, ambiguity) to enhance meaning 81

Skill 4.10   Maintains a formal style that is appropriate to task, purpose, and audience 81

Skill 4.11   Uses technology to produce and publish and to collaborate with other writers 82

COMPETENCY 5   WRITING NARRATIVES

Skill 5.1   Engages and orients the reader by elaborating a problem, conflict, or observation; establishes a point of view and introduces a narrator and characters 84

Skill 5.2   Uses techniques such as dialogue, description, reflection, and multiple plot lines to develop a story and its characters 85

Skill 5.3   Sequences events in such a way as to build toward an outcome; establishes tone and creates a coherent narrative 86

Skill 5.4   Uses precise vocabulary, interesting details, and description to convey experiences, setting, characters, and events... 87

Skill 5.5   Provides a conclusion that is clearly connected to the experiences, observations, and events of the narrative 87

Skill 5.6   Uses literary techniques such as allegory, stream of consciousness, irony, and ambiguity to affect meaning 87

Skill 5.7   Adapts voice and language for different contexts and audiences 88

Skill 5.8   Improves narrative writing by planning, revising, editing, and rewriting ... 88

COMPETENCY 6   RESEARCHING TO BUILD AND PRESENT KNOWLEDGE

Skill 6.1   Generates a research question and knows how to narrow down or broaden inquiry 90

Skill 6.2   Gathers relevant information from multiple sources (e.g., textual, digital, audio, visual, etc.)... 91

Skill 6.3   Assesses the validity or suitability of a source in terms of task, purpose, and audience 92

Skill 6.4   Integrates information into a text and maintains the flow of ideas........... 93

Skill 6.5   Avoids plagiarism and cites sources using standard methodology and formatting.. 95

COMPETENCY 7   SPEAKING AND LISTENING

Skill 7.1   Communicates effectively with audiences from diverse backgrounds and perspective 97

Skill 7.2   Collaborates in groups in discussions, decision-making, and project tasks. 98

Skill 7.3   Moves conversations forward by asking and responding to questions .. 101

Skill 7.4   Works to ensure that a range of perspectives are heard in group discussions 101

Skill 7.5   Clarifies, verifies, and challenges ideas and conclusions 102

Skill 7.6   Responds thoughtfully to diverse points of view; synthesizes claims and evidence on both sides of an issue; seeks to resolve contradictions; recognizes what additional information may be needed for research or to complete a task... 102

Skill 7.7   Integrates multiple sources to make informed decisions and find solutions. 104

Skill 7.8   Evaluates a speaker's point of view and assesses the speaker's stance, tone, and word choice... 104

Skill 7.9   Presents information to convey an organized, clear perspective; content, style, and language are appropriate to the audience and task.............. 105

Skill 7.10   Uses digital media successfully in presentations to enhance understanding and interest 107

COMPETENCY 8   LANGUAGE

Skill 8.1   Understands that conventions of English usage change over time and are sometimes contested 109

Skill 8.2   Has command of Standard English conventions in spelling, capitalization, and punctuation 111

Skill 8.3   Uses context clues to determine the meaning of unknown words and words with multiple meanings... 116

Skill 8.4   Uses patterns of word changes indicating different meanings and parts of speech to determine the meaning of unknown words 117

Skill 8.5   Understands figurative language, word relationships, and subtle difference in word meanings by interpreting context and analyzing denotative meanings 118

Skill 8.6   Understand the usage of verbs in the passive and active voices, imperative, interrogative, conditional, and subjunctive mood; uses verbs in different moods to create different effects 119

Skill 8.7   Is familiar with and uses domain-specific vocabulary at the college and career readiness level 124

Skill 8.8   Demonstrates ability to gather vocabulary knowledge 126

COMPETENCY 9   PEDAGOGICAL CONTENT KNOWLEDGE

Skill 9.1   Is able to assess whether a student is ready for a new learning goal related to analyzing informational or narrative texts 127

Skill 9.2   Designs effective instructional experiences that connect students' prior knowledge to new learning 127

Skill 9.3   Employs knowledge of instructional strategies to help students develop effective questions to further their learning about a topic in an informational or a literary text 128

Skill 9.4   Designs instructional approaches that help students to analyze interpretations of literary texts; helps students understand how each version interprets the text differently 130

Skill 9.5   Assists students in creating interpretive and responsive texts that demonstrate knowledge and understanding of connections between life and literary work 131

Skill 9.6   Employs effective assessment methods that measure and promote student learning 132

REFERENCES 137

SAMPLE TEST 138

CONSTRUCTED RESPONSE 167

ANSWER KEY 168

RATIONALES 169

About the Test

The New York State Teacher Certification Exam (NYSTCE) for English Language Arts (Field 003) is a computer-based test designed to ensure that English Language Arts educators have the content-area skills and knowledge of pedagogy necessary to teach effectively in New York State schools. The test covers topics including:

- The reading of literature and informational texts
- Writing of informational, persuasive, and narrative texts
- Research
- Speaking and listening
- Language
- Pedagogical approaches for the effective teaching of English Language Arts

The test includes selected-response items that measure content-area knowledge and one constructed-response that assesses pedagogical knowledge. In the constructed-response, candidates describe an instructional intervention strategy to address a learning difficulty or an instructional approach to help students achieve a learning goal. The response must include a rationale describing the relevance and appropriateness of the teaching strategy.

Selected-response questions make up 80% of the total test score, and the constructed-response accounts for the remaining 20%. Each question from the selected-response section has the same value in determining the final score.

The total test time is 3 hours and 15 minutes. While taking the test, candidates determine their own pace, but the following is the estimated breakdown of how time is allotted during the test:

- **Constructed-response** – approximately 60 minutes
- **Selected-response** - approximately 135 minutes

The table below shows the estimated breakdown of test questions:

Competency	Approximate number of questions	Approximate percentage of total score
Reading literature	15	13%
Reading informational texts	15	13%
Writing arguments	10	9%
Writing informative and explanatory texts	10	9%

Writing narratives	10	9%
Researching to build and present knowledge	10	9%
Speaking and listening	10	9%
Language	10	9%
Pedagogical content knowledge (constructed response)	1	20%

A passing score for the test is 520 or higher.

For test locations in New York or other states, please consult the NYSTCE website. The test can be taken throughout the year by appointment on Monday to Saturday.

Great Study and Testing Tips!

What to study in order to prepare for the subject assessments is the focus of this study guide but equally important is *how* you study.

You can increase your chances of truly mastering the information by taking some simple, but effective steps.

Study Tips:

1. **Some foods aid the learning process.** Foods such as milk, nuts, seeds, rice, and oats help your study efforts by releasing natural memory enhancers called CCKs (*cholecystokinin*) composed of *tryptopha*n, *choline*, and *phenylalanine*. All of these chemicals enhance the neurotransmitters associated with memory. Before studying, try a light, protein-rich meal of eggs, turkey, and fish. All of these foods release the memory enhancing chemicals. The better the connections, the more you comprehend.

Likewise, before you take a test, stick to a light snack of energy boosting and relaxing foods. A glass of milk, a piece of fruit, or some peanuts all release various memory-boosting chemicals and help you to relax and focus on the subject at hand.

2. **Learn to take great notes.** A by-product of our modern culture is that we have grown accustomed to getting our information in short doses (i.e., TV news sound bites or *USA Today*-style newspaper articles.)

Consequently, we've subconsciously trained ourselves to assimilate information better in *neat little packages*. If your notes are scrawled all over the paper, it fragments the flow of the information. Strive for clarity. Newspapers use a standard format to achieve clarity. Your notes can be much clearer through use of proper formatting. A very effective format is called the *"Cornell Method."*

Take a sheet of loose-leaf lined notebook paper and draw a line all the way down the paper about 1–2" from the left-hand edge.

Draw another line across the width of the paper about 1–2" up from the bottom. Repeat this process on the reverse side of the page.

Now look at the result. You have ample room for notes, a left margin for special emphasis items or inserting supplementary data from the textbook, a large area at the bottom for a brief summary, and a little rectangular space for just about anything you want. This should make your note-taking much more effective.

3. **Get the concept then the details.** Too often we focus on the details and don't gather an understanding of the concept. However, if you simply memorize only dates, places, or names, you may well miss the whole point of the subject.

A key way to understand things is to put them in your own words. If you are working from a textbook, automatically summarize each paragraph in your mind. If you are outlining text, don't simply copy the author's words.

Rephrase them in your own words. You'll remember your own thoughts and words much better than someone else's, and subconsciously tend to associate the important details to the core concepts.

4. **Ask Why?** Pull apart written material paragraph by paragraph and don't forget the captions under the illustrations.

Example: If the heading is "Stream Erosion," flip it around to read "Why do streams erode?" Then answer the questions.

If you train your mind to think in a series of questions and answers, not only will you learn more, but it also helps to lessen the test anxiety because you are used to answering questions.

5. **Read for reinforcement and future needs.** Even if you only have 10 minutes, put your notes or a book in your hand. Your mind is similar to a computer; you have to input data in order to have it processed. *By reading, you are creating the neural connections for future retrieval.* The more times you read something, the more you reinforce the learning of ideas.

Even if you don't fully understand something on the first pass, *your mind stores much of the material for later recall.*

6. <u>Relax to learn so go into exile</u>. Our bodies respond to an inner clock called biorhythms. Burning the midnight oil works well for some people, but not everyone.

If possible, set aside a particular place to study that is free of distractions. Shut off the television, cell phone, and pager, and exile your friends and family during your study period.

If silence bothers you, try background music. Light classical music at a low volume has been shown to aid in concentration over other types of music. Music that evokes pleasant emotions without lyrics is highly suggested. Try just about anything by Mozart. It relaxes you.

7. <u>Use arrows not highlighters</u>. At best, it's difficult to read a page full of yellow, pink, blue, and green streaks. Try staring at a neon sign for a while and you'll soon see that the horde of colors obscure the message.

A quick note, a brief dash of color, an underline, and/or an arrow pointing to a particular passage is much clearer than a horde of highlighted words.

8. <u>Budget your study time</u>. Although you shouldn't ignore any of the material, *allocate your available study time in the same ratio that topics may appear on the test.*

Testing Tips:

1. <u>Get smart, play dumb</u>. Don't read anything into the question. Don't make an assumption that the test writer is looking for something else than what is asked. Stick to the question as written and don't read extra things into it.

2. <u>Read the question and all the choices *twice* before answering the question</u>. You may miss something by not carefully reading, and then re-reading both the question and the answers.

If you really don't have a clue as to the right answer, leave it blank on the first time through. Go on to the other questions, as they may provide a clue as to how to answer the skipped questions. If later on, you still can't answer the skipped ones . . . **Guess.** The only penalty for guessing is that you *might* get it wrong. Only one thing is certain; if you don't put anything down, you will get it wrong!

3. <u>Turn the question into a statement</u>. Look at the way the questions are worded. The syntax of the question usually provides a clue. Does it seem more familiar as a statement rather than as a question? Does it sound strange?

By turning a question into a statement, you may be able to spot if an answer sounds right, and it may also trigger memories of material you have read.

4. <u>Look for hidden clues</u>. It's actually very difficult to compose multiple-foil (choice) questions without giving away part of the answer in the options presented. In most multiple-choice questions, you can often readily eliminate one or two of the potential answers. This leaves you with only two real possibilities and automatically your odds go to fifty-fifty for very little work.

5. <u>Trust your instincts</u>. For every fact that you have read, you subconsciously retain something of that knowledge. On questions that you aren't really certain about, go with your instincts. **Your first impression on how to answer a question is usually correct.**

6. <u>Mark your answers directly on the test booklet</u>. Don't bother trying to fill in the optical scan sheet on the first pass through the test.

Just be very careful not to miss-mark your answers when you eventually transcribe them to the scan sheet.

7. <u>Watch the clock</u>! You have a set amount of time to answer the questions. Don't get bogged down trying to answer a single question at the expense of 10 questions you can more readily answer.

Current Teaching Trends

Digital pedagogy and the use of 21st century teaching methods have shifted the landscape of teaching to create a bigger focus on student engagement. Student-centered classrooms now utilize technology to create efficiencies and increase digital literacy. Classrooms that once relied on memorization and the regurgitation of facts now push students to *create* and *analyze* material. The Bloom's Taxonomy chart below gives a great visual of the higher order thinking skills that current teachers are implementing in their learning objectives. There are also examples of the verbs that you might use when creating learning objectives at the assignment, course, or program level.

21st Century Bloom's Taxonomy

Lower- order			Higher- order		
Remember	Understand	Apply	Analyze	Evaluate	Create
• Define • Describe • Recall	• Classify • Explain • Summarize	• Determine • Organize • Use	• Deduct • Estimate • Outline	• Argue • Justify • Support	• Construct • Adapt • Modify

Most importantly, you'll notice that each of these verbs will allow teachers to align a specific assessment to assess the mastery of the skill that's being taught. Instead of saying "Students will learn about parts of speech," teachers will insert a measurable verb into the learning objective. The 21st century model uses S.M.A.R.T. (Specific, Measurable, Attainable, Realistic, Time-bound) assessment methods to ensure teachers can track progress and zero in on areas that students need to revisit before they have fully grasped the concept.

When reading the first objective below, you might ask yourself the following questions:

Students will:
1. Learn about parts of speech

How will they learn? How will you assess their learning? What does "learn" mean to different teachers? What does "learn" look like to different learning styles?

In this second example, the 21st century model shows specific ways students will use parts of speech.

Students will be able to:
1. Define parts of speech (lower)
2. Classify parts of speech (lower)
3. Construct a visual representation of each part of speech (higher)

Technology in the 21ˢᵗ Century Classroom

Student-centered classrooms now also rely heavily on technology for content delivery (PowerPoint, LMS) assessment (online quizzes) and collaborative learning (GoogleDrive). Particular to ESL classrooms, teachers can now record themselves speaking using lecture capture software. Students can then watch the video multiple times to ensure they've understood concepts. They have the ability to pause/rewind/replay any sections they are confused about, and they can focus on taking better notes while having the ability to watch the video a second or third time.

Online assessments also give students and teachers a better idea for comprehension level. These quick, often self-grading assessments give teachers more time to spend with students instead of grading. They eliminate human error and give teachers data needed to zero in on concepts that need to be revisited. For example, if 12 of 15 students got number 5 wrong, the teacher will know to discuss this concept in class. Online assessments may include listening, speaking, reading, and/or writing practice. This reinforces the content that was taught in the classroom and gives opportunity for practice at students' leisure. In addition, adaptable learning will help teachers by tracking user data to demonstrate learning gains. This can be completed in pre-posttest form, with conditionals within an assessment, or through small, formative assessments.

SMART Technologies, Inc. is a very popular company that creates software and hardware for educational environments. You may have heard of a "SmartBoard" before. These are promethean boards (interactive whiteboards) and are most commonly gained using grant money. They can be used as a projector for PowerPoints, their speakers can be used for audio practice, and their video options can allow you to "bring" a guest speaker into your classroom using videoconferencing, such as Skype. They record notes made on the whiteboard and record audio from lectures, which can then be saved and sent to students that were absent, or used to review for tests on varying concepts.

Google has created ample opportunity for secondary teachers in creating efficiencies for document sharing, assessment tools, and collaborative learning environments. Their drive feature can allow for easy transfer of assignment instructions, essays, and group projects. Slides can be used to create and post PowerPoints for students to have ongoing access. Forms is a great way to create quizzes, and the data can be sorted and manipulated in a number of ways. They can also be used for self-assessment, peer evaluation, and for pre-post analyses.

As technology continues to evolve, it's critical for teachers to continue to implement tools that make their classrooms more effective and efficient while also preparing students to successfully function in a technology-driven society. Through simple lessons and technology demonstrations, students will have a great start at applying technology skills in the outside world. The classroom is a great starting place for ESL students to learn how to use technology and how to practice their own reading, writing, listening, and speaking.

COMPETENCY 1   READING LITERATURE

Skill 1.1   Analyzes and understands the explicit meaning of literary texts

The earliest skills of literary analysis begin when we first learn to read. We are first asked to remember details of plot and characters. As our skills develop and the literary texts we encounter become more complex, we must draw more extensively on our background knowledge to interpret meaning, examine evidence, look for connections between ideas, and to separate opinions from fact.

Successfully determining the meaning of literary texts involves different strategies that can be used separately or combined.

Context
Context includes the author's feelings, beliefs, past experiences, goals, needs, and physical environment. The reader incorporates an understanding of how these elements may have affected the writing to enrich an interpretation of it. Knowledge of the time period and key events from that period can illuminate our understanding of what we read.

Symbols
Also referred to as a sign, a symbol designates something that stands for something else. In most cases, it is standing for something that has a deeper meaning than its literal denotation. Symbols can have personal, cultural, or universal associations. Use an understanding of symbols to unearth a meaning the author might have intended but not expressed, or even something the author never intended at all.

Essential terminology and literary devices germane to literary analysis include alliteration, allusion, antithesis, aphorism, apostrophe, assonance, blank verse, caesura, conceit, connotation, consonance, couplet, denotation, diction, epiphany, exposition, figurative language, free verse, hyperbole, iambic pentameter, inversion, irony, kenning, metaphor, metaphysical poetry, metonymy, motif, onomatopoeia, octava rima, oxymoron, paradox, parallelism personification, quatrain, scansion, simile, soliloquy, Spenserian stanza, synecdoche, terza rima, tone, and wit.

The more basic terms and devices, such as alliteration, allusion, analogy, aside, assonance, atmosphere, climax, consonance, denouement, elegy, foil, foreshadowing, metaphor, simile, setting, symbol, and theme are defined and exemplified in the English 5-9 Study Guide.

Antithesis: Balanced writing about conflicting ideas, usually expressed in sentence form. Some examples are "expanding from the center," "shedding old habits," and "searching never finding."

Aphorism: A focused, succinct expression about life from a sagacious viewpoint. Writings by Ben Franklin, Sir Francis Bacon, and Alexander Pope contain many aphorisms. "Whatever is begun in anger ends in shame" is an aphorism.

Apostrophe: Literary device of addressing an absent or dead person, an abstract idea, or an inanimate object. Sonneteers, such as Sir Thomas Wyatt, John Keats, and William Wordsworth, address the moon, stars, and the dead Milton. For example, in William Shakespeare's Julius Caesar, Mark Antony addresses the corpse of Caesar in the speech that begins: "O, pardon me, thou bleeding piece of earth / That I am meek and gentle with these butchers! / Thou art the ruins of the noblest man / That ever lived in the tide of times. / Woe to the hand that shed this costly blood!"

Blank Verse: Poetry written in iambic pentameter but unrhymed. Works by Shakespeare and Milton are epitomes of blank verse. Milton's Paradise Lost states, "Illumine, what is low raise and support, / That to the highth of this great argument I may assert Eternal Providence / And justify the ways of God to men."

Caesura: A pause, usually signaled by punctuation, in a line of poetry. The earliest usage occurs in Beowulf, the first English epic dating from the Anglo-Saxon era. "To err is human, // to forgive, divine" (Pope).

Conceit: A comparison, usually in verse, between seemingly disparate objects or concepts. John Donne's metaphysical poetry contains many clever conceits. For instance, Donne's "The Flea" (1633) compares a flea bite to the act of love; and in "A Valediction: Forbidding Mourning" (1633) separated lovers are likened to the legs of a compass, the leg drawing the circle eventually returning home to "the fixed foot."

Connotation: The ripple effect surrounding the implications and associations of a given word, distinct from the denotative or literal meaning. For example, the word "rest" in "Good night, sweet prince, and flights of angels sing thee to thy rest" refers to a burial.

Consonance: The repeated usage of similar consonant sounds, most often used in poetry. "Sally sat sifting seashells by the seashore" is a familiar example.

Couplet: Two rhyming lines of poetry. Shakespeare's sonnets end in heroic couplets written in iambic pentameter. Pope is also a master of the couplet; his Rape of the Lock is written entirely in heroic couplets.

Denotation: What a word literally means, as opposed to its connotative meaning.

Diction: The right word in the right place for the right purpose. The hallmark of a great writer is precise, unusual, and memorable diction.

Epiphany: The moment when the something is realized and comprehension sets in. James Joyce used this device in his short story collection The Dubliners.

Exposition: Fill-in or background information about characters meant to clarify and add to the narrative; the initial plot element that precedes the buildup of conflict.

Figurative Language: Not meant in a literal sense but to be interpreted through symbolism. Figurative language is made up of such literary devices as hyperbole, metonymy, synecdoche, and oxymoron. A synecdoche is a figure of speech in which the word for part of something is used to mean the whole; for example, "sail" for "boat," or vice versa.

Free Verse: Poetry that does not have any predictable meter or patterning. Margaret Atwood, e. e. cummings, and Ted Hughes write in this form.

Hyperbole: Exaggeration for a specific effect. For example, "I'm so hungry that I could eat a million of these."

Iambic Pentameter: The two elements in a set five-foot line of poetry. An iamb is two syllables, unaccented and accented, per foot or measure. Pentameter means five feet of these iambs per line or ten syllables.

Inversion: An atypical sentence order to create a given effect or interest. Bacon and Milton's work use inversion successfully. Emily Dickinson was fond of arranging words outside of their familiar order. For example in "Chartless" she writes "Yet know I how the heather looks" and "Yet certain am I of the spot." Instead of saying "Yet I know" and "Yet I am certain" she reverses the usual order and shifts the emphasis to the more important words.

Irony: An unexpected disparity between what is written or stated, and what is really meant or implied by the author. Verbal, dramatic and situational are the three literary ironies. Verbal irony is when an author says one thing and means something else. Dramatic irony is when an audience perceives something that a character in the literature does not know. Irony of situation is a discrepancy between the expected result and actual results. Shakespeare's plays contain numerous and highly effective use of irony. O. Henry's short stories have ironic endings.

Kenning: Another way to describe a person, place, or thing so, as to avoid prosaic repetition. The earliest examples can be found in Anglo-Saxon literature such as Beowulf and "The Seafarer." Instead of writing King Hrothgar, the anonymous monk wrote great Ring-Giver, or Father of his people. A lake becomes the swans' way, and the ocean or sea becomes the great whale's way. In ancient Greek literature, this device was called an "epithet."

Metaphysical Poetry: Verse characterization by ingenious wit, unparalleled imagery, and clever conceits. The greatest metaphysical poet is John Donne. Henry Vaughan and other 17th century British poets contributed to this movement as in Words, "I saw eternity the other night, like a great being of pure and endless light."

Metonymy: Use of an object or idea closely identified with another object or idea to represent the second. "Hit the books" means "go study." Washington, D.C. means the U.S. government and the White House means the U.S. president.

Motif: A key, oft-repeated phrase, name, or idea in a literary work. Dorset/Wessex in Hardy's novels and the moors and the harsh weather in the Bronte sisters' novels are effective use of motifs. Shakespeare's Romeo and Juliet represents the ill-fated young lovers' motif.

Onomatopoeia: Word used to evoke the sound in its meaning. The early Batman series used "pow," "zap," "whop," "zonk," and "eek" in an onomatopoetic way.

Octava Rima: A specific eight-line stanza of poetry whose rhyme scheme is abababcc. Lord Byron's mock epic, Don Juan, is written in this poetic way.

Oxymoron: A contradictory form of speech, such as jumbo shrimp, unkindly kind, or singer John Mellencamp's "It hurts so good."

Paradox: Seemingly untrue statement, which when examined more closely proves to be true. John Donne's sonnet "Death Be Not Proud" postulates that death shall die and humans will triumph over death, at first thought not true, but ultimately explained and proven in this sonnet.

Parallelism: A type of close repetition of clauses or phrases that emphasize key topics or ideas in writing. The psalms in the King James Version of the Bible contain many examples.

Personification: Giving human characteristics to inanimate objects or concepts. Great writers, with few exceptions, are masters of this literary device.

Quatrain: A poetic stanza composed of four lines. A Shakespearean or Elizabethan sonnet is made up of three quatrains and ends with a heroic couplet.

Scansion: The two-part analysis of a poetic line. Count the number of syllables per line and determine where the accents fall. Divide the line into metric feet. Name the meter by the type and number of feet. Much is written about scanning poetry. Try not to inundate your students with this jargon; rather, allow them to feel the power of the poets' words, ideas, and images instead.

Soliloquy: A highlighted speech, in drama, usually delivered by a major character expounding on the author's philosophy or expressing, at times, universal truths. This is done with the character alone on the stage, as in Hamlet's famous "To be or not to be" soliloquy.

Spenserian Stanza: Invented by Sir Edmund Spenser for use in The Faerie Queene, his epic poem honoring Queen Elizabeth I. Each stanza consists of nine lines, eight in iambic pentameter. The ninth line, called an alexandrine, has two extra syllables or one additional foot.

Stream of Consciousness: A style of writing which reflects the mental processes of the characters expressing, at times, jumbled memories, feelings, and dreams. James Joyce, Virginia Woolf, and William Faulkner use stream of consciousness in their writings.

Terza Rima: A series of poetic stanzas use the recurrent rhyme scheme of aba, bcb, cdc, ded, and so forth. The second-generation Romantic poets - Keats, Byron, Shelley, and, to a lesser degree, Yeats - used this Italian verse form, especially in their odes. Dante used this stanza in The Divine Comedy.

Tone: The discernible attitude inherent in an author's work regarding the subject, readership, or characters. Swift's or Pope's tone is satirical. Boswell's tone toward Johnson is admiring.

Skill 1.2   Is able to make logical inferences about the meaning of literary texts

Inference draws on similar strategies to help the reader to determine meaning but goes beyond stated meaning to examine what may not be immediately obvious about the meaning of a text. We infer meaning based upon evidence in a text such as:

- What we know about a character;
- What we know about the time period;
- What we can tell about relationships between characters; and
- What we can tell about the relationship between events in a text.

Inference is an essential skill in literary analysis, as many complex texts have multiple layers of meaning and multiple possible interpretations. Fundamentally, inference follows a line of logic. Interpretive responses result in inferences about character development, setting, or plot; analysis of style elements - metaphor, simile, allusion, rhythm, tone; outcomes derivable from information provided in the narrative; and assessment of the author's intent. Interpretive responses are made verbally or in writing.

An inference is drawn from an inductive line of reasoning. The most famous one is "all men are mortal," which is drawn from the observation that everyone a person knows has died or will die and that everyone else concurs in that judgment. It is assumed to be true and for that reason can be used as proof of another conclusion: "Socrates is a man; therefore, he will die."

Sometimes the inference is only assumed proven when it is not reliably true in all cases, such as "ageing brings physical and mental infirmity." Reasoning from that inference, many companies will not hire anyone above a certain age. Actually, being old does not necessarily imply physical and/or mental impairment. There are many instances where elderly people have made important contributions that require exceptional ability.

In fiction, figurative language, elements of plot, small details or even the omission of events may support the reader's inferences about meaning.

In Shelley's poem "Ozymandias" much of the meaning is implied.

> I met a traveller from an antique land
> Who said: "Two vast and trunkless legs of stone
> Stand in the desert . . . Near them, on the sand,
> Half sunk, a shattered visage lies, whose frown,
> And wrinkled lip, and sneer of cold command,
> Tell that its sculptor well those passions read
> Which yet survive, stamped on these lifeless things,
> The hand that mocked them, and the heart that fed:
> And on the pedestal these words appear:
> 'My name is Ozymandias, king of kings:
> Look on my works, ye Mighty, and despair!'
> Nothing beside remains. Round the decay
> Of that colossal wreck, boundless and bare
> The lone and level sands stretch far away."

On a surface level, this is a simple tale of a stranger remembering a statue he found in the desert. Why is this important? Why did Shelley find this necessary to recount?

To answer this, we need to look past what is literally stated to find what is implied. We can infer that the pedestal once referred to some grander structure, a monument perhaps, or maybe a castle or city. The face and pillars, at the very least, likely towered above the desert sometime in the past, depicting their fearsome subject for all to see. Surely this Ozymandias must have been wealthy to erect such a large sculpture, and it is telling that he wished to be depicted with a commanding sneer. A sculptor, who either feared or greatly revered his subject, carved the face. Ozymandias fancied himself a conqueror, one who would inspire awe in all who saw his monument.

But it did not last. The monument is crumbling; the desert around it is bare. Even this traveler from his "antique land" knows nothing of great Ozymandias except what he read on some plinth in the desert. Why did Ozymandias fade from memory? Who can say? Whatever great and terrible things Ozymandias accomplished, it was not enough to save him or his memory from the ravages of time.

The pedestal thus becomes sadly ironic – whereas once the mighty may have despaired upon seeing a fearsome monument that dwarfed them, today they will despair upon seeing that even the "king of kings", Ozymandias, has been forgotten for all time. Shelley is trying to teach us that even the mightiest of conquerors can die and be forgotten. Time waits for no man.

Skill 1.3   Is able to cite evidence from a text to support an argument about the meaning of a literary text

The first essential principle in the writing of an analysis of a literary selection is a thorough reading and understanding of the work. Once the writer feels that the author's intent is clearly understood, the writer should then determine the thesis statement through analyzing the work. The thesis will probably be a declaration of the purpose of the author in the work, itself. For example, if one were analyzing Mitch Albom's The Five People You Meet in Heaven, the thesis for the analysis might be as follows: "The theme of this story is that living to serve others gives meaning to the end of one's life."

However, the writer can make a meaningful point by focusing on other aspects of the story. For example, the style of a writer like Ernest Hemingway is so unusual and significant that the thesis might focus on a stylistic aspect of one of his stories. Setting may play a special role in a story and might make a good thesis for analysis. In fact, any aspect of the story can be useful for this kind of paper. This choice is important and will drive how the analysis is developed.

Once the thesis is decided, the next steps just naturally fall in line. The first step is a search for passages that support or relate to the proposed theme. Even before the thesis has been decided upon, the writer should have been taking notes, possibly on the pages of the book itself. Once the thesis is determined, the student will go back through the work, look at the notes already made, and add or adjust them to make sure adequate material is available to support the thesis of the analysis. Specifics are important here as are details if the analysis is to be complete and effective. In this second reading, the thesis might change—either to an entirely different one or to a variation of the first one.

Presenting supportive material is not sufficient; it must be organized in a way that is logical and reasonable to the reader of the analysis. In other words, the writer should develop a preliminary outline of the final paper. The structure of the outline may be in a different order than the examples in the work itself. One from later in the book might be relevant to an earlier one. The earlier one might foreshadow a later one, for instance.

Locating and organizing the evidence to support an interpretation of a literary work is a process that takes practice and support. Teaching students to read as if they were going to write an analysis of a work is an essential part of the process as it helps them to develop the habits of reading critically, noting passages that support their own interpretations of a work. Teachers support this analytical frame of mind through questioning and discussion, allowing students to formulate opinions that may change over time as they delve deeper into a literary work. Exploring literature is in part an intuitive process, but developing and articulating an interpretation successfully requires a logical, analytical approach.

Remember also that this is a recursive process. Nothing is permanent until the paper is ready to be handed in. Ideas and concepts will be seen on the second and third readings that were not apparent the first time through, and the writer must feel free to make changes that make the point clearer or stronger. Even the thesis or the aspect of the story that will be the focus of the analysis is open to change until the last stage of the writing process. Students sometimes have difficulty coming to a decision, so encourage them with setting time limits for themselves, making the decisions and completing the various steps required to write a successful paper.

Helping students become successful writers of literary analyses depends on several factors. They should have plenty of experience in analysis in class. The short story is a good way to help students develop the confidence that they can compose this kind of analytical writing, which requires independent reasoning. Using the short story as the basis for a writing course gives students more opportunities to go through the analysis process and gives them more opportunities to practice their analytical skills. The role of the teacher is to continually teach the principles but also to encourage independent thinking in these matters, even to accept sometimes less-than-perfect analyses.

Ultimately, the analysis should be the convictions arrived upon as a result of the reading and understanding the text. This is a good opportunity to help students begin to take responsibility for what they write—an important objective for a writing course.

Skill 1.4   Recognizes the theme(s) of a literary text

Theme in a work of fiction is similar to a thesis in an essay. It's the underlying idea that can be used to interpret the work as a whole. In a literary work, the reader may identify more than one possible theme since complex works often deal with multiple themes. The novel, *The Handmaid's Tale* by Margaret Atwood, for example, deals with the role of women in modern society as well as the ways in which the individual may resist oppression.

Identifying and supporting an argument about theme requires careful reading and should take into account the other aspects of the story before a firm decision is made with regard to the point of the story. Different analysts will come to different conclusions about what a story means. Very often the thesis of an analytical essay will be the writer's declaration of the theme according to an individual well-reasoned opinion.

Authors may set out to deliberately deal with a particular theme in their work. Others may simply set out to tell a story, and the theme may emerge in the telling of that story. Many times readers will identify themes that the author may not have envisioned when the original inspiration to tell the story struck.

Some common themes in literature include.

- Change vs. tradition
- Coming of age
- Empowerment

- Displacement
- The emptiness of pursuing a false dream
- The meaningless nature of life
- The futility of struggle
- The triumph of the individual in the face of adversity
- The individual vs. society
- The struggle to retain individuality in a society that seeks conformity
- The power of faith
- Greed as the cause of human downfall
- The struggle to do what is right
- The fight against injustice
- Loss of innocence
- The corrupting influence of power
- The fleeting nature of friendship/loyalty
- The power of progress
- Loss of innocence
- Vanity as downfall

The importance in identifying theme is not in choosing the 'right' one but in recognizing the elements in a literary work that support your analysis. Ten people reading the same book may identify ten different themes (and all of them may be correct).

See also Skill 1.3

Skill 1.5   Analyzes the connection between different elements of a literary text

All of the different elements of a literary work shape how we interpret it. Plot, character, setting, point of view, and language usage are some of the elements that affect our analysis of literature. His/her previous personal experiences, personal beliefs and even prior reading shape each person's interpretation. The key to creating a strong interpretation of literature is in supporting one's point of view with evidence and tying this evidence together.

Plot deals with what happens in the story and with the underlying conflicts. In a naturalist story, the conflicts may be between the protagonist and a hostile or indifferent world. Sometimes, the conflicts are between two characters, the protagonist and the antagonist; and sometimes the conflicts are internal—between two forces within an individual character that have created a dilemma. For example, a character may be torn between loyalty towards childhood friends and the ambition to tackle challenges and grow as an individual.

Once the conflicts have been determined, the pattern of action will hinge on how the story comes out. Who (or what) wins and who (or what) loses? If the protagonist struggles throughout the story but emerges triumphant in the end, the pattern is said to be rising. On the other hand, if the story is about the downfall of the major character, the story can be said to be falling.

Sometimes authors tell parallel stories in order to make their points. For example, in Count Leo Tolstoy's classic Anna Karenina, the unhappy extramarital affair of Anna Karenina and Count Vronsky is contrasted with the happy marriage of Lev and Kitty through the use of alternating chapters devoted to each couple. The plot consists of the progress of each couple: Anna and Count Vronsky into deeper neurosis, obsession, and emotional pain, and Lev and Kitty into deeper and more meaningful partnership through growing emotional intimacy, parenthood, and caring for members of their extended family.

In well-written novels, each part of the plot is necessary and has a purpose. For example, in Anna Karenina, a chapter is devoted to a horse race Count Vronsky participates in. This might seem like mere entertainment, but, in fact, Count Vronsky is riding his favorite mare, and, in a moment of carelessness in taking a jump, puts the whole weight of his body on the mare's back, breaking it. The horse must be shot. Vronsky loved and admired the mare, but being overcome by a desire to win, he kills the very thing he loves. Similarly, Anna descends into obsession and jealousy as their affair isolates her from society and separates her from her child, and ultimately kills herself. The chapter symbolizes the destructive effect that Vronsky's love, coupled with inordinate desire, has upon what and whom he loves.

Other authors use repetitious plot lines to reveal the larger story over time. For example, in Joseph Heller's tragic-comedy Catch-22, the novel repeatedly returns to a horrific incident in an airplane while flying a combat mission. Each time the protagonist, Yossarian, recalls the incident, more detail is revealed. The reader knows from the beginning that this incident is key to why Yossarian wants to be discharged from the army, but it is not until the full details of the gruesome incidents are revealed late in the book that the reader knows why the incident has driven Yossarian almost mad. Interspersed with comedic and ironic episodes, the book's climax (the full revealing of the incident) remains powerfully with the reader, showing the absurdity, insanity, and inhumanity of war. The comic device of Catch-22, a fictitious army rule from which the title is derived, makes this point in a funny way: Catch-22 states that a soldier cannot be discharged from the army unless he is crazy; yet, if he wants to be discharged from the army, he is not crazy. This rule seems to embody the insanity, absurdity, and inhumanity of war.

Characters are developed in many ways. Sometimes the writer simply tells the reader what kind of person this is. More often, however, the reader is left to deduce the characteristics from dialogue with others; with what other characters think or say about him/her; with description—what the character looks like, tall, short, thin, plump, dark-haired, gray-haired, etc. The techniques a writer uses to define character are called characterization, and a student writer will usually deal with these matters when writing an analysis.

Setting can be a period of time, like the 1930s, for example. It can also be a place, either a real place like a particular city or a fictional place like a farm or a mansion. It can also be emotional; some of Truman Capote's stories are set in an atmosphere of fear and danger, and the effectiveness of the story depends on that setting. An analysis should deal with the function of the setting in the story. For example, if it were set in a particular period of time like *The Great Gatsby* is, would the story be different if it were set in a different period of time? A setting can sometimes function as a symbol, so the writer should be looking for that as a possibility.

Point of view seems simple on the surface, but it rarely is in a story. In fact, Wallace Hildick wrote *Thirteen Types of Narrative* to explain point of view in literature. The most common ones are first person narrator objective in which the person telling the story only records his/her observations of what is happening. In this point of view, the only clues as to what the characters are like come from the narrator. The attitude of the narrator toward the theme or the characters will be an important part of the story and should be dealt with in an analysis. Sometimes, it's apparent that the narrator's view does not square with reality. In this case, the narrator becomes unreliable and the reader must determine what is real and what is not. If a writer uses this device, it's extremely important that the analyst points it out and analyzes what it does for the story.

The first person narrator may know what one or more of the characters are thinking and that will be important to the analysis of the story. If the narrator knows this, how did he/she acquire the knowledge? The most logical way is that that character or those characters told the story to the narrator in the first place.

Third person objective is another common form of development. In this point of view, there is no narrator. An unseen observer tells the story. The reader does not know what anyone is thinking, only what is being said and described.

Third person omniscient is also fairly common. In this point of view, the story is being told by an unseen observer, but the observer is able to know what at least one person is thinking, sometimes called limited omniscient point of view. The reader may also know what most or all of the characters are thinking, and this point of view is simply called third-person omniscient.

A complex literary work may lend itself to a multi-faceted analysis in which these different elements all play a role in shaping understanding of the overall work. Teaching students to recognize the interplay of different elements in a work is an ongoing and complex process.

Skill 1.6 Analyzes and interprets the meaning of language in a text (figurative, symbolic, context-specific, etc.)

Language as a medium of communication is often open to interpretation because it is imprecise. This is true in literature, though the degree to which language plays a role in analyzing a work varies based on the writer's style, the particular work, and/or the genre of writing. Shakespeare is perhaps the classic example of English language writers whose use of language is absolutely essential to the understanding of a work.

Shakespeare made extensive use of figurative of language, symbolism, double entendres, rhyme, and specific word choice to layer meaning in fascinating but complex ways. Seen on a continuum, Shakespeare may be at one end in terms of use of language, but language plays an important role in understanding many major works.

Poetry, one of the most layered forms of communication, is embedded with meaning. For students to enjoy and appreciate poetry, they should be able to peel away the layers to find the depth of meaning. One way they can do this is by understanding the techniques poets use.

Imagery
Imagery can be described as a word or sequence of words that refers to any sensory experience—that is, anything that can be seen, tasted, smelled, heard, or felt on the skin or fingers. While prose writers may also use these images, they are most distinctive of poetry. The poet intends to make an experience available to the reader. In order to do that, the poet must appeal to one of the senses. The most-often-used one, of course, is the visual sense. The poet will deliberately paint a scene in such a way that the reader can see it. However, the purpose is not simply to stir the visceral feeling but also to stir the emotions. A good example is "The Piercing Chill" by Taniguchi Buson (1715-1783):

The piercing chill I feel:
My dead wife's comb, in our bedroom,
Under my heel . . .

In only a few short words, the reader can feel many things: the shock that might come from touching the corpse, a literal sense of death, the contrast between her death and the memories he has of her when she was alive. Imagery might be defined as speaking of the abstract in concrete terms, a powerful device in the hands of a skillful poet.

Symbolism
A symbol is an object or action that can be observed with the senses in addition to its suggesting many other things. The lion is a symbol of courage; the cross a symbol of Christianity; the color green a symbol of envy.

These can almost be defined as metaphors because society agrees on the one-to-one meaning of them. Symbols used in literature are usually of a different sort. They tend to be private and personal; their significance is only evident in the context of the work where they are used. Background knowledge about the time period, author, or politics of the work can help in identifying symbolism in fiction. A good example of a symbol in poetry is the mending wall in Frost's poem. A symbol can certainly have more than one meaning, and the meaning may be as personal as the memories and experiences of the particular reader. In analyzing a poem or a story, students should identify the symbols and their possible meanings.

Looking for symbols is often challenging, especially for novice poetry readers. However, these suggestions may be useful: First, pick out all the references to concrete objects such as a newspaper, black cats, or other nouns. Note any that the poet emphasizes by describing in detail, by repeating, or by placing at the very beginning or ending of a poem. Ask yourself, what is the poem about? What does it add up to? Paraphrase the poem and determine whether the meaning depends upon certain concrete objects. Then ponder what the concrete object symbolizes in this particular poem.

Look for a character with the name of a prophet who does little but utter prophecy or a trio of women who resemble the Three Fates. A symbol may be a part of a person's body such as the eye of the murder victim in Poe's story *"The Tell-Tale Heart"* or a look, a voice, or a mannerism.

Allusion

An allusion is very much like a symbol, and the two sometimes tend to run together. An allusion is defined by Merriam Webster's Encyclopedia of Literature as "an implied reference to a person, event, thing, or a part of another text." Allusions are based on the assumption that there is a common body of knowledge shared by poet and reader and that a reference to that body of knowledge will be immediately understood. Allusions to the Bible and classical mythology are common in Western literature on the assumption that they will be immediately understood. This is not always the case, of course. T. S. Eliot's *The Wasteland* requires research and annotation for understanding. He assumed more background knowledge on the part of the average reader than usually exists. However, when Michael Moore on his web page headlines an article on the war in Iraq: "Déjà Fallujah: Ramadi surrounded, thousands of families trapped, no electricity or water, onslaught impending," we may recognize that he is referring first of all to a repeat of the human disaster in New Orleans caused by Hurricane Katrina. Here, however, the "onslaught" is not a storm but an invasion by American and Iraqi troops.

The use of allusion is a sort of shortcut for poets. They can use an economy of words and count on meaning to come from the reader's own experience.

Figurative Language

Figurative language is also called figures of speech. If all figures of speech that have ever been identified were listed, it would be a very long list. However, for purposes of analyzing poetry, a few are sufficient.

Alliteration: The repetition of consonant sounds in two or more neighboring words or syllables. In its simplest form, it reinforces one or two consonant sounds.

Example: Shakespeare's Sonnet #12:

When I do count the clock that tells the time.

Some poets have used more complex patterns of alliteration by creating consonants both at the beginning of words and at the beginning of stressed syllables within words.

Example: Shelley's "Stanzas Written in Dejection Near Naples":

The City's voice itself is soft like Solitude's

Bathos: A ludicrous attempt to portray pathos—that is, to evoke pity, sympathy, or sorrow. It may result from inappropriately dignifying the commonplace, elevated language to describe something trivial, or greatly exaggerated pathos.

Climax: A number of phrases or sentences are arranged in ascending order of rhetorical forcefulness. Example from Melville's Moby Dick:

All that most maddens and torments; all that stirs up the lees of things; all truth with malice in it; all that cracks the sinews and cakes the brain; all the subtle demonisms of life and thought; all evil, to crazy Ahab, were visibly personified and made practically assailable in Moby Dick.

Euphemism: The substitution of an agreeable or inoffensive term for one that might offend or suggest something unpleasant. Many euphemisms are used to refer to death to avoid using the real word such as "passed away," "crossed over," or nowadays "passed."

Hyperbole: Deliberate exaggeration for effect or comic effect. An example from Shakespeare's *The Merchant of Venice*:

Why, if two gods should play some heavenly match
And on the wager lay two earthly women,
And Portia one, there must be something else
Pawned with the other, for the poor rude world
Hath not her fellow.

Irony: Expressing something other than and particularly opposite the literal meaning such as words of praise when blame is intended. In poetry, it is often used as a sophisticated or resigned awareness of contrast between what is and what ought to be and expresses a controlled pathos without sentimentality. It is a form of indirection that avoids overt praise or censure. An early example: the Greek comic character Eiron, a clever underdog who by his wit repeatedly triumphs over the boastful character Alazon.

Malapropism: A verbal blunder in which one word is replaced by another similar in sound but different in meaning. This derives from Sheridan's Mrs. Malaprop in *The Rivals* (1775). Thinking of the geography of contiguous countries, she spoke of the "geometry" of "contagious countries." Meaning the "pinnacle of perfection," she describes someone as "the pineapple of perfection."

Metaphor: Indirect comparison between two things with the use of a word or phrase that denotes an object or action in place of another to suggest a comparison between them. While poets use them extensively, they are also integral to everyday speech. For example, chairs are said to have "legs" and "arms", although we know that humans and other animals have these appendages.

Parallelism: The arrangement of ideas in phrases, sentences, and paragraphs that balance one element with another of equal importance and similar wording. An example from Francis Bacon's Of Studies: "Reading maketh a full man, conference a ready man, and writing an exact man."

Personification: Human characteristics are attributed to an inanimate object, an abstract quality, or animal. Examples: John Bunyan wrote characters named Death, Knowledge, Giant Despair, Sloth, and Piety in his Pilgrim's Progress. The metaphor of an arm of a chair is a form of personification. Carl Sandburg, in his poem "Fog," writes "The fog comes / on little cat feet. // It sits looking / over harbor and city / on silent haunches / and then moves on."

Onomatopoeia: The naming of a thing or action by a vocal imitation of the sound associated with it such as buzz or hiss or the use of words whose sound suggests the sense. A good example: from "The Brook" by Tennyson:

I chatter over stony ways,
In little sharps and trebles,
I bubble into eddying bays,
I babble on the pebbles.

Oxymoron: A contradiction in terms deliberately employed for effect. It is usually seen in a qualifying adjective whose meaning is contrary to that of the noun it modifies such as "wise folly."

Simile: Direct comparison between two things using "like," "as," such as." For example: "My love is like a red-red rose."

Poets use figures of speech to sharpen the effect and meaning of their poems and to help readers see things in ways they have never seen them before. Marianne Moore observed that a fir tree has "an emerald turkey-foot at the top." Her poem makes us aware of something we probably had never noticed before. The sudden recognition of the likeness yields pleasure in the reading.

Figurative language allows for the statement of truths that more literal language cannot. Skillfully used, a figure of speech will help the reader see more clearly and focus upon particulars. Figures of speech add many dimensions of richness to our reading and understanding of a poem; they also allow many opportunities for worthwhile analysis. The approach to take in analyzing a poem on the basis of its figures of speech is to ask the question: What does it do for the poem? Does it underscore meaning? Does it intensify understanding? Does it increase the intensity of our response?

Skill 1.7   Recognizes the impact that language and word choice can have on a text

See also 1.6

A writer's use of language and even specific words can have a profound effect on our reaction to and interpretation of literary works. Word choice can evoke an emotional response just as figurative uses of language can prompt us to 'feel' what the narrator or writer want us to experience. Students need support in developing the skills to recognize the impact of language and word choice, especially as they transition from less complex, plot-driven young adult literature to more sophisticated work in the upper grades.

Generally it is easy for us to identify 'bad' word choice but harder to use language powerfully. In avoiding bad word choice, there are some clear things to avoid.

Redundancy or repetition
Good writers vary their phrasing and word choice. They vary word order and sentence structure to change pace and rhythm. Many also make use of a thesaurus to find synonyms for common words that enliven and enrich the language of their work.

Clichés
Certain phrases enter the language and are wonderful to hear and read at first, but after a while we simply tire of them. Others are considered hackneyed and overly sentimental. Once this happens we generally prefer not to see them in the books we read. Good writers have a sense of original language and tend to avoid clichéd phrasing.

Examples:

- At the end of the day
- Dead as a doornail
- Pushing the envelope
- Bent out of shape
- All bets are off
- Nerves of steel
- No man is an island
- See eye to eye
- Sharp as a tack
- Hard as nails

Wordiness

Wordiness is also a trait that most writers seek to avoid. Marcel Proust's *In Search of Lost Time* is praised for its incredibly elaborate descriptions, but most writers are not the masters of language that Proust was. Whereas he could describe eating a madeleine in glorious detail, we would generally say that being verbose is not a sought after trait in writing.

An excerpt from Proust:

> *She sent out for one of those short, plump little cakes called 'petites madeleines,' which look as though they had been moulded in the fluted scallop of a pilgrim's shell. And soon, mechanically, weary after a dull day with the prospect of a depressing morrow, I raised to my lips a spoonful of the tea in which I had soaked a morsel of the cake. No sooner had the warm liquid, and the crumbs with it, touched my palate, a shudder ran through my whole body, and I stopped, intent upon the extraordinary changes that were taking place. An exquisite pleasure had invaded my senses, but individual, detached, with no suggestion of its origin.*

Skill 1.8   Analyzes the way in which authors' choices affect meaning and structure

Students can sometimes almost see literary works as living things with their own specific characteristics. Characters are like people with personalities and backgrounds that shape who they are. In analyzing literature, however, it is important to note that a literary work is the product of the author's choices. Characters are who they are because of the decisions of the writer. Romeo was not born to be impetuous and prone to acting on impulse out of love; he was that way because Shakespeare wrote him that way.

Writers' choices about plot, character, language, meaning, and even narrative structure shape our understanding of their work. This does not mean that they have thought through all the potential meanings of a story, but it does mean that the way in which they choose to tell the story shapes our interpretation of it. The children's story of the Three Little Pigs in its traditional telling reminds young children of the importance of responsibility and careful work.

In Jon Scieszka and Lane Smith's retelling, *The True Story of the Three Little Pigs*, the story is reframed. By choosing a different perspective, they call into question the original version by telling the story from the wolf's point of view. Rather than a villain, there is now ambiguity around the wolf's role. Is he a villain, or simply misunderstood?

A piece of writing is an integrated whole. It's not enough to just look at the various parts; the total entity must be examined. It should be considered in two ways:

- As an emotional expression of the author

- As an artistic embodiment of a meaning or set of meanings

This is what is sometimes called tone in literary criticism.

In their writings, authors exhibit their individual beliefs, values, prejudices, and emotions. They tell their reader about the world as they see it, thus revealing aspects of their own personalities. By reading their works, the audience sees the authors' personal values and emotions embodied within the work. However, authors don't reveal everything in a single work. Sometimes, writers will be influenced by a desire to have a piece of work accepted. They may be motivated by the topics that appear to be current or by the interests and desires of the readers. These can destroy a work or make it less than it might be. Sometimes the best works are not commercial successes in the generation when they were written but are discovered at a later time and by another generation.

Choice of materials
Some characters have qualities that are attractive while others are repugnant. What an author shows in a setting will often indicate what the interests are. The writer's interpretation: The writer may be explicit, telling us directly about what is being felt. On the other hand, the writer may be implicit and feelings of a character come through in the description. For example, the use of "smirked" instead of "laughed" suggests a different attitude; "minced," "stalked," or "marched," instead of walked paint different pictures. The reader is asked to join the writer in the feelings expressed about the world and the things that happen in it. The tone of a piece of writing is important in a critical review of it.

Style, in literature, means a distinctive manner of expression and applies to all levels of language, beginning at the phonemic level—word choices, alliteration, and assonance. It continues to the syntactic level—length of sentences, choice of structure and phraseology, patterns, and, it extends even beyond the sentence to paragraphs and chapters. What is distinctive about this writer's use of these elements?

In Steinbeck's *Grapes of Wrath*, for instance, the style is quite simple in the narrative sections and the dialogue stays true to regional dialect. Because the emphasis is on the story—the narrative—the author's style is straightforward, for the most part. He tells the story, shining a light on the uncomfortable reality of what it was like to be a poor family in the Depression. However, within some chapters he varies his style. He uses symbols and combines them with description that is realistic. He sometimes shifts to a crisp, repetitive pattern to underscore the beeping and speeding of cars. By contrast, some of sections within chapters are lyrical, almost poetic in their realism.

These shifts in style reflect the attitude of the author toward the subject matter. S/he may intend to make a deliberate statement through their writing, and s/he uses a variety of styles to strengthen the point.

A writer makes decisions about language usage, dialogue, characters' temperaments, and plot. Based on what a writer does, we may identify and sympathize with a character who does bad things or judge a character based on his/her language. We may come to love a character that commits crimes or to hope that the character upholding the law fails. Adept authors can cause us to root for almost anyone based on what they include and what they omit. All these choices affect our view and understanding of literature.

Skill 1.9   Recognizes how techniques such as satire, irony, sarcasm, etc. can shape and contribute to an author's message

See also 1.1

Writers can make a powerful point using techniques such as satire, irony, sarcasm, and understatement.

Irony is an unexpected disparity between what is written or stated and what is really meant or implied by the author. Verbal, dramatic and situational are the three literary ironies. Verbal irony is when an author says one thing and means something else. Dramatic irony is when an audience perceives something that a character in the literature does not know. Irony of situation is a discrepancy between the expected result and actual results. Shakespeare's plays contain numerous and highly effective use of irony. *O. Henry*'s short stories have ironic endings.

Irony is often 'missed' by students, especially when they are unfamiliar with the technique. Discussion, questioning and close reading will generally help students learn to watch for it. Especially as they develop a deeper understanding of character, they will learn to see that some characters are more likely to 'speak' with an ironic voice, often to highlight the truth.

Sarcasm employs sharp, cutting remarks, often to make fun of someone or something. It also frequently involves irony in that the writer/speaker may say something but mean something entirely different. Students are usually familiar with sarcasm (and can be quite expert at it) but may confuse it with irony. Though there are similarities, irony is generally more subtle and elaborated.

Satires can often be seen as shining a light on the flaws or shortcomings of a society or institution. Successful satires often make us laugh at the ridiculousness of a situation. George Orwell's *Animal Farm* satirized the Soviet Union under Stalin; in the novel farm animals stage a revolution against their human masters only to have the pigs establish themselves as new masters through manipulation and, eventually, the threat of violence.

Understatement is used to draw attention to something by deliberately making it seem unimportant. This can be done to humorous effect (as in the famous Monty Python and the Holy Grail when the knight responds that 'It's just a flesh wound' after losing his arm in a fight) or to draw attention to tragedy. In *Romeo and Juliet,* when Mercutio describes his mortal injury as being "not so deep as a well nor so wide as a church door but enough," we know that his wound is fatal.

These techniques are often difficult for students to master but easier to learn to recognize. Understanding how authors employ them to convey meaning, often subtly, is an important skill.

Skill 1.10   **Is familiar with important works of American literature from the 18th, 19th, and 20th centuries; recognizes how different texts from the same period may deal with a similar topic**

Although American literature does not have a history as long as that of other countries, it is still rich and diverse. As the country has developed, its literature has reflected the changing cultural and historical trends shaping the country. Writers explored both the strengths and ideals of the United States while others examined the ways in which American society has at time failed to live up to its promise. Issues of racism, discrimination, class, and corruption have been fodder for some of the great works of American writing. Simply put, American writing has always been a reflection of the historical, social, ethnic, political and economic environment of the time.

Below is a handy chart laying out some of the most important formative works in American literature.

Author	Time Period	Contributions & Significant Works
John Winthrop	16th Century	English Puritan lawyer; leading contributor and first governor of the Massachusetts Bay colony *A Model of Christian Charity* *The History of New England*
Anne Bradstreet	17th Century	American Puritan; first woman recognized as an accomplished New World Poet; first female writer in North America to be published *Another* *Another II* *The Prologue* *To My Dear and Loving Husband*

John Edwards	18th Century	Protestant preacher; influential theologian and philosopher "Sinners in the Hands of an Angry God" (sermon) *The End for Which God Created the World* *The Life of David Brainerd* *Religious Affections*
Phillis Wheatley	18th Century	First published African American poet; native to West Africa *Poems on Various Subjects, Religious and Moral*
James Fenimore Cooper	19th Century	Writing influenced by experience working in the US Navy; many of his works referenced life at sea *The Spy* *Leatherstocking Tales*
Frederick Douglass	19th Century	African-American social reformer; escaped slave; leader of abolitionist movement *Narrative of the Life of Frederick Douglass, An American Slave* *My Bondage and My Freedom*
Thomas Jefferson	19th Century	Founding father; former president of the United States; principal author of the Declaration of Independence
Edgar Allen Poe	19th Century	Poet; short story author; Boston native "The Raven" "A Dream Within a Dream"
Abraham Lincoln	19th Century	Former President of the United States; abolished slavery; assassinated Emancipation Proclamation
Nathaniel Hawthorne	19th Century	Dark romance short story author; Salem, MA native *The Scarlet Letter* *Twice-Told Tales* *The House of Seven Gables*

Ralph Waldo Emerson	19th Century	Leader of the transcendentalist movement; poet; essayist; highly influential to the American romantic movement *Essays: First Series* *Essays: Second Series* "Nature" "Uriel" "The Snow-Storm"
Henry David Thoreau	19th Century	Leader of the transcendentalist movement; poet and essayist known for writing about nature and natural history *Walden* "Civil Disobedience"
Walt Whitman	19th Century	Leader in creation of free verse; poet; essayist; journalist; displayed views from transcendentalism and realism; self-published *Leaves of Grass* *Franklin Evans*
Herman Melville	19th Century	Renaissance poet, short story writer, and novelist; spent years at sea before becoming a writer *Typee* *Moby Dick*
Emily Dickinson	19th Century	Prolific Romantic poet; thousands of poems found hidden in her room upon her death *The Complete Poems of Emily Dickinson*
Mark Twain	19th Century	Novelist; known for writing about southern culture *The Adventures of Tom Sawyer* *Adventures of Huckleberry Finn*
Stephen Crane	19th Century	Protestant Methodist poet, short story writer, and novelist; demonstrated realism, naturalism, and impressionism in his works *The Red Badge of Courage* *Maggie: A Girl on the Streets*

		War is Kind
Harriet Beecher Stowe	19th Century	Author of over 30 books; abolitionist; fought for women's rights *Uncle Tom's Cabin*
Kate Chopin	19th Century	Short story and novel writer; known for fiction; accepted to many prestigious magazines *The Awakening*
Henry James	19th Century	Realist; known for narrative fiction *The Portrait of a Lady*

18th Century

The earliest American literature reveals the development of a distinct national identity, separate from that of Great Britain. Shaped by their experiences and environment, writers began to explore what it meant to be American and to slowly develop their own literary tradition.

The Colonial Period

William Bradford's excerpts from *The Mayflower Compact* relate vividly the hardships of crossing the Atlantic in such a tiny vessel, the misery and suffering of the first winter, the approaches of the American Indians, the decimation of their ranks, and the establishment of the Bay Colony of Massachusetts.

"If ever two were one, then surely we.   If ever man were loved by wife, then thee."

Anne Bradstreet's poetry relates colonial New England life. From her journals, modern readers learn of the everyday life of the early settlers, the hardships of travel, and the responsibilities of different groups and individuals in the community, Early American literature also reveals the commercial and political adventures of the Cavaliers who came to the New World with King George's blessing.

William Byrd's journal, *A History of the Dividing Line*, concerning his trek into the Dismal Swamp separating the Carolinian territories from Virginia and Maryland makes quite lively reading. A privileged insider to the English Royal Court, Byrd, like other Southern Cavaliers, was given grants to pursue business ventures.

The Revolutionary Period

There were great orations such as Patrick Henry's Speech to the Virginia House of Burgesses -- the "Give me liberty or give me death" speech - and George Washington's Farewell to the Army of the Potomac. Less memorable and thought rambling by modern readers are Washington's inaugural addresses.

The **Declaration of Independence**, the brainchild predominantly of Thomas Jefferson, with some prudent editing by Ben Franklin, is a prime example of neoclassical writing -- balanced, well crafted, and focused.

Epistles include the exquisitely written, moving correspondence between John Adams and Abigail Adams. The poignancy of their separation - she in Boston, he in Philadelphia - is palpable and real.

The 19th Century

Nathaniel Hawthorne and Herman Melville are the preeminent early American novelists, writing on subjects definitely regional, specific and American, yet sharing insights about human foibles, fears, loves, doubts, and triumphs.

Hawthorne's writings range from children's stories to adult fare of dark, brooding short stories such as "Dr. Heidegger's Experiment," "The Devil and Tom Walker," and "Rappaccini's Daughter." His masterpiece, *The Scarlet Letter*, takes on the society of hypocritical Puritan New Englanders, who ostensibly left England to establish religious freedom but who have been entrenched in judgmental finger wagging. They ostracize Hester and condemn her child, Pearl, as a child of Satan. Great love, sacrifice, loyalty, suffering, and related epiphanies add universality to this tale. The House of the Seven Gables also deals with kept secrets, loneliness, societal pariahs, and love ultimately triumphing over horrible wrong.

Herman Melville's great opus, *Moby Dick*, follows a crazed Captain Ahab on his Homeric odyssey to conquer the great white whale that has outwitted him and his whaling crews time and again. The whale has even taken Arab's leg and, according to Ahab, wants all of him. Melville recreates in painstaking detail and with insider knowledge of the harsh life of a whaler out of New Bedford, by way of Nantucket. For those who don't want to learn about every guy rope or all parts of the whaler's rigging, Melville offers up the succinct tale of Billy Budd and his Christ-like sacrifice to the black and white maritime laws on the high seas. An accident results in the death of one of the ship's officers, a slug of a fellow, who had taken a dislike to the young, affable, shy Billy. Captain Vere must hang Billy for the death of Claggert but knows that this is not right. However, an example must be given to the rest of the crew so that discipline can be maintained.

Edgar Allan Poe creates a distinctly American version of romanticism with his 16-syllable line in "The Raven," the classical "To Helen," and his Gothic "Annabelle Lee." The horror short story can be said to originate from Poe's pen. "The Tell-Tale Heart,"

"The Cask of Amontillado," "The Fall of the House of Usher," and "The Masque of the Red Death" are exemplary short stories. The new genre of detective story also emerges with Poe's "Murders in the Rue Morgue."

Writers such as Harriet Beecher Stowe used literature to shine a light on the ills of American society. With *Uncle Tom's Cabin* she sought to highlight the injustice of slavery. By exposing the horrible truth of how the institution of slavery exploited and abused people, she hoped to turn American to the Abolitionist cause. Authors such as Kate Chopin and Louisa May Alcott explored essential ideas about the roles of women in society while creating compelling novels.

American Romanticism has its own offshoot in the transcendentalism of Ralph Waldo Emerson and Henry David Thoreau. One wrote about transcending the complexities of life; the other, who wanted to get to the marrow of life, pitted himself against nature at Walden Pond and wrote an inspiring autobiographical account of his sojourn, aptly titled On Walden Pond. He also wrote passionately on his objections to the interference of government on the individual in "On the Duty of Civil Disobedience."

Emerson's elegantly crafted essays and war poetry still validate several important universal truths. Probably most remembered for his address to Thoreau's Harvard graduating class, "The American Scholar," he defined the qualities of hard work and intellectual spirit required of Americans in their growing nation.

The 20th Century

The start of the twentieth century begins the period of modern literature. American writers continued to distinguish themselves in drama, poetry, fiction, and nonfiction. American literature continued to reflect the issues of American society and the growing interconnectedness that came with globalization. American voices in literature came to influence literature around the world.

Author	Time Period	Significant Works & Contributions
Charlotte Perkins Gilman	19th Century	Novelist; short story writer; poet; feminist; lecturer for social reform "The Yellow Wallpaper"
Gertrude Stein	20th Century	Writer and poet; contributor to the modernist era *Three Lives* *How to Write*

Edith Wharton	20th Century	Novelist; short story writer; Pulitzer Prize winner; known for writing depictions of an affluent lifestyle *The Age of Innocence*
T.S. Eliot	20th Century	Poet; social critic; leader of the Modernist era; Nobel prize winner "The Love Song of J. Alfred Prufrock" *Four Quartets*
William Faulkner	20th Century	Author of novels, short stories, essays, plays, and poetry; Nobel Prize winner; known for incorporating stories about southern culture *As I Lay Dying* *The Sound and the Fury*
Langston Hughes	20th Century	Harlem Renaissance leader; athor of poems and novels; social activist *Let America be America Again* *The Ways of White Folks*
Eugene O'Neill	20th Century	Nobel prize winner; playwright; plays were known for incorporating elements of realism *Beyond the Horizon* *Anna Christie* *Strange Interlude*
Gwendolyn Brooks	20th Century	First African American woman to win the Pulitzer Prize for poetry; Teacher; Poet *Negro Hero* *Annie Allen*
Ernest Hemingway	20th Century	Writer of novels and short stories; Pulitzer Prize winner; Nobel Prize winner *A Farewell to Arms* *The Sun Also Rises* *For Whom the Bell Tolls*

James Baldwin	20th Century	Author of novels, poems, and plays; social justice activist; *Notes of a Native Son*
Toni Morrison	21st Century	Novelist; feminist; Nobel Prize Winner; Pulitzer Prize winner; known for speaking out against racism and sexism *Beloved*
Maya Angelou	21st Century	Poet, Civil Rights Activist *I Know Why the Caged Bird Sings*
Louise Erdrich	21st Century	Novelist; poet; children's book author; known for inclusion of Native American culture *The Plague of Doves*

American Drama

The greatest and most prolific of American playwrights include the following:

Eugene O'Neill, *Long Day's Journey into Night, Mourning Becomes Electra*, and *Desire Under the Elms*
Arthur Miller, *The Crucible, All My Sons*, and *Death of a Salesman*
Tennessee Williams, *Cat on a Hot Tin Roof, The Glass Menagerie*, and *A Streetcar Named Desire*
Lorraine Hansberry, *A Raisin in the Sun*
Edward Albee, *Who's Afraid of Virginia Woolf? Three Tall Women*, and *A Delicate Balance*

American Fiction

The diversity of the American experience has shaped American literature in countless ways. Different writers from different backgrounds have explored themes sometimes closely tied to identity while others have delved into personal experience. Rich, layered, and powerful works have emerged from some of the biggest challenges to American society. Some of the greatest American novels of the 20th century have dealt with:

- Racism
- Inequality
- The rights of women
- Slavery and its effects
- The effects of colonization

- The experience of immigrants as they adapted to and shaped American society
- Poverty and class
- The struggle for equality
- Sexual identity

Some examples of renowned American novelists of the 20th century include these authors:

Toni Morrison: *Beloved, The Bluest Eye*
John Updike: *Rabbit Run* and *Rabbit Redux*
Sinclair Lewis: *Babbitt* and *Elmer Gantry*
Alice Walker: *The Color Purple, The Temple of My Familiar*
John Steinbeck: *Cannery Row, The Grapes of Wrath*
Zora Neale Hurston: *Their Eyes Were Watching God*
F. Scott Fitzgerald: *The Great Gatsby* and *Tender Is the Night*
Gary Soto: *Tale of Sunlight*
Louise Erdrich: *Love Medicine, The Round House*
Richard Wright: *White Man, Listen!* and *Native Son*
Ernest Hemingway: *A Farewell to Arms* and *For Whom the Bell Tolls*
William Faulkner: *The Sound and the Fury* and *Absalom, Absalom*
Leslie Marmon Silko: *Gardens in the Dunes, Ceremony*
Cormac McCarthy: The Border Trilogy
Sandra Cisneros: *The House on Mango Street* and short story collections

[Note that here are too many important writers to try and create a comprehensive list.]

American Poetry

The poetry of the twentieth century is multifaceted, as represented by Edna St. Vincent Millay, Marianne Moore, Richard Wilbur, Langston Hughes, Maya Angelou, and Rita Dove. Robert Frost's New England motifs of snowy evenings, birches, apple picking, stone wall mending, hired hands, and detailed nature studies relate universal truths in exquisite diction, polysyllabic words, and rare allusions to either mythology or the Bible.

As a teacher, one of the most important elements of teaching English Language Arts is establishing the connection between literature and society. Some of the greatest works in American literature are closely tied to the most pressing issues of their time while others explore the human experience and the struggles of the individual. Still others do both.

American authors made significant contributions to changing their world with their prose, poetry, and drama. Whether they focused inward on their own part of the globe or focused outward on their place in the world, these authors provide students a broad and deep view into American life.

Local Color

Local color is defined as the presenting of the peculiarities of a particular locality and its inhabitants. This genre began primarily after the Civil War, although there were certainly precursors such as Washington Irving and his depiction of life in the Catskill Mountains of New York. However, the local colorist movement is generally considered to have begun in 1865, when humor began to permeate the writing of those who were focusing on a particular region of the country.

Samuel L. Clemens (Mark Twain) is best known for his humorous works such as "The Notorious Jumping Frog of Calaveras County." The country had just emerged from its "long night of the soul," a time when death, despair, and disaster had preoccupied the nation for almost five years. It's no wonder that the artists sought to relieve the grief and pain and lift spirits nor is it surprising that their efforts brought such a strong response. Mark Twain is generally considered to be not only one of America's funniest writers but one who also wrote great and enduring fiction.

Other examples of local colorists who used many of the same devices are George Washington Cable, Joel Chandler Harris, Bret Harte, Sarah Orne Jewett, and Harriet Beecher Stowe.

Slavery

One of the best known of the early writers who used fiction as a political statement about slavery is Harriet Beecher Stowe, author of *Uncle Tom's Cabin*. This was her first novel, and it was published first as a serial in 1851 then as a book in 1852. This anti-slavery book infuriated Southerners. However, the 1850 Fugitive Slave Law that made it legal to indict those who assisted runaway slaves angered Stowe herself. It also took away rights not only of the runaways but also of the free slaves. She intended to generate a protest of the law and slavery. It was the first effort to present the lives of slaves from their standpoint.

Stowe cleverly used depictions of motherhood and Christianity to stir her readers. When President Lincoln finally met her, he told her it was her book that started the war.

Many writers used the printed word to protest slavery:

Frederick Douglass
William Lloyd Garrison
Benjamin Lay, a Quaker
Jonathan Edwards, Connecticut theologian
Susan B. Anthony

The efforts to achieve real equality in the United States were also reflected in American writing. Different writers captured different elements of the struggle for civil rights. Though their perspectives on how to reach the goal of equality for all Americans sometimes differed, writers inspired people to see the struggle as an essential part of realizing and fulfilling the promises of America.

David Halberstam, who had been a reporter in Nashville at the time of the sit-ins by eight young black college students that initiated the protest movement that eventually led to the Civil Rights Act, wrote *The Children*, published in 1998 by Random House, for the purpose of reminding Americans of their courage, suffering, and achievements. Congressman John Lewis, Fifth District, Georgia, was one of those eight young men who has gone on to a life of public service. Halberstam records that when older black ministers tried to persuade these young people not to pursue their protest, John Lewis responded: "If not us, then who? If not now, then when?"

Some examples of literature of the period:

James Baldwin: *Blues for Mister Charlie*
Martin Luther King: *Where Do We Go from Here?*
Langston Hughes: *Fight for Freedom: The Story of the NAACP*
Eldridge Cleaver: *Soul on Ice*
Malcolm X: *The Autobiography of Malcolm X*
Leroi Jones: *Home*

Vietnam
An America that was already divided over the Civil Rights movement faced even greater divisions over the war in Vietnam. Those who were in favor of the war and who opposed withdrawal saw it as the major front in the war against communism. Those who opposed the war and who favored withdrawal of the troops believed that it would not serve to defeat communism and was a quagmire.

Though set in the last years of World War II, Catch-22 by Joseph Heller was a popular anti-war novel that became a successful movie of the time.

Authors Take Sides on Vietnam, edited by Cecil Woolf and John Bagguley, is a collection of essays by 168 well-known authors throughout the world. *Where is Vietnam?* edited by Walter Lowenfels consists of 92 poems about the war.

Many writers were publishing works for and against the war, but the genre that may have had the most impact was rock music. Bob Dylan was an example of the musicians of the time. His music represented the hippie aesthetic and brilliant, swirling colors and hallucinogenic imagery and created a style that came to be called psychedelic. Some other bands that originated during this time and became well-known for their psychedelic music, primarily about the Vietnam War in the early years, are the Grateful Dead, Jefferson Airplane, Big Brother, Sly and the Family Stone. In England, the movement attracted the Beatles and the Rolling Stones.

Immigration
This has been a popular topic for literature from the time of the Louisiana Purchase in 1804. The recent *Undaunted Courage* by Stephen E. Ambrose is ostensibly the autobiography of Meriwether Lewis but is actually a recounting of the Lewis and Clark expedition. Presented as a scientific expedition by President Jefferson, the expedition

was actually intended to provide maps and information for the opening up of the west. A well-known novel of the settling of the west by immigrants from other countries is *Giants in the Earth* by Ole Edvart Rolvaag, himself a descendant of immigrants.

John Steinbeck's *Cannery Row* and *Tortilla Flats* reflect the lives of Mexican migrants in California. Amy Tan's *The Joy Luck Club* deals with the problems faced by Chinese immigrants.

Skill 1.11 **Is knowledgeable about different literary genres and a wide variety of work from various time periods, cultures, and countries (including the United States)**

See also 1.10

A complete understanding of the long history of literature is impossible. Some major influences on modern writing stand out, however. Different regions of the world have had powerful impacts on literature around the world at different times. Writers from different literary traditions have, at different times, been at the vanguard of innovation in writing. Their ideas and styles have spread to different countries and regions regardless of language. While each of these may continue to have a powerful literary culture, their wider influence may wax and wane over time.

The **epic** is one of the major forms of narrative literature, which chronologically retells the life of a mythological person or group of persons. This genre has become uncommon since the early 20th century, although the term has been used to define certain extraordinarily long prose works and films. Usually a large number of characters, multiple settings, and a long span of time are features that lead to its designation as an epic. This change in the use of this term might indicate that some prose works of the past might be called epics although they were not composed or originally understood as such.

The epic was a natural manifestation of oral poetic tradition in preliterate societies where the poetry was transmitted to the audience and from performer to performer by purely oral means. It was composed of short episodes, each of equal status, interest, and importance, which facilitated memorization. The poet recalls each episode and uses it to recreate the entire epic.

Some Ancient Epics:

The Iliad and the Odyssey, both ascribed to Homer
Lost Greek epics ascribed to the Cyclic poets:
Trojan War cycle
Theban Cycle
Argonautica by Apollonius of Rhodes
Mahabharata and Ramayana, Hindu mythologies

Aeneid by Virgil
Metamorphoses by Ovid
Argonautica by Gaius Valerius Flaccus
Some Medieval Epics (500-1500)
Beowulf (Anglo-Saxon mythology)
Bhagavata Purana (Sanskrit "Stories of the Lord")
Divina Commedia (The Divine Comedy) by Dante Alighieri
The Canterbury Tales by Geoffrey Chaucer
Alliterative Morte Arthure
Some Modern Epics (from 1500)
The Faerie Queene by Edmund Spenser (1596)
Paradise Lost by John Milton (1667)
Paradise Regained by John Milton (1671)
Prince Arthur by Richard Blackmore (1695)
King Arthur by Richard Blackmore (1697)
The Works of Ossian by James MacPherson (1765)
Hyperion by John Keats (1818)
Don Juan by George Gordon Byron, 6th Baron Byron (1824)

An ode is generally a long lyric poem and as a form or poetry or song has an extensive history. Though odes vary in topic and occasionally structure, three forms have risen to the foreground in literature. These three forms are identifiable by their different features, and all odes carry characteristics that line up somewhere among the three. They may contain parts from one form and pieces from another, but this is generally true. The two best-known and best-established ode forms are the Pindaric and the Horatian odes of the Greek and Roman traditions respectively.

Named after a 5th century B.C. Greek poet Pindar, the Pindaric ode consists of a triadic structure, which emulates the musical movement of the early Greek chorus. Though infrequently attempted in English, some examples do exist. The Roman poet Horace is credited for the Horatian form, which typically has equal-length stanzas with the same rhyme scheme and meter. The Horatian ode, unlike the Pindaric ode, also has a tendency to be personal rather than formal.

Pastoral odes differ from others mostly in subject matter. "Pastoral" designates a literary work that has to do with the lives of shepherds or rural life and usually draws a contrast between the innocence and serenity of the simple life and the discomforts and corruptions of the city and especially court life. The poet's moral, social, and literary views are usually expressed.

In John Keats' short career, his writing shifted from the popular sonnet form to the older form of the ode toward the end of his life. His "Ode on a Grecian Urn," which is about a piece of pottery, is a twist on the pastoral theme. He focuses on the natural scene that is pictured on the urn. Instead of a concern with the disturbing forces of the world as with most pastoral works, he uses the sculptured panel on the urn as a sort of "frozen pastoral" and makes his statement about what is valuable and real.

Some Pastoral Odes:

"Intimations of Immortality" by William Wordsworth
"Ode to a Nightingale" by John Keats
"Ode to Psyche" by John Keats
"Ode to the West Wind" by Percy Bysshe Shelley

The Upanishads are Hindu treatises that deal with broad philosophic problems. The term means "to sit down near" and implies sitting at the feet of a teacher. There are approximately 108 that record views of many teachers over a number of years.

Read chronologically, they exhibit a development toward the concept of a single supreme being and suggest ultimate reunion with it. Of special philosophical concern is the nature of reality.

Their appearance in Europe in the early 19th century captured the interest of philosophers, particularly in Germany. The work of Arthur Schopenhauer is reflective of the Upanishads.

Virgil (Publius Vergilius Maro, later called Virgilius and known in English as Virgil or Vergil, October 15, 70 BC/September 21, 19BC) was a Latin poet, author of the Eclogues, the Georgics, and the Aeneid. The Aeneid is a poem of twelve books that became the Roman Empire's national epic.

Virgil has had a strong influence on English literature. Edmund Spenser's The Faerie Queene reflects that influence. It was also the model for John Milton's Paradise Lost, not only in structure but also in style and diction. The Augustan poets considered Virgil's poetry the ultimate perfection of form and ethical content. He was not so popular during the Romantic period, but Victorians such as Matthew Arnold and Alfred, Lord Tennyson rediscovered Virgil and were influenced by the sensitivity and pathos that had not been so appealing to the Romantics.

Germany
German poet and playwright Friedrich von Schiller is best known for his history plays William Tell and The Maid of Orleans. He is a leading literary figure in Germany's Golden Age of Literature. Also from Germany, Rainer Maria Rilke, the great lyric poet, is one of the poets of the unconscious, or stream of consciousness. Germany also has given the world Herman Hesse, (*Siddhartha*), Gunter Grass (*The Tin Drum*), and perhaps the best known of all German writers, Johann Wolfgang von Goethe (*Faust*).

Scandinavia has encouraged the work of Hans Christian Andersen in Denmark, who advanced the fairy tale genre with such wistful tales as "The Little Mermaid" and "Thumbelina." The social commentary of Henrik Ibsen in Norway startled the world of drama with such issues as feminism (The Doll's House and Hedda Gabler) and the effects of sexually transmitted diseases (The Wild Duck and Ghosts). Sweden's Selma Lagerlof is the first woman to ever win the Nobel Prize for literature. Her novels include

Gosta Berling's Saga and the world-renowned *The Wonderful Adventures of Nils*, a children's work.

Russia
Russian literature is vast and monumental. Who has not heard of Fyodor Dostoevsky's *Crime and Punishment* or *The Brothers Karamazov*, or Count Leo Tolstoy's *War and Peace*? These are examples of psychological realism. Dostoevsky's influence on modern writers cannot be overly stressed. Tolstoy's *War and Peace* is the sweeping account of the invasion of Russia and Napoleon's taking of Moscow, abandoned by the Russians. This novel is called the national novel of Russia. To further advance Tolstoy's greatness: his ability to create believable, unforgettable female characters, especially Natasha in *War and Peace* and the heroine of *Anna Karenina*. Pushkin is famous for great short stories; Anton Chekhov for drama, (*Uncle Vanya, The Three Sisters, The Cherry Orchard*); Yevtushenko for poetry (*Babi Yar*).

France
France has a multifaceted canon of great literature that is universal in scope, almost always championing some social cause: the poignant short stories of Guy de Maupassant; the fantastic poetry of Charles Baudelaire (*Fleurs du Mal*); and the groundbreaking lyrical poetry of Rimbaud and Verlaine. France's drama category is represented best with Rostand's Cyrano de Bergerac, and the neo-classical dramas of Racine and Corneille (El Cid). The great French novelists include Andre Gide, Honore de Balzac (*Cousin Bette*), Stendel (*The Red and the Black*), the father/son duo of Alexandre Dumas (*The Three Musketeers* and *The Man in the Iron Mask.*

Victor Hugo is the Charles Dickens of French literature, having penned the masterpieces, *The Hunchback of Notre Dame* and the French national novel, *Les Miserables*. The stream of consciousness of Proust's *Remembrance of Things Past*, and the Absurdist theatre of Eugene Ionesco (*The Rhinoceros*) attest to the groundbreaking genius of the French writers.

Spain
Spain's great writers include Miguel de Cervantes (*Don Quixote*) and Juan Ramon Jimenez. The anonymous national epic *El Cid* has been translated into many languages.

Italy
Italy's great writers include Virgil, who wrote the great epic, *The Aeneid*; Giovanni Boccaccio (*The Decameron*); and Dante Alighieri (*The Divine Comedy*).

Ancient Greece
Greece will always be foremost in literary assessments for Homer's epics, *The Iliad* and *The Odyssey*. No one, except Shakespeare, is more often cited. Add to these the works of Plato and Aristotle for philosophy; the dramatists Aeschylus, Euripides, and Sophocles for tragedy, and Aristophanes for comedy. Greece is one of the cradles not only of democracy, but of literature as well.

East Asia

The classical Age of Japanese literary achievement includes the father Kiyotsugu Kanami and the son Motokiyo Zeami who developed the theatrical experience known as No drama to its highest aesthetic degree. The son is said to have authored over 200 plays, of which 100 still are extant.

Katai Tayama (*The Quilt*) is touted as the father of the genre known as the Japanese confessional novel. He also wrote in the "ism" of naturalism. His works are definitely not for the squeamish.

The "slice of life" psychological writings of Ryunosuke Akutagawa gained him acclaim in the western world. His short stories, especially "Rashomon" and "In a Grove," are greatly praised for style as well as content.

China, too, has a long, rich literary tradition. Li Po, the T'ang dynasty poet from the Chinese Golden Age, revealed his interest in folklore by preserving the folk songs and mythology of China. Po further enables his reader to enter into the Chinese philosophy of Taoism and to know this feeling against expansionism during the T'ang dynastic rule. Back to the T'ang dynasty, which was one of great diversity in the arts, the Chinese version of a short story was created with the help of Jiang Fang. His themes often express love between a man and a woman.

Central American/Caribbean Literature

The Caribbean and Central America encompass a vast area and cultures that reflect oppression and colonialism by England, Spain, Portugal, France, and The Netherlands. The Caribbean writers include Samuel Selvon from Trinidad and Armando Valladares of Cuba. Central American authors include dramatist Carlos Solorzano, from Guatemala, whose plays include *Dona Beatriz, The Hapless, The Magician*, and *The Hands of God*.

South American Literature

Chilean Gabriela Mistral was the first Latin American writer to win the Nobel Prize for literature. She is best known for her collections of poetry, *Desolation and Feeling*. Chile was also home to Pablo Neruda, who, in 1971, also won the Nobel Prize for literature for his poetry. His twenty-nine volumes of poetry have been translated into more than 60 languages, attesting to his universal appeal. *Twenty Love Poems* and *Song of Despair* are justly famous. Isabel Allende carries on the Chilean literary standards with her acclaimed novel, *House of Spirits*. Argentine Jorge Luis Borges is considered by many literary critics to be the most important writer of his century from South America. His collections of short stories, *Ficciones*, brought him universal recognition. Also from Argentina, Silvina Ocampo, a collaborator with Borges on a collection of poetry, is famed for her poetry and short story collections, which include *The Fury* and *The Days of the Night*. In the works of Gabriel García Márquez, the world became familiar with magic realism and his work went on to influence generations of writers in Latin America and beyond.

Russian Literature

Boris Pasternak won the Nobel Prize (*Dr. Zhivago*). Aleksandr Solzhenitsyn (*The Gulag Archipelago)* is only recently back in Russia after years of exile in Vermont. Ilya Varshavsky, who creates fictional societies that are dystopias- or the opposite of utopias- and represents the genre of science fiction.

French Literature

French literature is defined by the **existentialism** of Jean-Paul Sartre (*No Exit, The Flies, Nausea*), Andre Malraux, (*The Fall*), and Albert Camus (*The Stranger, The Plague*), the recipient of the 1957 Nobel Prize for literature. Feminist writings include those of Sidonie-Gabrielle Colette, known for her short stories and novels, as well as Simone de Beauvoir.

Slavic Nations

Austrian writer Franz Kafka (*The Metamorphosis, The Trial*, and *The Castle*) is considered by many to be the literary voice of the first-half of the twentieth century. The poet Vaclav Havel represents the Czech Republic. Slovakia has dramatist Karel Capek (R.U.R.) and Romania is represented by Elie Wiesel (*Night*), a Nobel Prize winner.

Asia

Asia has many modern writers who are being translated for the western reading public. India's Krishan Chandar has authored more than 300 stories. Rabindranath Tagore won the Nobel Prize for literature in 1913 (*Song Offerings*). R. K. Narayan, India's most famous writer (*The Guide*), is interested in mythology and legends of India. Santha Rama Rau's work *Gifts of Passage* is her true story of life in a British school where she tries to preserve her Indian culture and traditional home.

Revered as Japan's most famous female author, Fumiko Hayashi (*Drifting Clouds*) by the time of her death had written more than 270 literary works.

In 1968 the Nobel Prize for literature was awarded to Yasunari Kawabata (*The Sound of the Mountain, The Snow Country*) considered to be his masterpieces. His Palm-of-the-Hand Stories take the essentials of Haiku poetry and transform them into the short story genre.

Modern feminist and political concerns are written eloquently by Ting Ling, who used the pseudonym Chiang Ping-Chih. Her stories reflect her concerns about social injustice and her commitment to the women's movement.

North American Literature

North American literature is divided between the United States, Canada, and Mexico. Canadian writers of note include Margaret Atwood, (*The Handmaid's Tale)*; Alice Munro, a remarkable short story writer; Rohinton Mistry and Joseph Boyden. Mexican writers include 1990 Nobel Prize winning poet, Octavio Paz, (*The Labyrinth of Solitude*) feminist Rosario Castellanos (*The Nine Guardians*), and Carlos Fuentes (*Christopher Unborn, The Death of Artemio Cruz*).

Africa

African literary greats include South Africans Nadine Gordimer (Nobel Prize for literature) and Peter Abrahams (*Tell Freedom: Memories of Africa*), an autobiography of life in Johannesburg. Chinua Achebe (*Things Fall Apart*) and the poet, Wole Soyinka, hail from Nigeria. Mark Mathabane wrote an autobiography, *Kaffir Boy,* about growing up in South Africa. Egyptian writer, Naguib Mahfouz, and Doris Lessing from Zimbabwe, write about race relations in their respective countries. Because of her radical politics, Lessing was banned from her homeland and the Union of South Africa, as was Alan Paton whose seemingly simple story, *Cry, the Beloved Country*, helped highlight the injustice of apartheid to the rest of the world.

Great Britain has had a large influence on American literary traditions. With a common language and its role as colonial 'parent' to the United States, Great Britain influenced early American writers both in terms of style and theme. Later, as the country sought to establish itself as an independent country, the fight for freedom from Great Britain inspired some of America's great early thinkers and writers. Later, as close allies the two countries shared many of the same experiences (wars, industrialization, an increasingly diverse society) that affected both countries' writers.

The following chart documents some of the milestones in British literature.

Author	Time Period	Significant Works & Contributions
Unknown	~700-1000 AD	Old English epic poem from the Anglo-Saxon period; the exact date is unknown, and the author is also a mystery; arguably the oldest poem ever written in Old English "Beowulf"
The Gawain poet / Unknown	14th Century	Poems written in Middle English; author unknown; *Pearl* *Sir Gawain and the Green Knight*
Geoffrey Chaucer	15th Century	Poet; known as the "Father of English literature"; arguably the best poet of the Middle Ages *The Canterbury Tales*
Sir Thomas Malory	15th Century	Knight; author of the first prose piece in English *Le Morte d'Arthur*

| William Shakespeare | 17th Century | Arguably the best poet and dramatist of all time; known for wit and tragedy

Sonnets
Hamlet
Romeo and Juliet
A Midsummer Night's Dream |
|---|---|---|
| John Donne | 17th Century | Poet; known for love poems, religious poems, and sonnets

"An Anatomy of the World" |
| John Milton | 17th Century | Poet; best known for writing in blank verse

Paradise Lost |
| Samuel Johnson | 18th Century | Poet; essayist; literary critic; known for being a devout Anglican; influencer of Modern English

A Dictionary of the English Language |
| Alexander Pope | 18th Century | Poet; known for satirical writing style

Essay on Criticism
The Rape of the Lock |
| Jonathan Swift | 18th Century | Poet; essayist; Anglo-Irish; known as master of satire

Gulliver's Travels |
| William Blake | 19th Century | Poet; contributor to the Romantic Age

Songs of Innocence
Milton |
| William Wordsworth | 19th Century | Poet; leader of the Romantic Movement

Lyrical Ballads |

Samuel Taylor Coleridge	19th Century	Poet; leader of the Romantic Movement *The Rime of the Ancient Mariner*
Jane Austen	19th Century	Best known for writing about women's roles in affluent English communities *Sense and Sensibility* *Pride and Prejudice*
Percy Shelley	19th Century	Romantic poet; husband of Mary Shelley; known for radical content *Ode to the West Wind*
Mary Wollstonecraft	18th Century	Women's rights activist; feminist *A Vindication of the Rights of Woman*
Lord Byron	19th Century	Poet; leader of the Romantic Movement *Don Juan*
John Keats	19th Century	Romantic poet; known for imagery and odes "Ode to a Nightingale"

The reign of Elizabeth I ushered in a renaissance that led to the end of the medieval age. It was a very fertile literary period. The exploration of the new world expanded the vision of all levels of the social order from royalty to peasant, and the rejection of Catholicism by many in favor of a Christianity of their own opened up whole new vistas to thought and daily life. The manufacture of cloth increased, driving many people from the countryside into the cities, while the population of London exploded, creating a metropolitan business center. William Caxton brought printing to England in the 1470s and literacy increased from 30% in the 15th century to over 60% by 1530. These seem dramatic changes, and they were, but they were occurring gradually.

The Italian Renaissance had a great influence on the Renaissance in England, and early in the 16th century, most written works were in Latin. It was assumed that a learned person must express his thoughts in that language. However, there began to emerge a determination that vernacular English was valuable in writing, and it began to be defended. Elizabeth's tutor, Roger Ascham, for example, wrote in English.

Luther's theses in 1517 brought on the Reformation and eventually the breakup of western Christendom. Once the Church's monolithic role in society was broken, the secularization of society gradually followed. It also led, in many European countries, to the establishment of the king or queen as the head of this new/old church. This also brought about a new feeling that being religious was also being patriotic and promoted nationalism.

The ascension of Elizabeth to the throne also followed a very turbulent period regarding succession, and she ruled for 45 peaceful years, which allowed arts and literature to flourish.

Elizabeth happened to have very shrewd political instincts. She identified with her country as no previous ruler had and that in itself brought on a period of intense nationalism. She was a symbol of Englishness. The defeat of the Spanish Armada in 1588 was the direct result of the strong support she had from her own nation.

Drama was the principal form of literature in this age. Religious plays had been a part of the life of England for a long time, particularly the courtly life. But in the Elizabethan age, they became more and more secular and were created primarily for courtly entertainment. By the '60s, Latin drama, particularly the tragedies of Seneca and the comedies of Plautus and Terence began to wield an influence in England. Courtyards of inns became favorite places for the presentation of plays, but in 1576, the Earl of Leicester's men constructed their own building outside the city and called it The Theatre. Other theatres followed. Each had its own repertory company, and performances were for profit but also for the queen and her court. It is said that Shakespeare wrote *The Merry Wives of Windsor* at the specific command of the queen, who liked Falstaff and wanted to see him in love. It was also for the courtly audience that poetry was introduced into drama.

Shakespeare and Marlowe dominated the late 1500s, and at the turn of the century, only a few years before Elizabeth's death, Ben Jonson began writing his series of satirical comedies. Court favor was notoriously precarious and depended on the whims of the queen and others. Much of the satire of the period reflects the disappointment of writers like Edmund Spenser and John Lyly and the superficiality and treachery of the court atmosphere. "A thousand hopes, but all nothing," wrote Lyly, "a hundred promises, but yet nothing."

However, not all literature from the period was dictated by the court. The middle classes were developing and had their own style. Thomas Heywood and Thomas Deloney catered to bourgeois tastes.

Greene had sixteen different patrons from seventeen books whereas Shakespeare had a satisfactory relationship with the Earl of Southampton and didn't need to seek other support. Publishers would also sometimes pay for a manuscript, which they would then own. Unfortunately, if the manuscript did not meet approval with all who could condemn it—the court, the religious leaders, prominent citizens—it was the author who was culpable. Very few became as comfortable as Shakespeare did. His success was not only in writing, however, but also from his business acumen.

Writing was seen more as a craft than as an art in this period. There was not great conflict between art and nature, little distinction between literature, sports of the field, or the arts of the kitchen.

Balance and control were important in the England of this day; this is reflected in the writing, the poetry in particular. The sestina, a form in which the last words of each line in the first stanza are repeated in a different order in each of the following stanzas, became very popular. Verse forms range from the extremely simple four-line ballad stanza through the rather complicated form of the sonnet to the elaborate and beautiful eighteen-line stanza of Spenser's Epithalamion.

Sonnets were called "quatorzains." The term "sonnet" was used loosely for any short poem. Quatorzains are fourteen-line poems in iambic pentameter with elaborate rhyme schemes. However, Chaucer's seven-line rhyme royal stanza also survived in the 16th century. Shakespeare used it in "The Rape of Lucrece", for example. An innovation was Spenser's nine-line stanza, called the Spenserian stanza, as used in "The Faerie Queene".

As to themes, some of the darkness of the previous period can still be seen in some Elizabethan literature, like for example in Shakespeare's *Richard II*. At the same time, a spirit of joy, gaiety, innocence, and lightheartedness can be seen in much of the most popular literature, and pastoral themes became popular. The theme of the burning desire for conquest and achievement was also significant in Elizabethan thought.

Some important writers of the Elizabethan Age:

Sir Thomas More (1478-1535)
Sir Thomas Wyatt the Elder (1503-1542)
Edmund Spenser (1552-1599)
Sir Walter Raleigh (1552-1618)
Sir Philip Sidney (1554-1586)
John Lyly (1554-1606)
George Peele (1556-1596)
Christopher Marlowe (1564-1593)
William Shakespeare (1564-1616)

The Industrial Revolution in England began with the development of the steam engine. However, the steam engine was only one component of the major technological, socioeconomic, and cultural innovations of the early 19th century that began in Britain and spread throughout the world. An economy based on manual labor was replaced by one dominated by industry and the manufacture of machinery. The textile industries also underwent very rapid growth and change. Canals were being built, roads were improving, and railways were being constructed.

Steam power (fueled primarily by coal) and powered machinery (primarily in the manufacture of textiles) drove the remarkable amplification of production capacity. All-metal machine tools were developed by 1820 making it possible to produce more machines.

The date of the Industrial Revolution varies according to how it is viewed. Some say that it began in the 1780s and wasn't fully perceived until the 1830s or 1840s. Others maintain that the beginning was earlier, about 1760, and began to manifest visible changes by 1830. The effects spread through Western Europe and North America throughout the 19th century, eventually affecting all major countries of the world. The impact on society has been compared to the period when agriculture began to develop and the nomadic lifestyle was abandoned.

The first Industrial Revolution was followed immediately by the Second Industrial Revolution around 1850, when the progress in technology and world economy gained momentum with the introduction of steam-powered ships and railways and eventually the internal combustion engine and electrical power generation.

In terms of what was going on socially, the most noticeable effect was the development of a middle class of industrialists and businessmen and a decline in the landed class of nobility and gentry. While working people had more opportunities for employment in the new mills and factories, working conditions were often less than desirable. Exploiting children for labor wasn't new—it had always existed—but it was more apparent and perhaps more egregious as the need for cheap labor increased. In England, laws regarding employment of children began to be developed in 1833. Another effect of industrialization was the enormous shift from hand-produced goods to machine-produced ones and the loss of jobs among weavers and others. This resulted in violence against the factories and machinery beginning in about 1811.

Eventually, the British government took measures to protect industry. Another effect was the organization of labor. Because laborers were now working together in factories, mines, and mills, they were better able to organize to gain advantages they felt they deserved.

Conditions were bad enough in these workplaces that the energy to bring about change was significant and eventually trade unions emerged. Laborers quickly learned to use the weapon of the strike to get what they wanted. The strikes were often violent and, while the managers usually gave in to most of the demands made by strikers, the animosity between management and labor was endemic.

The mass migration of rural families into urban areas also resulted in poor living conditions, long work hours, extensive use of children for labor, and a polluted atmosphere.

Another effect of industrialization of society was an increased division of labor. One person now often stayed at home and looked after the home and family and the other went off to work, a very different configuration from an agriculture-based economy where the entire family was usually involved in making a living. Eventually, gender roles began to be defined by the new configuration of labor in this new world order.

The application of industrial processes to printing brought about a great expansion in newspaper and popular book publishing. This, in turn, was followed by rapid increases in literacy and eventually because of demands from mass political participation.

Romanticism, the literary, intellectual, and artistic movement that occurred along with the Industrial Movement was actually a response to the increasing mechanization of society, an artistic hostility to what was taking over the world. Romanticism stressed the importance of nature in art and language in contrast to the monstrous machines and factories. Blake called them the "dark, satanic mills" in his poem "And Did Those Feet in Ancient Time."

This movement followed on the heels of the Enlightenment period and was, at least in part, a reaction to the aristocratic and political norms of the previous period. Romanticism is sometimes called the Counter-Enlightenment. It stressed strong emotion, made individual imagination the critical authority, and overturned previous social conventions. Nature was important to the Romanticists and it elevated the achievements of misunderstood heroic individuals and artists who participated in altering society.

Some British/Scottish Romantic Writers:

William Blake
Lord George Gordon Byron
Samuel Taylor Coleridge
John Keats
Walter Scott
Percy Bysshe Shelley
William Wordsworth

Other Romantic Writers:

E. T. A. Hoffmann (German)
Ludwig Tieck (German)
Johann Wolfgang von Goethe (German)
Victor Hugo (French)
Alexander Pushkin (Russian)

James Fenimore Cooper (American)
Emily Dickinson (American)
Washington Irving (American)
Henry Wadsworth Longfellow (American)
Edgar Allan Poe (American)

World War I, also known as The First World War, the Great War, and The War to End All Wars, raged from July 1914 to the final Armistice on November 11, 1918. It was a world conflict between the Allied Powers led by Great Britain, France, Russia, and the United States (after 1917) and The Central Powers, led by the German Empire, the Austro-Hungarian Empire, and the Ottoman Empire. It brought down four great empires: The Austro-Hungarian, German, Ottoman, and Russian. It reconfigured European and Middle Eastern maps.

More than nine million soldiers died on the various battlefields and nearly that many more in the participating countries' home fronts as a result of food shortages and genocide committed under the cover of various civil wars and internal conflicts. However, even more people died of the worldwide influenza outbreak at the end of the war and shortly after than died in the hostilities. The unsanitary conditions engendered by the war, severe overcrowding in barracks, wartime propaganda interfering with public health warnings, and migration of so many soldiers around the world, contributed to the outbreak becoming a pandemic.

The experiences of the war led to a collective national trauma afterwards for all the participating countries. The optimism of the 1900s was entirely gone and those who fought in the war became what are known as "the Lost Generation" because they never fully recovered from their experiences. For the next few years, memorials continued to be erected in thousands of European villages and towns.

Certainly a sense of disillusionment and cynicism became pronounced, and nihilism became popular. The world had never before witnessed such devastation, and the depiction in newspapers and on movie screens made the horrors more personal.

War has always spawned creative bursts, and this one was no exception. Poetry, stories, and movies proliferated. In fact, it's still a fertile subject for art of all kinds, particularly literature and movies. In 2006, a young director by the name of Paul Gross created, directed, and starred in Passchendaele, based on the stories told him by his grandfather, who was haunted all his life by his killing of a young German soldier in this War to End All Wars.

Some literature based on World War I:

"The Soldier," poem by Rupert Brooke
Goodbye to All That, autobiography by Robert Graves
"Anthem for Doomed Youth" and "Strange Meeting," poems by Wilfred Owen, published posthumously by Siegfried Sassoon in 1918

"In Flanders Fields," poem by John McCrae
Three Soldiers, novel by John Dos Passos
Journey's End, play by R. C. Sherriff
All Quiet on the Western Front, novel by Erich Maria Remarque
Death of a Hero, novel by Richard Aldington
A Farewell to Arms, novel by Ernest Hemingway
Memoirs of an Infantry Officer, novel by Siegfried Sassoon

The dissolution of the British Empire, the most extensive empire in world history and for a time the foremost global power, began in 1867 with its transformation into the modern Commonwealth. Dominion status was granted to the self-governing colonies of Canada in 1867, to Australia in 1902, to New Zealand in 1907, to Newfoundland in 1907, and to the newly-created Union of South Africa in 1910.

Although the Allies won the war and Britain's rule expanded into new areas, the heavy costs of the war made it less and less feasible to maintain the vast empire. Economic losses as well as human losses put increasing pressure on the Empire to give up its far-flung imperial posts in Asia and the African colonies. At the same time, nationalist sentiment was growing in both old and new Imperial territories. It was fueled partly by their troops' contributions to the war and the anger of many non-white ex-servicemen at the racial discrimination they had encountered during their service.

The rise of anti-colonial nationalist movements in the subject territories and the changing economic situation of the world in the first half of the 20th century challenged an imperial power now increasingly preoccupied with issues nearer home. The Empire's end began with the onset of the Second World War when a deal was reached between the British government and the Indian independence movement, whereby India would cooperate and remain loyal during the war but afterwards they would be granted independence. Following India's lead, nearly all of the other colonies would become independent over the next two decades.

The changing global status of Great Britain was reflected in its literature. Furthermore, immigration to Britain changed the demographics of society, bringing new voices, new experiences, and new styles into the long tradition of British writing.

Skill 1.12 Recognizes and interprets different points of view from literary works from countries other than the United States

See 1.11

Throughout history, the politics of each culture are reflected in its literature. Developments in technology, philosophy, and language can be charted through familiarity with each culture's body of work. An understanding of major developments in world literature provides insights on the different perspectives and viewpoints of major events both in history and in modern society. At times of major technological innovation, for example, literature can both reflect anxiety about the changes as well as excitement about what the future holds. Major events such as colonization and wars often highlight contrasting perspectives and can be glimpsed through literature from different countries and cultures.

Chinua Achebe's *Things Fall Apart* uses literature to examine colonialism from the point of a Nigerian village and, in particular, Okonkwo, a successful and respected resident of the fictional town of Umuofia. In this 1958 novel, the reader sees the upending of a way of life because of the colonizing forces of Great Britain. Values, beliefs, and power structures are swept away and replaced by a new way – a way that does not value traditions or the people who have built them.

Similarly, Canadian author Joseph Boyden's *The Orenda* depicts the destruction of the Huron way of life by the arrival of French colonists. The forces of religion, capitalism, disease, and local rivalries decimate the traditional order and end in the uprooting of the Huron nation. Rather than statistics about the effects of disease on populations and facts about the role of missions in colonization, Boyden's novel attempts to bring to life the perspectives and stories of the people affected. Though fiction, this is one of the great powers of fiction.

Both books are classic examples of the ways in which literature can bring to life a radically different view of the world than the one we are used to. Rather than the heroic stories of 'settling' the land or 'bringing civilization', the reader sees that there is another story to be told.

This ability to reveal another side of things is one of the great powers of literature. Many readers who would not likely explore history texts to find another analysis of historical events will see an entirely different viewpoint through literature. One benefit of being a reader in the 21st Century is greater likelihood of encountering literature from other countries and cultures. More works are translated and published in multiple countries, bringing new voices and perspectives.

A few well-known books from around the world (and the topics they give us insight about) include:

- *The Kite Runner* (modern history of Afghanistan)
- *How the Soldier Repairs the Gramophone* (Bosnian perspective on the Bosnian War)
- *In the Shadow of the Banyan* (a Cambodian's perspective on the Khmer Rouge)
- *Balzac and the Little Chinese Seamstress* (living through the Cultural Revolution)
- *Our Lady of the Assassins* (the drug conflict in Colombia from the perspective of a middle aged man who has recently returned home)
- *White Tiger* (wealth and poverty in India)

These works give us a different perspective on the issues and events we may see in the news media.

In many ways, literature can allow readers to 'pull back the curtain' and see the truth (or at least another side of things). Just as in *The Wizard of Oz* we often learn about one side of things – the greatness of certain individuals or events – and great writers often have the power to introduce us to look at things in a new light.

Skill 1.13 **Understands and recognizes how an author may draw on or be inspired by other works by other authors**

See 1.10, 1.11, and 1.12

Literature is a reflection of its time, but each author is influenced by the work of her/his predecessors. Modern writers, for example, still incorporate themes and ideas from early religious works. *Fifteen Dogs* by André Alexis examines the nature of what it means to be human, an age-old topic of philosophy, poetry, essay and fiction, by depicting the meddling of Hermes and Apollo.

The stories and language of Shakespeare have inspired generations of poets and novelists who have adopted elements of his style or reinterpreted and retold his stories. Chaucer and Plutarch, as well as the history, inspired Shakespeare. *Julius Caesar*, inspired by one of ancient Rome's most famous leaders, uses Caesar's rule as a vehicle for exploring themes of honor, loyalty, and patriotism. *Antony and Cleopatra*, another of his great tragedies, examines political intrigue while also brings to life a great love story.

Margaret Atwood has in turn retold Shakespeare's *The Tempest* as a prose novel in *Hag-Seed*. Her work was one in series by the Hogarth Shakespeare project which commissioned contemporary writers like Jeanette Winterson, Gillian Flynn, Tracy Chevalier, and Edward St. Aubyn have drawn inspiration from Shakespeare's plays to tell modern stories. Each author has found fodder for novels exploring contemporary issues in works from the 16th Century.

Jane Austen, whose novels examine and comment upon the society of the landed gentry in Britain at the end of the 18th Century, has inspired major retellings of her works. Joanna Trollope has tackled *Sense and Sensibility*, Val McDermid has written a new version of *Northanger Abbey,* and Curtis Sittenfeld has reworked *Pride and Prejudice*. That does not even include the zombie thriller *Pride and Prejudice and Zombies*. Each writer has seen in Austen's examinations of class and the role of women themes that resonate in modern literature.

These works are directly inspired reimaginings of important literary works by other authors. Far more are less directly connected but still clearly influenced. *Cold Mountain*, by Charles Frazier, is set during the American Civil War shares much in common with *The Odyssey*, Homer's epic poem likely written near the end of the 8th century B.C. C.S. Lewis drew inspiration from the Bible for *The Lion, the Witch, and the Wardrobe* and his other Narnia works.

The Bronte sisters were groundbreaking novelists in the 1840s and 1850s and their works went on to inspire generations of writers both in Britain and around the world. T.S. Eliot referred to a 'dead poets' society' to describe the ways in which every generation of poet changed and interpreted the traditions of the writers who came before. In his 1919 essay "Tradition and the Individual Talent" he writes of loyalty to tradition and the ways new writers recognize tradition but avoid repetition by building something new.

Upton Sinclair and Harriet Beecher Stowe influenced writing in different ways. They used their writing to shine a light on societal injustices and problems. This not only inspired political movements but also later generations of writers. The social responsibility of the writer can often give voice to the voiceless. Every social movement in modern American history has been reflected in (or been inspired by) literature.

James Joyce's *Ulysses* contains many parallels to the *Odyssey*. As a leader of the Modernist movement in twentieth century literature, his influence spread considerably. In his time and beyond, Joyce had an impact on such writers as:

- Samuel Beckett
- Jorge Luis Borges
- John Updike
- Salman Rushdie
- Joseph Campbell

William Faulkner influenced Gabriel García Márquez, the famed Colombian writer. His work in turn influenced whole generations of writers around the world. Hamid Ismailov, from Uzbekistan, notes that García Márquez inspired a whole generation of writers in the Soviet Union. The style and themes of his work spread far beyond his country, his region (Latin America), or even his language (Spanish). In short, no writing exists in a vacuum.

Given that literature so often deals with experiences shared by many people, it is not surprising that writers are influenced and inspired by those who come before them. These influences, both stylistic and thematic, wax and wane. Some influences are direct while others are subtle. What is inescapably true today is that the powerful spread of ideas and information means that the influence of good writing will spread far and wide. A broad understanding of literary traditions and of history helps us to understand the connections and relationships between great writers and their works.

A small selection of influential writers:

Author	Time Period	Significant Works & Contributions
Charles Dickens	19th Century	Fiction writer; arguably the best author of the Victorian Era *Oliver Twist*

		Great Expectations *A Tale of Two Cities*
Emily Brontë	19th Century	Teacher, poet, and novelist; contributor to the Victorian Era *Wuthering Heights*
Charlotte Brontë	19th Century	Oldest Brontë sister; novelist and poet; contributor to the Victorian Era *Jane Eyre*
Matthew Arnold	19th Century	Victorian poet; known for highly intellectual writing "Dover Beach"
William Butler Yeats	20th Century	Poet; Nobel Prize winner; arguably one of the best poets in the 20th Century; known for lyrical poetry; Protestant; Anglo-Irish *The Green Helmet and Other Poems*
James Joyce	20th Century	Irish novelist and poet; highly influential author in the 20th Century *Dubliners* *A Portrait of the Artist as a Young Man*
George Bernard Shaw	20th Century	Playwright; Anglo-Irish; Nobel Prize winner *Man and Superman* *Pygmalion*
Virginia Woolf	20th Century	Author and journalist; leader of Modernist Era *Mrs. Dalloway* *To the Lighthouse*

Dylan Thomas	20th Century	Welsh poet; known for erratic writing "Do not go gentle into that good night"
Doris Lessing	21st Century	Poet, novelist, and short story writer; Nobel Prize winner; feminist *The Golden Notebook*
Seamus Heaney	21st Century	Irish poet and playwright; Nobel Prize winner; known for describing the struggle of living in Northern Ireland as a Catholic *Wintering Out*

Skill 1.14   Sees the connection between modern literary work and works from other eras, religions, and cultures

See 1.10, 1.11, 1.12 and 1.13

In addition to the explanations in the skills noted above, this table contains some of the earliest key works that have continued to shape literary writing and are still read widely today. Even though some are religious texts, their influence extends beyond religious writing.

Author	Time Period	Significant Works & Contributions
Unknown	~1800-2000 B.C.	The Gilgamesh epic Epic poem about a heroic man created by gods
Unknown	~600-1500 B.C.	The Vedas Hindi poems, hymns, prayers, and religious stories sacred to the Vedic religion. *The Rig Veda* *Sama Veda* *Yajur Veda* *Atharva Veda*

Unknown	~300-600 B.C.	The Old Testament Collection of religious writings; first section of the Bible; sacred to Christians; originally written in Hebrew; Moses is assumed author
Unknown	~50-200 A.D.	The New Testament Collection of religious writings; second section of the Bible; sacred to Christians; originally written in Greek; eight wise men assumed authors
Muhammad	~600 C.E.	Qur'an Religious text of Islam; sacred to Muslim faith; written in Arabic; assumed author is Muhammad
Murasaki Shikibu	2nd Century	Novelist and poet from Japan; lady-in-waiting at the Imperial court during the Heian period. *The Tale of Genji*
Omar Khayyám	2nd Century	Iranian poet, mathematician, scholar, philosopher, and astronomer; greatly contributed to the Middle Ages; said to have written over one thousand poems *The Rubáiyát of Omar Khayyám*
Rumi	13th Century	Persian Sunni Muslim poet; Islamic scholar, theologian; arguably the greatest poet of mystic poetry *Maṭnawīye Ma'nawī*
Dante Alighieri	13th Century	Italian poet; contributor to the late Middle Ages; known for love poems *De vulgari eloquentia*

English Language Arts

COMPETENCY 2   READING INFORMATIONAL TEXTS

Skill 2.1   Analyzes the meaning of informational texts using evidence and examples

A written document can be expected to have a thesis—either expressed or derived. To discover the thesis, the reader must ask what point the writer intended to make. The writing can also be expected to be organized in some logical way and to contain additional points that support or establish that the thesis is valid. Writers must include and readers must be able to identify details and/or examples that will support the author's point. Analyzing this evidence is essential to determining the overall meaning of any informational text.

If the reader only needs to know the gist of a written document, skimming to identify important statements and key words to deduce the basic content and message of the document may be sufficient. If the reader needs a deep grasp of how the writer has achieved his or her purpose in the document, a careful reading to identify not only main ideas but also supporting evidence is necessary. This approach will help to reveal how the thesis is developed, resulting in a greater understanding of the author's purpose and method of development.

A more In-depth type of reading requires the reader to scrutinize each phrase and sentence, looking first for the thesis and then for the topic sentences in the paragraphs that develop the thesis, while at the same time, looking for connections such as transitional devices which provide clues to the direction the reasoning is taking. This type of reading also requires the reader to identify the differences between main ideas and specific details within paragraphs.

Informational texts often include many features that guide the reader in building meaning and understanding. Whether they are magazine articles, academic papers, textbooks, or nonfiction books each has elements that facilitate the reader's ability to find examples and evidence. Some of these text features include:

- Table of contents
- Infographics to display information and statistics
- Index
- Sidebars
- Definitions

Learning to use these features can make it easier to find information and to analyze texts.

Structurally oriented graphic organizers can help students identify and remember main ideas. For example, graphic organizers can help students identify cause and effect, compare and contrast, question and answer, and understanding general and temporal descriptions of information or events. Organizing notes in this way helps readers identify both the main points in the piece and the relevance of specific details used to elaborate on those points.

When the time comes to write about informational texts, these graphic organizers (and the habits of reading that they help build) support the use of evidence for analysis. The organizers are an important way of building understanding, and once an understanding of how to find information is established, most readers can engage in independent analysis.

Skill 2.2   Makes inferences based on evidence from the text

Readers must also be able to infer meaning that is not explicitly stated in a text. Ideas, opinions, and judgments are examples of elements that frequently implied in a text. A discerning reader is able to infer meaning from both what is omitted from and text and what is included in the text.

To draw inferences and make conclusions, a reader must use prior knowledge and apply it to the current situation. A conclusion or inference is never stated. You must rely on your common sense. An example of making inferences and drawing conclusions can be seen in the following fairly simple passage.

The Smith family waited patiently around carousel number 7 for their luggage to arrive. They were exhausted after their 5-hour trip and were anxious to get to their hotel. After about an hour, they realized that they no longer recognized any of the other passengers' faces. Mrs. Smith asked the person who appeared to be in charge if they were at the right carousel. The man replied, "Yes, this is it, but we finished unloading that baggage almost half an hour ago."

From the man's response we can infer that:

(A) The Smiths were ready to go to their hotel.
(B) The Smiths' luggage was lost.
(C) The man had their luggage.
(D) They were at the wrong carousel.

Since the Smiths were still waiting for their luggage, we know that they were not yet ready to go to their hotel. From the man's response, we know that they were not at the wrong carousel and that he did not have their luggage. Therefore, though not directly stated, it appears that their luggage was lost. Choice (B) is the correct answer.

There are often patterns to the types of incorrect inferences readers make. A fallacy is an error in reasoning and to recognize one, students will need to develop stronger analytical and critical thinking skills.

A common fallacy in reasoning is the post hoc ergo propter hoc ("after this, therefore because of this") or the false-cause fallacy. These occur in cause/effect reasoning, which may either go from cause to effect or effect to cause.

They happen when an inadequate cause is offered for a particular effect; when the possibility of more than one cause is ignored; and when a connection between a particular cause and a particular effect is not made.

An example of a post hoc: Our sales shot up thirty-five percent after we ran that television campaign; therefore the campaign caused the increase in sales.

It might have been a cause, of course, but more evidence is needed to prove it.

An example of an inadequate cause for a particular effect: An Iraqi truck driver reported that Saddam Hussein had nuclear weapons; therefore, Saddam Hussein is a threat to world security.

More causes are needed to prove the conclusion.

An example of ignoring the possibility of more than one possible cause: John Brown was caught out in a thunderstorm and his clothes were wet before he was rescued; therefore, he developed influenza the next day was because he got wet.

Being chilled may have played a role in the illness, but Brown would have had to contract the influenza virus before he came down with it, whether or not he had gotten wet.

An example of failing to make a connection between a particular cause and an effect assigned to it: Anna fell into a putrid pond on Saturday; on Monday she came down with polio; therefore, the pond caused the polio.

This, of course, is not acceptable unless the poliovirus is found in a sample of water from the pond. A connection must be proven.

Skill 2.3   Recognizes the central idea of informational texts

Successfully determining the main idea of a text is an essential component of reading comprehension. It is based on an understanding both of the organization of a text and on an understanding of the writer's purpose. Using text type characteristics can help readers quickly identify a text's purpose and intended audience. Taking a closer look at features and structures can help readers quickly identify a text's central idea. Being able to evaluate an informational text quickly to determine purpose, audience and main idea is an invaluable reading comprehension skill for research, debate, and discussion. Additionally, identifying these aspects of the text can help readers better understand future informational texts they read and while laying a foundation for writing informational texts.

News and magazine articles, for example, usually contain the central idea at the start. With academic articles, abstracts usually summarize the main point or findings included in the text in one or two paragraphs at the start.

Being able to recognize central ideas is also a key element in the research process. Even with good search queries, with innumerable sources to choose from, the reader may have to wade through many possible texts to find relevant information. Recognizing the main idea quickly saves time and moves the research and writing process along. One way to build this skill is to work on the ability to summarize texts. Paraphrasing is the art of rewording text. The goal is to maintain the original purpose of the statement while translating it into your own words. Your newly generated text must capture the essential meaning of the original succinctly. In this case it is valuable to concentrate on the meaning, not on the words. Do not change concept words, special terms, or proper names.

Another strategy for recognizing main idea involves using questions such as:

- Can I tell the main idea based on the title?
- Does the first paragraph introduce the main idea?
- What topic keeps coming up in the text?
- What details are related to the main idea?
- Are there examples that illustrate the main idea?

From these questions, building towards a summary can help in self-evaluating comprehension of the main idea.

When students are organized, study models help teach students to locate main ideas and supporting details, to recognize sequential order, to distinguish fact from opinion, and to determine cause/ effect relationships. One such model is the SQ3R method, a technique that enables students to learn the content of even large amounts of text (Survey, Question, Read, Recite, and Review Studying),

Teacher-guided activities that require students to organize and to summarize information based on the author's explicit intent are pertinent strategies in middle grades. Evaluation techniques include oral and written responses to standardized or teacher-made worksheets.

Summarizing in progressively shorter stages can help with finding the central idea and summarizing it. Starting first with a paragraph and eventually moving on to just one sentence forces the reader to zero in on the core meaning and essential message of a text. This can be done orally or in writing.

SQR3
Method

Skill 2. 4   Analyzes how an author develops an idea or event in an informational text

Just as students can learn to identify informational text types by their characteristics, they can learn to identify features and structures of those key texts. When they are able to do this, they can use their analysis of features and structures to better comprehend the text.

Some common features and structures of informational texts, particularly expository texts are headings, sub-headings, indexes, tables of contents, links to sources or more information or definitions (digital texts), etc. Another feature, particularly of modern news and magazine articles, is to start with an illustrative anecdote. The anecdote lays the groundwork or sets the stage for the rest of the article to explain the main idea using additional details or analysis.

Students can use these features to find the information they need. In addition, if students are aware that the structure of the text is cause and effect or a temporal sequence, it can help them better comprehend the key concepts they are learning. Even younger children can use these strategies to look at labels and diagrams to enhance comprehension and to read informational texts that are organized around alphabets and counting, i.e. *Ben Franklin: His Wit and Wisdom from A–Z.*

Even with literary non-fiction texts, the same strategies can be applied. If students need to skim read and know that the structure is narrative, they know that they are supposed to read from beginning to end and can focus on key words, key ideas and their response to the text; using different comprehension strategies than they would use for an expository text.

After identifying the main ideas in informational texts and paragraphs, readers need to analyze the reasoning and arguments. Readers must be able to connect the topics in paragraphs to the main idea and to be able to trace the reasoning of the argument or thesis. In addition, readers should look for evidence or examples to support these points.

Using textual features and structures to identify the central idea can help readers closely trace the evolution of that idea or thesis through arguments and evidence. Readers can use tools like graphic organizers and/or mind maps to record essential information so that they can evaluate the arguments and evidence to form their own opinions on the thesis.

It is essential that readers are able to analyze the relevance and importance of evidence and examples and to determine if there is enough of each to convincingly support the main idea of the informational text. Students can do this without checking for credibility - it is an important skill to do first. Does the main idea make sense? Do the reasons or arguments follow the main idea? Do the evidence or examples support the reasons? Graphic organizers, discussions with teachers and/or in small groups can greatly facilitate these types of skills so that students are able to do this more and more independently.

Skill 2.5   Is able to summarize an informational text

See also Skill 2.3 (particularly on how to practice summarizing informational texts)

Being able to summarize an informational text involves several important reading comprehension skills. The reader must be able to identify the main idea and also recognize the key information that supports it. With complex texts this can be a difficult process, but it is an essential part of comprehension. Sifting through large amounts of information and detail to focus only on the essential elements of a text is invaluable.

In debate, discussion, research and writing, we have to quickly synthesize information and present it in summary form. This often happens without the ability to refer to the text directly, so the reader must be able to accurately recall the core meaning and significance.

In doing research, the reader must be able to quickly summarize/synthesize the main idea of the text in order to determine relevance. Whether a text is important to the understanding of a topic or provides a new perspective on it is an essential skill. Determining whether a secondary source accurately summarizes a primary source is a part of the process for doing research successfully. Increasingly, because of digital tools and internet research, we have access to primary sources. Whereas in the past we often had to rely on someone else's interpretation of speeches, documents, and events, today we can compare them. Knowing if something is an accurate depiction can help us decide whether a source is worth considering.

If they don't, the reader may need to find a new secondary source, or even change their opinion or topic because their purpose or objective is not as clear.

Readers will also want to employ this skill when reading news so that if something doesn't make sense to them, they can do more research to find a credible source. Comparing and contrasting coverage of important events (both modern and historical) helps the reader to assess credibility and to interpret the author's point of view.

There are many strategies readers can use to determine the accuracy of a summary including comparing their notes (from a graphic organizer) to the summary in question. Readers can also summarize a text after they read it and compare/contrast that with the summary provided. Or, they can go backwards and read the summary first and then the article or primary source, using the same tools. It is essential to remember that these are reading strategies that should focus solely on the texts and not on other factors.

Skill 2.6   Discerns the meaning of key words and phrases in informational texts including figurative, connotative and technical meanings

In everyday language, we attach affective meanings to words unconsciously; we exercise more conscious control of informative connotations. In reading, one must come not only to grasp the definitions of words but also to become more conscious of the affective connotations and how we process these connotations. Terms like 'educational reform', for example, have very different connotations when used by different writers. Whereas one writer may use the term to advocate for charter schools, another writer may refer to a move towards standards-based grading.

Similarly, figurative language and technical language play a key role in determining meaning with informational texts. Though we often associate figurative language more with fiction and poetry, it also plays a role in many informational texts.

Figurative language (**see also 1.6**) may add an additional layer of meaning and/or help connect to a larger idea. The 'cloud that hung over the election campaign' can, for example, suggest that there was an element of dispute about the campaign or a hint of scandal that persisted throughout the course of the election cycle. Figurative language can sometimes provide us with a shorthand for understanding bigger ideas.

Technical language is often specific to a field of study, a profession, or an industry. It may use familiar words in unfamiliar ways or use entirely new words to refer to things related to that field. Domain or subject area specific texts often make extensive use of technical language, and the reader must be prepared to determine meaning through context or, if necessary, to look up key terms.

Even in reading daily news stories, we will find references to terminology from domains like economics (gross domestic product, producers price index), physics (dark matter, neutrino, quantum theory), technology (domain name, IP address, cryptography), and art (Neo-Classical, baroque, avant-garde). Many of these can be determined through context and/or previous experience, but one must also be ready to acknowledge that we need to seek outside information.

Understanding the way figurative language is used illuminates and informs the reader (and enlivens writing).

Skill 2.7   Examines how a writer uses key terms

See Skill 2.6

Skill 2.8   Analyzes the effectiveness of the structure an author uses to explain or support an argument

It is not just the word choices and phrasing that support the effectiveness and clarity of a text. Meaning is also supported through structure. The organization of ideas works hand in hand with the language choices of the author to support an argument or the explanation of information and ideas. Some text types come with clear structural explanations.

Standard essays in English, for example, are expected to start with a paragraph explaining the author's central idea or thesis. In subsequent paragraphs, the author is expected to support that idea with evidence and examples. If specific evidence is cited, there are clear expectations about how citation should be done. Finally, the author is supposed to close with a conclusion that reinforces his/her central idea while also tying the supporting evidence together.

In evaluating nonfiction writing, it's important to also evaluate its structure. We determine whether an author successfully articulated a point of view or explained key ideas in large part based on whether the writing 'fits' together. That is, we look to see whether the pieces fit together as a whole to create a clear explanation or argument.

Often we can assess whether a piece of writing is well organized by asking specific questions that are geared towards a particular mode of presentation. A sample of these questions follows:

- What is the central idea or questions?
- How is the central idea or question answered?
- Is the purpose of the writing clear?
- What evidence or examples does the writer use to answer the central question or to explain the central idea?
- Are there facts? Examples? Anecdotes? Quotes?

Often writers use comparison to articulate a point. In this case the reader looks to see whether the writer has provided enough information to show similarity (or highlighted enough differences to contrast multiple ideas). Organization of information and arguments is essential to successful nonfiction writing.

Skill 2.9   Can determine the author's point of view and purpose

Most texts are not entirely objective. News reporting, which in the strictest sense involves just reporting what happened, incorporates choices of language, of what is included, of what is excluded and of what is important. Two writers reporting on the same incident may highlight different events, different people, or use different language to describe something. These may be deliberate choices to provoke a reaction from the reader, or they may be unconscious choices. Good readers are aware of the factors that may shape or reveal an author's point of view and/or purpose.

The way in which something is written may also have to do with purpose. In addition to trying to explain the risks of climate change, for example, a writer may be trying to urge governments to take action to stop it. This purpose may shape the writer's language, highlighting the urgency of doing something sooner rather than later. Similarly, a writer may be trying to gain readers or followers on social media, leading to different word choices intended to grab a reader's attention. Understanding purpose is an important part of comprehension.

Determining point of view and purpose often has to do with distinguishing between fact and opinion. Facts are statements that are verifiable. Opinions are statements that must be supported in order to be accepted. Facts are used to support opinions. For example, "Jane is a bad girl" is an opinion. However, "Jane hit her sister with a baseball bat" is a fact upon which the opinion is based. Judgments are opinions—decisions or declarations based on observation or reasoning that express approval or disapproval. Facts report what has happened or exists and come from observation, measurement, or calculation. Facts can be tested and verified whereas opinions and judgments cannot. They can only be supported with facts.

Most statements cannot be so clearly distinguished. "I believe that Jane is a bad girl" is a fact. The speaker knows what he/she believes. However, it obviously includes a judgment that could be disputed by another person who might believe otherwise. Judgments are not usually so firm. They are, rather, plausible opinions that provoke thought or lead to factual development.

Fact vs. Opinion
Charts like the one below can be useful in distinguishing facts and opinions.

	Text Details & Direct Quotes From the Text	Explain How You Know the Details are Facts or Opinions
Facts		
Opinions		
http://www.greece.k12.ny.us/instruction/ela/6-12/Tools/factvsopinion.pdf		

Conclusions

Conclusions are drawn as a result of a line of reasoning. Whether inductive or deductive, a conclusion is an analysis of what the data means. Given all the facts, all the opinions, all the details, the reader can draw a conclusion.

With informative expository texts, evidence is essential in showing or proving something. The writer must include examples, citations, quotations, and facts that support an idea. Furthermore, the evidence must be organized in a way that the reader comes to the same conclusion as the writer. As readers, we quickly recognize when there seems to be a lack of information or evidence. As writers, we must learn to do the same thing.

Determining an author's point of view and/or purpose involves many of the same skills as those used in analyzing literature. The reader examines language, structure, and details to form an opinion and uses those features to support his/her analysis (if needed).

Skill 2.10 Recognizes how author's craft can contribute to the persuasiveness of an informational text

See also 1.8

Similar to fiction and poetry, an author's choices shape our understanding and reaction to the writing. Word choice, structure, and tone may provoke reactions of anger, of sympathy, or of pride (among others). We may feel moved to action or to contemplate the future by a piece of writing depending on how the elements the writer chooses to highlight. Authors may build an argument slowly by using evidence, or capture our attention a powerful anecdote. Some writers may appeal to logic while others appeal to emotion.

Skill 2.11 Analyzes different sources of information in different formats (visual, quantitative, etc.) to solve a problem or answer a question

Visuals are an effective and dynamic way to add meaning to a text. They can clarify meaning, emphasize important data, summarize points, and add visual appeal. More often, they are a supplement to the written text rather than standing independent. Learning how to interpret the data in various graphics is an important skill for students.

When children learn to read, they are also learning to interpret graphics. In an article on visual literacy development in young children, authors articulated a theory that children develop graphic concepts along with print concepts. Some of these basic concepts are summarized below.

Graphics can be used to identify or show:

Action:	Graphics can be used to show flow or interactions
Relevance/	Supporting ideas in written text
Extensions:	Providing additional information to readers
Importance:	Highlighting the most important information in a text
Intention:	Illustration with communicative purpose within a text (political cartoon)
Partiality:	Not everything written in the text is illustrated

Tables

Tables depict exact numbers and other data in rows and columns. Those that simply store descriptive information in a form available for general use are called repository tables. They usually contain primary data, which simply summarize raw data. They are not intended to analyze the data, so any analysis is left to the reader or user of the table. A good example of a repository table would be a report of birth statistics by the federal Health and Human Services Department. An analytical table, on the other hand, is constructed from some sort of analysis of primary or secondary data, possibly from a repository table or from the raw data itself. An example of an analytical table would be one that compares birth statistics in 1980 to birth statistics in 2005 for the country at large. It might also break the data down into comparisons by state.

Graphs

Graphs depict trends, movements, distributions, and cycles more readily than tables. While graphs can present statistics in a more interesting and comprehensible form than tables, they are less accurate. For this reason, the two will often be shown together.

Maps

While the most obvious use for maps is to locate places geographically, they can also show specific geographic features such as roads, mountains, and rivers. They can also show information according to geographic distribution such as population, housing, or manufacturing centers.

Illustrations

A wide range of illustrations, such as pictures, drawings, and diagrams, may be used to illuminate the text in a document. They also may be a part of a graphic layout designed to make the page more attractive.

Some possibilities for the analysis of data whether presented in tables, charts, graphs, maps, or other illustrations are as follow:

- Qualitative descriptions: Would drawing conclusions about the quality of a particular treatment or course of action be revealed by the illustration?
- Quantitative descriptions: How much do the results of one particular treatment or course of action differ from another one, and is that variation significant?
- Classification: Is worthwhile information derived from breaking the information down into classifications?

- Estimations: Is it possible to estimate future performance on the basis of the information in the illustration?
- Comparisons: Is it useful to make comparisons based on the data?
- Relationships. Are relationships between components revealed by the scrutiny of the data?
- Cause-and-effect relationships: Is it suggested by the data that there were cause-and-effect relationships that were not previously apparent?
- Mapping and modeling: If the data were mapped and a model drawn up, would the point of the document be demonstrated or refuted?

Questions to ask regarding an illustration: Why is it in this document? What was the writer's purpose in putting it in the document and why at this particular place? Does it make a point clearer? What implications are inherent in a table that shows birth statistics in all states or even in some selected states? What does that have to do with the point and purpose of this piece of writing? Is there adequate preparation in the text for the inclusion of the illustration? Does the illustration underscore or clarify any of the points made in the text? Is there a clear connection between the illustration and the subject matter of the text?

Skill 2.12 Assesses whether information is sufficient and relevant in determining whether an argument is valid

Effective argumentative discourse is based on the strengths of the writer's support. Using reliable and relevant facts, an argument can convince or motivate.

An argument is a generalization that is proven or supported with facts. If the facts are not accurate, the generalization remains unproven. Using inaccurate "facts" to support an argument is called a fallacy in reasoning.

Accuracy
Some factors to consider in judging whether the facts used to support an argument are accurate are as follows:

Are the facts current or are they out of date? For example, if the proposition "birth defects in babies born to drug-using mothers are increasing," then the data must include the latest that is available.

Another important factor to consider in judging the accuracy of a fact is its source. Where was the data obtained, and is that source reliable?

The calculations on which the facts are based may be unreliable. Before using a piece of derived information, can you repeat the results by making your own calculations?

Relevance

Even facts that are true and have a sharp impact on the argument may not be relevant to the case at hand. Health statistics from an entire state, for example, may have no relevance, or little relevance, to a particular county or zip code. Statistics from an entire country cannot be used to prove very much about a particular state or county.

An analogy can be useful in making a point, but the comparison must match up in all characteristics or it will not be relevant. Analogies should be used very carefully. It is often just as likely to destroy an argument, as it is to strengthen it.

Importance

The importance or significance of a fact may not strengthen an argument. For example, using the case of a single false conviction is likely not enough to convince people that an overhaul of the justice is necessary. Though the evidence may be true, it may not be important enough by itself to persuade a reader. They may achieve a positive reaction, but they will not prove that one solution is better than another. If enough cases were cited from a variety of geographical locations, the information might be significant.

Sufficiency

How much is enough? Generally speaking, in standard persuasive essay formats, three strong supporting facts are usually considered enough to establish the thesis of an argument. If those three examples are not specific to the writer's conclusion, however, they may still be insufficient. For example:

Conclusion: All green apples are sour.

Evidence 1) When I was a child, I bit into a green apple from my grandfather's orchard, and it was sour.

Evidence 2) I once bought green apples from a roadside vendor, and when I bit into one, it was sour.

Evidence 3) My grocery store had a sale on green Granny Smith apples last week, and I bought several, only to find that they were sour when I bit into one.

The fallacy in the above argument is that the sample was insufficient. A more exhaustive search of literature will probably turn up some green apples that are not sour.

Sometimes more than three arguments are too many. On the other hand, it's not unusual to hear public speakers, particularly politicians, who will cite a long litany of facts to support their positions.

Skill 2.13   Analyzes important U.S. historical and literary documents to determine theme, purpose and text features

See other skills from Competency 2

In analyzing historical and literary documents from another time period it may be more difficult to determine meaning. What we consider standard features of texts (organizational, linguistic, etc.) may have changed substantially over the years. Furthermore, references may be unfamiliar and language style quite different. Though the same skills are involved in analysis, greater care, research, and time may be necessary.

Key documents from U.S. that are important in the language arts classroom include:

- The Declaration of Independence
- The Constitution
- The Federalist Papers
- The Bill of Rights
- Washington's Farewell Address
- The Monroe Doctrine
- What to the Slave is the Fourth of July?
- Dred Scott v. Sandford
- Emancipation Proclamation
- The Gettysburg Address
- I Have a Dream
- Great Society speech

These documents are of course important in American history, but they also have great significance in literature. They have inspired writers, they have inspired social movements, and they have in many cases attempted to capture elements of what it means to be American.

Skill 2.14   Analyzes texts related to diverse cultures and viewpoints

See other skills from Competency 2

Analyzing texts from different cultures and viewpoints involves the same skills as outlined in the rest of Competency 2. The reader must, however, be cognizant that the topic is unfamiliar, that they are lacking background knowledge, and that they may not be as well-equipped to make judgments about relevance or accuracy. Further research or consultation may be necessary to successfully analyze and interpret texts in this situation.

COMPETENCY 3   WRITING ARGUMENTS

Skill 3.1   Is able to introduce a claim, demonstrate its significance, and make it stand out from alternate claims

A persuasive text can generally be described as a text that is constructed to make you do, think or want something. Depending on the purpose and the audience, writers choose the appropriate form of persuasive writing to get their points across. Sometimes the form and purpose of a persuasive composition is given to a writer, as in an ad writer or a student in a history class, in which case the writer identifies the audience for the writing and crafts the text to reach them.

Some forms of persuasive writing include: editorials, essays, speeches, letters, songs, poems, advertisements, personal opinion writing, etc.

The structure of a persuasive essay, regardless of length, is fairly consistent and expected by readers. Beginning with a thesis paragraph, the writer relays the main idea of the essay and introduces the topic. The next several paragraphs of the essay support the main idea, using examples that give credence to the main idea. At times, writers may use the compare-and-contrast organizational style that gives "counterpoints" at the end of the supporting paragraphs to show recognition of the opposite argument.

In other persuasive text such as speeches, the writer may take longer to express point of view, building slowly by laying the groundwork. Once the position is clear, however, the need to support the claim or arguments is the key to a successful speech.

A persuasive text has the general features of a claim with support and appeals to convince the reader. Appeals in persuasive texts can be emotional, logical, personal or stylistic or a combination of any or all of these. An analysis of a novel arguing for a certain interpretation would rely on logic and evidence. An editorial about freedom of the press might rely on a mix of emotional appeal and historical evidence to make a claim. The focus in a persuasive piece is trying to convince or persuade the reader, so knowing the audience is an essential aspect of an effective piece of writing.

Introduction and Main Idea or "Thesis" of the Essay

The first or topic paragraph that answers a question or expresses the writer's position, lays out an argument, and presents brief highlights of how the writer plans support for that argument. This first paragraph makes a claim (statement) and shows how the composition will support it. Typically, this paragraph should only be five or six sentences long - so from the very beginning, thoughts must be well-organized.

The most common introductory sentences (usually two at the beginning of this paragraph) begin to set the tone and topic for a reader. The writer defines the central idea from the start and then builds support for it. "Frankenstein was not a monster, but rather a representation of the ills in society" is an example of a strong main idea that could be supported by passages in Mary Shelley's book as well as other writings of that time. It clearly and plainly states what the reader will learn in the paper.

The best introductory paragraphs avoid three mistakes: First, they don't restate the question either directly or paraphrased. Next, they focus on the argument - not why the argument is being made. The "why" is all background that feeds the paper, but is NOT the paper. For the final 'mistake' to avoid, introductions do not include a quote or statement of what someone else has said. Introductions stay focused on what the writer's thoughts and ideas are while quotes make up part of the evidence for the writer's argument and should fall in the body paragraphs.

Skill 3.2   Can sequence claims, reasons and evidence

The sequencing of arguments in persuasive writing is important in constructing a logical, compelling claim. Though appeals to emotion can be powerful features of persuasive writing, the structure is expected to be logical and to methodically lay out the writer's reasoning. Without a strong structure, many arguments fall flat or are considered open to criticism.

A common framework involves three argument/reasons or pieces of evidence to support a claim. People are often accustomed to reading lists of three. When considering that studies have shown repeatedly that it takes a person six times to hear a message in order to believe it, this three-fold format makes sense. Each of the three support ideas has two sub-supporting prongs that uphold or illustrate the supporting idea - that makes six points to support your main idea.

Writers often include six or seven specific examples to support their central idea. Each then falls into a type of category. This gives three paragraphs in order to support the introductory thesis paragraph and each of these support paragraphs has two examples to support the topic of each paragraph. Each paragraph should go back to the thesis to address the central point, ensuring that there is support for the main idea (and not just restating it).

Continuing with the Frankenstein example, where the generalization of societal ills incorporated the supportive categories of boundaries, grotesqueness and secrecy/shame, the writer might include two points that helped create these categories:

> Point 1 - Boundaries
> > Sub-point A: isolation or alienation from society
> > Sub-point B: perspectives alter viewpoint(s)' interpretation
> Point 2 - Grotesqueness
> > Sub-point C: delusions of personal grandeur and lack of self-reflection
> > Sub-point D: personal assumptions based on appearance
> Point 3 - Secrecy/shame

Sub-point E: shame of rejection, which leads to revenge
Sub-point F: madness compels Victor to create his own reality

Use your knowledge of the book and the sub-points to determine the strongest one (the one you can write about the most easily and with the most confidence). You should shift the order of the list so that this identified strong point now is the last grouping. You may even reorder the sub-points within the point, to help ensure the final sub-point in each paragraph is the strongest. While your list may appear differently, your list may now appear as follows:

Skill 3.3   Develops claims and counterclaims thoroughly; provides evidence and points out the strengths and weaknesses of both

Another potential structure in persuasive writing involves point/counterpoint. Developing claims and counterclaims can be tricky and involves careful planning. The writer has to anticipate both sides of an argument and, eventually, how to refute one of them.

This structure can be written by alternating supporting points and counterpoints all by explaining all the reasons 'for' and then all the reasons 'against' (block all of one side of the argument and then block all of the other side of the argument) - ensuring that the strongest arguments, just as before, are incorporated at the end of the composition.

If, for example, the writer is comparing two people and how they performed their jobs - authors, politicians, characters or whomever - the block method is probably best suited for that persuasion. The author takes the points for each, but lists Author A with all of her/his qualities on the topics and then provides Author B with all of her/his qualities on the same points. In this way, the writer blocks the points one, two and three for each person being compared, and the transitions explain the differences in the second person's outline by using such phrases as "compared to Author A, Author B said..." or "unlike Author A, Author B thought it important to focus on..." to relate the blocks to each other.

Persuasive arguments should engage a reader to follow a train of thought to reach a conclusion, but these two methods take much more energy, focus and commitment on the part of the author. The Block method in this particular style results in a composition that appears "A, A and A whereas B, B and B yield to conclusion that [A or B] was..." and the effort must be focused on showing the differences on these pieces and how or why one is preferred or the other option. The Point/Counterpoint method requires that the writer keep the reader engaged and wanting to read further as the "argument ball" goes back and forth between support, and the final "shot" is the one that cinches support for the main idea. Once the support 'pieces' are completed, the writer moves to the final step of the essay.

In argument writing of this type, the writer concludes by demonstrating conclusively why one side of the argument is correct. One side's evidence should clearly be more convincing than the other, which allows the writer to definitively take a side.

Skill 3.4 **Anticipates the concerns, knowledge level, and perspective of an audience**

To write a successful persuasive argument, it is important to understand one's audience. If the anticipated audience has extensive background knowledge in a subject, for example, they will quickly lose interest (or perhaps even feel resentful) if a writer feels it is necessary to include basic details about a topic. Conversely, if the intended audience is unfamiliar with a topic, the writer can 'lose' the audience by focusing on a high level, in-depth analysis of a topic.

Similarly, if a writer is trying to persuade an audience that consists of people who work in the oil industry of the need to reduce consumption of fossil fuels in order to address climate change, they must be careful not to be seen as demonizing the oil industry as the cause of the problem. Rather, a successful argument might include calls for a gradual transition to different energy sources while providing support for workers who need retraining. If appealing to politicians, a writer might reference their responsibility to the long-term health and prosperity of the country.

The writer must learn to adapt their writing to the needs of their audiences. One way to do this is to determine the values, needs, constraints, and demographics of their audience.

Values: What is important to this group of people? What is their background and how will that affect their perception of your arguments? If you are encouraging people to view things in a different way, an appeal to compromise might be effective. If trying to convince people to sacrifice, an appeal to 'goodness' may be effective.

Needs: Find out in advance what the audience's needs are. Why are they reading your writing? Find a way to satisfy their needs.

Constraints: What might hold the audience back from being fully engaged in what you are saying, agreeing with your point of view, or processing what you are trying to say? These could be political reasons, which make them wary of your ideology from the start, or knowledge reasons, in which the audience lacks the appropriate background information to grasp your ideas. Avoid this last constraint by staying away from technical terminology, slang, or abbreviations that may be unclear to your audience.

Demographic information: Demographics include age, gender, education, religion, income level and other countable characteristics. Arguing for greater support for public schools to an audience of seniors might be more successful if it referenced the need to provide for future generations or noted the strong support for community schools they enjoyed as children. An argument on the same topic to wealthy families who may or may not send their children to public schools might emphasize the shared responsibility of all citizens to ensure an educated populace for the good of society.

After determining audience, writers should decide which one (or more) of the following appeals:

Personal: using the author's personality to sway the reader
Emotional: using and/or triggering the reader's' emotions to sway the reader
Logical: Using science, statistics, or logical arguments to sway the reader.
Stylistic: using language (figurative, stylistic devices, word choice) to sway the reader.

Start where the readers are, and then take them where you want to go.

Skill 3.5 Creates a clear relationship between claims/counterclaims, reasons, and evidence

See Skill 3.3

Skill 3.6 Develops a conclusion that clearly relates to an argument

The final piece of a story is always the most memorable - for good or bad. In a persuasive essay it is important that your conclusion is NOT a mirror image of the introduction with only a few word changes. Rather, it is essential to give a slightly modified thesis, building upon facts and sub-points used. It's strongest when the writer is able to state the thesis in another manner, summarizing quickly and giving the reader something positive to consider for the future.

To restate the main idea used with the previous Frankenstein example, we can adjust the main idea to reflect the generalized supportive points. For example, we may wrap the conclusion around the main sentence for this paragraph as "The monster was a manifestation of personal flaws - shame, alienation, outrageous ego - and Shelley compelled the reader to reflect on how environment/nature shapes the development of a person and society's acceptance of things that are different."

This statement takes the reader back to what was included in the body, but in a different phrasing and actually gives the action item of how to read the story without asking a question. [In general it is strongly discouraged to use a question.] A strong conclusion practically begs the reader to ask themselves if they are smart enough to think of it in the manner in which the persuasive essay has.

In a trial, the closing arguments allow the attorneys to link the evidence together and tell the jury, based on that evidence, how they should decide. The conclusion of a successful written argument is similar. It is much more concise, but its purpose is very similar.

The conclusion is what the readers will remember. For you, the writer, it's your last chance to persuade the reader and to demonstrate how powerful your argument is. It is the last thing they see before deciding whether an argument is compelling. Good writing makes it count - restating in a different way why the argument was oriented in such a way and wrapping up the ideas neatly.

The list below can guide you in writing effective conclusions.

- Link the conclusion to the first paragraph. You may even use a phrase or key word from your introduction.
- Simple, direct language can be particularly effective in a conclusion.
- Avoid 'speaking' to the reader (i.e., do not use *you*).
- Consider including the implications of your argument – how your analysis or interpretation for example connect with a larger issue.
- In general, avoid using quotes in the conclusion.
- Try not to use phrases such as *in conclusion* or *to summarize*. These are short cuts that undermine the effectiveness of your writing.

Skill 3.7   Develops an argument through planning, writing, revision, and rewriting

As in all other forms of writing, planning, writing, revision, and rewriting are essential elements of persuasive writing. All successful writers go through these stages. Although with persuasive writing this is equally true, as the writer refines an argument to be as powerful, concise and compelling as possible.

In developing the central message of a persuasive piece of writing, it's often best to form an outline (or "mind map"). Any time there is a limited timeframe to finish writing, the few minutes spent organizing one's thoughts are very beneficial because it saves time later on. Most people need to write an outline (or type it out) and not rely on what they can track in their head (that makes it too easy for errors, and the hard copy allows you to check off when you complete that discussion area in your essay).

To create an outline, brainstorm things about the topic first. Start with potential thesis statements and try to come up with examples of facts/reasons that support that point of view. Successful writer revisit this list, considering better ideas and then finding specific facts or data to elaborate on a claim. The outline guides the writing of the argument and can allow the writer to visualize how different elements of evidence will fit together as part of a cohesive whole.

This process is the strongest way to form a persuasive argument. When you have taken a few minutes to draft the outline, when you reach the concluding portion, it is fairly easy to determine if you have indeed identified the correct thesis or you should change it; it's much simpler to do before you get deep into writing.

Tone is an important element to consider in revising persuasive arguments. It is important to read the audience well. In an attempt not to sound too 'bossy' about a topic, you don't want to sound like you are unsure. Conversely, you do not want to sound arrogant or pedantic. Having a second person read your work is an effective way to strike the right tone.

After writing, it is common to seek feedback about the clarity of ideas and the efficacy of the supporting arguments. Another reader may notice gaps in the argument that don't stand out to you because they seem obvious. Since the argument is yours, you may not see the 'holes' in the evidence. Someone who is not immersed in your thinking may need clarification; this is a good sign that you need to add to your argument.

Sometimes additional research is needed to find stronger examples. At other times, a counterpoint may be anticipated, allowing the writer to refine and improve his/her argument. These stages of planning, writing, revising, and rewriting are essential parts of the writing process.

COMPETENCY 4   WRITING INFORMATIVE AND EXPLANATORY TEXTS

Skill 4.1   Writes a clear introduction that establishes what is to follow

The purpose of an expository writing text can be to inform about, explain or describe an event, a person, a thing or a place. Facts, examples, statistics, and information are presented in a formal manner. The tone is direct and the delivery objective rather than subjective. There are many forms of expository writing and each one brings with it a specific structure.

Expository writing forms include but are not limited to:

- Description
- Classification
- Process-based or how-to
- Compare/contrast
- Cause and effect
- Problem and solution

When beginning to write an expository text, writers should have a purpose and a form in mind.

Informative texts share elements in common with persuasive texts. Rather than trying to convince the reader of a particular point of view, however, the writer of an informative text seeks to clearly explain a topic. Beginning with a thesis paragraph, the writer relays the main idea of the essay and introduces the topic. The informative essay introduction may state the importance of the topic or may simply describe the topic.

An essay on measures to combat climate change may begin with a paragraph explaining why researchers feel that taking action to stop climate change is important before going on to explain different proposals to combat it. Though there may be an element of opinion here, the focus is on giving information rather than picking a side. The information speaks for itself rather than being used as part of an appeal to do or to believe something. The writer might demonstrate that action to address climate change is necessary would not directly say so.

Introduction and Main Idea of the Essay

The first topic paragraph should clearly establish what the rest of the piece would be about. Typically, this paragraph should only be five or six sentences long - so from the very beginning, thoughts must be well-organized. The writer must clearly establish what the rest of the piece will be about and may also include purpose.

Once a topic is assigned or chosen, the next step is to begin preliminary research. Those materials may come from the writer's own experience, and the best way to collect them is in prewriting—simply putting on paper whatever is there by way of past experience relevant to the topic; observations concerning it; newspaper articles or books that have been read on the topic; and television or radio presentations related to the topic.

The writer needs to keep in mind the need to make a statement about the topic—to declare something about it. Very often, once the writer has gone through this exercise, getting his/her own ideas and thoughts down on paper, a thesis or several theses may emerge. If not, then it is time to continue research on the topic.

Introductions generally seek to accomplish the following goals.

- Clearly define the topic
- Lay out a 'map' of sorts of the types of evidence that will follow
- Be engaging and make the reader want to continue

In most cases for academic purposes, the introduction does not include a quote or citation. Instead the introduction relies on the voice of the writer.

See also 3.1

Skill 4.2   Organizes ideas, concepts, and information so that different elements build on each other

Subsequent paragraphs elaborate on the topic. Using the previously mentioned example of measures to combat climate change, the paragraphs that follow the introduction might go on to do the following:

- Explain a proposal to deal with climate change
- Describe the research that has been done regarding that proposal
- Share information about the result so far
- Explain another proposal
- Describe related research regarding that proposal

The structure continues to build not towards an argument (as in a persuasive piece) but towards a full understanding of what proposals are being considered (again, using the same example) to combat climate change. The different sections are linked by a common thread, established in the introduction, and go on to explain related ideas and information.

The essential thing to remember is that the ideas must be organized so that the reader's knowledge steadily builds. The writer takes care to fully explain one element before moving on to another. By the end of an informative piece of writing, the reader may in fact be persuaded to act, to believe something, or to support something, but informative writing does not explicitly set out to persuade the reader. Instead, it strikes a much more objective tone.

Just as when one learns about the importance of coral reefs as habitats for breeding fish and comes to believe that reefs must be protected because of the facts presented, there is no argument that they must be protected. That is left for the reader to decide based on evidence. Persuasive arguments generally state a position and argue for it.

Some things to consider include unity (everything tied to the initial idea laid out in the introduction), coherence (the way different elements fit together as part of a whole), and emphasis (the attention given to different elements based on importance).

Unity

All ideas must relate to the controlling thesis. At the simplest level, this means that all sentences must develop the topic sentence of a paragraph. By extension, then, all paragraphs must develop the thesis statement of the essay; all chapters must develop the main idea of the book; all ideas must develop the argument.

Coherence

One way to achieve unity is to show the relationships between ideas by using transitional words, phrases, sentences, and paragraphs. Using coordinating conjunctions (for, and, nor, but, or, yet, so), subordinating conjunctions (because, since, whenever), or transitional adverbs (however, therefore) is an effective way to show logical order and thus create coherence. Another way to show relationships between ideas is to use an appropriate strategy (spatial, chronological, cause and effect, classification, comparison/contrast) to arrange details.

Emphasis

Use strategic placement of arguments to emphasize the significance of the ideas. In direct order, the main ideas are stated first and then supported by reasons or details. In indirect order, the support is provided first (in either increasing or decreasing order of importance) and leads to a well-defended argument.

The table below provides a general guide to the organizational structure of common types of informational writing.

Form	Structure
Description	Explanation of features of a person, place, thing or event organized by general features or in chronological order (if an event)
Classification	Break a large topic down into smaller pieces, starting from the general to the specific
How-to	List explanations of how to do something in either numeric (like a recipe) or chronological order (the writing process)

Compare/Contrast	Usually comparing two ideas, events, people or things - organized by similarities and differences
Cause/Effect	Relationship between two events, usually organized by cause and then effect
Problem/Solution	Organized by defining and explaining a problem and then offering one or more solutions

Skill 4.3   **Develops a topic by selecting relevant facts, details, definitions, quotations and other examples**

See also Skill 4.2

As noted in Skill 4.2, the structure of the piece is organized to inform the reader by logically explaining different elements of the topic. Each section should contain facts, quotes, and other details to help the reader understand the topic thoroughly. Continuing with the example of proposals to combat climate change, below are some ideas of the type of information that might be incorporated into the different sections.

- A definition of greenhouse gases and its acronym
- Statistic about the amount of greenhouse gases produced by cars in a typical American city
- Cost of electric vehicle
- Quote from a producer of electric vehicles about their potential
- Description of how solar panels work
- Explanation of a particular city that has installed large numbers of solar panels

Though you may know these things yourself, you cannot assume that your reader does. You must inform at the same time that you demonstrate your knowledge of the topic. Using and citing sources demonstrates that what you are saying is not simply your opinion, but rather the product of much thought and evidence.

Though a writer could likely explain several different proposals to combat climate change in general terms, the addition of details like statistics, quotes, and examples are necessary to truly inform the reader (and to show that the writer knows what s/he is talking about).

In shorter informational texts, a rule of thumb is that each body paragraph should be organized around a concrete piece of evidence. Each one should include a quotation, an example, or a fact that helps explain the topic. This would mean one citable source per body paragraph. In longer pieces, evidence would likely be spread out more and more time would be taken to explain it. One particularly valuable approach is to explain the importance or significance of the evidence. Such as:

- The implications it holds
- Its relationship to other evidence
- Its value
- The ways in which it can be used

Continuing with example of proposals to combat climate change, one paragraph might discuss a new solar panel manufacturing process. The following paragraph might include a statistic about lower costs, and the next might include a quotation about the breakthrough's impact.

Selecting relevant information involves many choices, not least of which includes determining valid sources (**see Competency 6**). At the same time, you must also be flexible in the information you select. This is a fluid process and you may spend a big part of discarding or reshuffling the information you find. Despite the widespread of digital tools, there are still some people who prefer to use note cards with their evidence on them because they can physically move them around as they conceptualize the form their writing will take.

Skill 4.4   Uses varied transitions and syntax to clearly link ideas in different sections of a text

Transitional words and phrases are designed to lead the reader forward and through a piece of writing. Such words as "therefore," "however," "even so," and "although" are clues to connections between one part of the writing and another. Phrases sometimes substitute for words. Some examples include "in the case of," "in the long run," and "looking back." These transitional words and phrases clarify the nature of the connection as seen in the following examples.

To show time or order: afterwards, then, first, finally
To show contrast: however, but, although
To show additional ideas: furthermore, and, moreover
To show example: for instance, for example, as in the case of

Another example of a transitional sentence could be, "Not all projects have been so successful." This could refer to the previous information and prepares for the next paragraph, which will be about an unsuccessful project. This next transitional sentence is a little more forthright: "The cost of these proposed projects - and who will pay for them - may jeopardize their implementation."

Another fairly simple and straightforward transitional device is the use of numbers or their approximation. Words like, 'first', 'initially', 'second' may help to sequence ideas and information, but these should be used cautiously to avoid overuse.

An entire paragraph may be transitional in purpose and form. In *Darwiniana*, Thomas Huxley used a transitional paragraph:

So much, then, by way of proof that the method of establishing laws in science is exactly the same as that pursued in common life. Let us now turn to another matter (though really it is but another phase of the same question), and that is, the method by which, from the relations of certain phenomena, we prove that some stand in the position of causes toward the others.

The paragraph serves as a transition to another point or idea. The reader has a reasonable idea of what the writer will pursue next. Students often struggle with transitions, and it is worthwhile to illustrate successful examples of transitions (phrases, words, etc.) by using mentor texts.

Common transitional words and phrases can often be grouped into categories. The table below indicates a small sampling of them.

Time	Addition	Contrast	Illustration	Effect
after	In addition	however	For example	therefore
following	finally	though	To illustrate	thus
subsequently	moreover	In contrast	As evidenced by	consequently
during	furthermore	nevertheless	specifically	As a result

Using transitions well also involves varying their use. A thesaurus or quick internet search will reveal a huge number of options.

Skill 4.5 Uses precise, domain-specific language to help explain or inform about a topic

Successful informative writing includes words and terminology specifically related to the topic. Just as the writer (as noted in 4.4) could likely describe in general terms several proposals related to combatting climate change, they could also do so without using specific terms. The effect, however, would not be particularly interesting or informative, and the reader would likely come having learned nothing.

This is one of the hallmarks of writing for an academic purpose. The writer is supposed to immerse himself/herself in the topic and develop expertise in it. If the writing is about climate change, then the language should reflect that used by people who work in the field. If the topic is economics, then the writer should 'speak' the language of economics.

As an example, the writer could talk generally about ways in which humans have impacted the environment, but using the term 'Anthropocene' (a term many scientists use to describe the age in which we are living) gives a greater sense of the scale of change that researchers are warning about and more weight to the information being shared. Defining the terms and explaining its importance put the reader strengthens the readers understanding of your topic.

Successfully using this type of domain-specific language requires learning on the part of the writer, research, and often clear definitions of terms for the reader.

Skill 4.6   Writes conclusions that support the information presented

See also Skill 3.6

For many writers, conclusions are the hardest thing to write. After all the work of gathering evidence, explaining it, and linking it together, the conclusion can feel like something that is just tacked on at the end of an informative piece. It should, however, be seen as the last opportunity to leave the reader with something important.

Aristotle taught that the conclusion should strive to do five things:

1. Inspire the reader with a favorable opinion of the writer.
2. Amplify the force of the points made in the body of the paper.
3. Reinforce the points made in the body.
4. Rouse appropriate emotions in the reader.
5. Restate in a summary way what has been said.

The conclusion may be short or it may be long depending on its purpose in the paper. Recapitulation, a brief restatement of the main points or certainly of the thesis, is a common part of effective conclusions. A good example is a court trial where an attorney would review the main points, tying together all the information previously shared.

In an informative piece, the writer would generally refer back to the main idea and make a larger point about it. Using the same example proposal to combat climate change, the conclusion might read something like this:

With competing proposals to tackle climate change, individuals, businesses, and government leaders will have to make some difficult decisions. Costs, feasibility, and the ability of researchers to 'sell' their ideas to the public will all play a role in the final outcome. In the meantime, people with beachfront property may be watching the sea warily.

In this example, it begins with a reference to the original premise of the piece (explaining different proposals to tackle climate change). It also acknowledges the people involved in making decisions about the proposals. From there it refers to factors in the decision. The final sentence is meant to leave the reader with the impression that climate change is a lingering threat in the future.

The list below can guide you in writing effective conclusions.

- Link the conclusion to the first paragraph. You may even use a phrase or key word from your introduction.
- Simple, direct language can be particularly effective in a conclusion.
- Avoid 'speaking' to the reader (i.e., do not use *you*).
- Consider including the implications of your argument – how your analysis or interpretation for example connect with a larger issue.
- In general, avoid using quotes in the conclusion.
- Try not to use phrases such as *in conclusion* or *to summarize*. These are short cuts that undermine the effectiveness of your writing.

Skill 4.7   Improves writing by planning, revising, editing, and rewriting

See Skill 3.7

Skill 4.8   Selects evidence from literature or literary nonfiction to support analysis and interpretation

See also Skill 1.3

Successfully selecting evidence from literature or literary nonfiction texts starts with careful reading. The writer must read the texts with an eye towards the writing to come. This usually means annotating a text while reading it, looking for passages, ideas, and quotes that would support an interpretation.

Since we usually formulate or interpretations of literary texts as we read, there are several key strategies to pursue when working with students. First and perhaps most important, encourage reading with a critical eye through ongoing discussion and questioning about the text. By making the analysis part of the process of reading, students will be looking for passages to support topics of discussion.

Using these passages later on is much easier if there is a methodical way of keeping track of them while reading. This annotation can take many forms. Some prefer notes in the margins; others like to highlight or underline. With digital tools, it is also easy to do this electronically, saving passages in cloud-based services like Diigo (with attributions already properly formatted!) to be used when writing.

The process must be recursive as well. Our impressions of characters, of the significance of events, and our predictions of what things mean will change. Taking time to look back while reading to see how the significance of our original annotations has changed is important.

Skill 4.9   Employs techniques from different literary genres (e.g., allegory, irony, ambiguity) to enhance meaning

See also Skills 1.1 and 1.9

Informative writing can be beautiful in the same way that literature can. It can also incorporate many different literary devices. Though this may be an advanced stage in informative, expository writing, it can valuable.

Allegories are stories with characters representing virtues and vices. Allegories may be read on either of two levels, the literal and the symbol. George Orwell's *Animal Farm* is an allegory about the abuses of totalitarianism. In informative texts, an allegory might be an anecdote that illustrates or represents a larger point. In the climate change example, the island nation of the Republic of Kiribati could be used to represent the future many countries face.

Irony involves expressing something other than and particularly opposite the literal meaning such as words of praise when blame is intended. In expository texts, irony may be used as a sophisticated or resigned awareness of contrast between what is and what ought to be. This could be used to highlight the shortcomings of a leader, for example.

Ambiguity, when something is open to more than one interpretation, may be useful in expository, informative texts if the writer wants to show that no particular course of action is clear. Ambiguity might be a powerful tool in an essay about the guilt or innocence of someone accused of a crime. The writer could easily lie out the evidence and, by not taking a specific side, make the point that in deciding someone's guilt, juries have a tremendous responsibility.

Skill 4.10   Maintains a formal style that is appropriate to task, purpose, and audience

See Skill 3.4

Listening to students sitting on the steps that lead into the building that houses their classrooms, teachers will hear dialogue that may be wholly unfamiliar. The student who is writing a story for an audience of his/her peers will need to know and understand the peculiarities of that discourse to be very effective with them. Tailoring language for audience is something we do constantly in conversations with friends, colleagues, employers etc.

Take this opportunity to teach the concept of jargon. Writing to be read by a lawyer is different than writing to be read by a medical doctor. Writing for parents is different than writing for school administrators. Not only are the vocabularies different, but also the formality/informality of the discourse will need to be adjusted.

In general, informational expository texts are written in a formal style. Factors to consider in determining formality are vocabulary, sentence length and construction, and use of contractions. This does not mean that this type of writing should be overly complex or difficult to understand; instead it means that the style is not conversational. The writer generally tries to achieve an authoritative tone, demonstrating his/her knowledge of the topic.

Some stylistic features of informative writing that support a more formal tone include:

- Lack of 'flowery' language – Informative writing can include beautiful language (and even figurative language as noted previously), but it tends to avoid the appearance of striving for beautiful description or emotional language. The goal is, again, to be authoritative and let facts speak.
- Leave feelings out of it – When you are writing an informative piece, this does not mean you don't have an opinion about the topic. In fact you probably do. But that opinion is left out of what you write. Your point of view comes through in the facts and examples you include (and what you exclude). To strike the right tone, avoid any language that seems like opinion.
- No 'I' – Informational writing, in general, does not make use of the first person.

Keeping these points in mind will help maintain the proper level of formality in your writing.

Skill 4.11   Uses technology to produce and publish and to collaborate with other writers

It has never been easier to publish work and collaborate with others. There are countless venues for publishing work (blogs, platforms like Medium.com, digital newspapers, websites, etc.). Writers can include images, video, links to other sources, and audio in ways that newspapers would have only dreamed of a few years ago. Publication allows writers to reach an authentic audience and get feedback on their work.

To see the potential of informational writing, check some of the major newspapers' feature articles. Papers like the *New York Times* offer feature articles that are true multimedia experiences. The text is often supplemented with:

- Mini documentaries
- Photo essays
- Audio interviews with subjects from the articles
- Links to past articles on the topic
- Links to background information

Collaboration as well has changed dramatically. Cloud-based document sharing (Dropbox, Drive, OneDrive, etc.) allows people to work on the same documents, share ideas, and edit each other's work. Collaboration within and beyond the classroom is a powerful part of the writing process.

Students can easily work with peers in multiple ways: They can divide sections of a written piece, edit each other's work, make comments, and add media. It's a level of cooperation that seemed unthinkable not too long ago.

Informative vs
Explanitory writing.
How do I teach different forms to students?

COMPETENCY 5   WRITING NARRATIVES

Skill 5.1   Engages and orients the reader by elaborating a problem, conflict, or observation; establishes a point of view and introduces a narrator and characters

It is important to have a purpose and choose a form when composing a narrative text. A general definition of narrative writing is that it relates an experience using a temporal structure. The narrative can be a fictional story or it can convey a personal experience of the author or someone they know or narrate an event that the author or someone they know has experienced.

Narrative writing can be descriptive by centering on a person, place, or object, using sensory words to create a mood or impression and arranging details in a chronological or spatial sequence. Narrative writing can be developed using an incident or anecdote or a related series of events.

Some forms of narrative writing include: story, novel, autobiography, biography, memoir, personal essay, etc.

When a writer has a purpose and a narrative form in mind, they are ready to choose a topic or subject.

There is no formula for a good narrative, but there are established elements that should be part of any narrative work. Different writers, even different genres, develop certain characteristics more than others, but these elements are still part of just about every narrative.

The elements of narrative vary in importance and development. Some narratives are mainly plot-driven while others are character studies. Stories can be so tightly constructed that all elements work together to develop the theme and entertain the reader. Although readers can certainly enjoy a story without an in-depth understanding of these elements, they can develop a deeper appreciation for those works that display the author's talent and writing skill.

The **problem or conflict** in a narrative is usually what drives the piece. Conflict can be between characters, between the characters and some external force (such as in a survival story), or even be internal (a character dealing with guilt or responsibility, for example). Most narratives move towards a resolution of the conflict (though this does not mean that the problem is 'solved', just that there is an end result).

Narrator(s) and point of view

Narratives can have more than one narrator (the person telling the story), but the most important thing is to establish a narrative point of view clearly. If narrative perspective switches (which is common), making a clear separation between the perspectives is essential (such as by chapter or section breaks). There is nothing more frustrating for a reader than to wonder 'who is talking now?"

Character is portrayed in many ways: description of physical characteristics, dialogue, interior monologue, the thoughts of the character, the attitudes of other characters toward this one, and so on. Descriptive language depends on the ability to recreate a sensory experience for the reader.

If the description of the character's appearance is a visual one, then the reader must be able to see the character. What's the shape of the nose? What color are the eyes? How tall or how short is this character? Thin or chubby? How does the character move? How does the character walk? Writers choose terms that will create a picture for the reader. It's not enough to say the eyes are blue, for example. What kind of blue? Often the color of eyes is compared to something else to enhance the reader's ability to visualize the character.

A good test of characterization is the level of emotional involvement of the reader in the character. If the reader is to become involved, the description must provide an actual experience—seeing, smelling, hearing, tasting, or feeling. In the following example, Isaac Asimov deftly describes a character both directly and indirectly.

Skill 5.2   Uses techniques such as dialogue, description, reflection, and multiple plot lines to develop a story and its characters

Dialogue is one of the most powerful methods at a writer's disposal for creating a character and developing a story. It is the way we 'hear' a character and can create subtle impressions about their outlook on the world, their sense of humor, their intelligence, and even the way they feel about themselves. Dialogue will reflect characteristics countless characteristics; the ability to portray the speech of a character can make or break a story.

The kind of person the character is in the mind of the reader is dependent on impressions created by description and dialogue. How do other characters feel about this one as revealed by their treatment of him/her, their discussions of him/her with each other, or their overt descriptions of the character? For example, "John, of course, can't be trusted with another person's possessions."

Description of people and places shape narratives in powerful ways. Description can be oriented towards sensory input - what the reader would see, hear, feel, etc. - or towards action. Using words that capture the sense of what is happening (e.g., *screamed* vs. *said*) help develop the story as well.

Setting can be visual, temporal, psychological, or social; descriptive words are often used here also. In Edgar Allan Poe's description of the house in "The Fall of the House of Usher", as the protagonist/narrator approaches it, the air of dread and gloom that pervades the story is caught in the setting and sets the stage for the story. A setting may also be symbolic, as it is in Poe's story, where the house is a symbol of the family that lives in it. As the house disintegrates, so does the family.

The language used in all of these aspects of a story—plot, character, and setting—work together to create the mood of a story. Poe's first sentence establishes the mood of the story: "During the whole of a dull, dark, and soundless day in the autumn of the year, when the clouds hung oppressively low in the heavens, I had been passing alone, on horseback, through a singularly dreary tract of country; and at length found myself, as the shades of the evening drew on, within view of the melancholy House of Usher."

Multiple plot lines (**also described in Skill 5.3**) increase the complexity of a narrative. They are also much more like real life in that our lives are shaped by events that happen out of our direct 'range'. For example, the decision to postpone a test in class may change the 'story' of what students will do after school.

Skill 5.3   Sequences events in such a way as to build toward an outcome; establishes tone and creates a coherent narrative

Narrative writing, whether personal essay, memoir, or short story depends heavily on time as a deeper structure because in all cases, the author is conveying a story, fictional or otherwise. Stories have beginnings, middles and ends. Events and experiences have starting points, midpoints and endpoints in space and time, even though we may think about them long after they occur.

Writers can choose to tell their stories by starting at the beginning, in chronological order, or by starting in medias res (in the middle of action) and use flashbacks to narrate the backstory.

In making a decision about organizational structures to use in narrative texts, writers should consider purpose and audience. Even if a narrative text is related in chronological order, it still needs a hook or a reason for the reader to keep reading. If the audience is older and/or contemplative, vivid descriptions of setting may do the trick. If the audience is in middle school, starting with a provocative line of dialogue or event will make them want to read more.

Plot is sometimes called "action", or the sequence of the events. Narratives depend on a clear sequence of events so that the reader is not left wondering what is happening. The most common narrative structure involves a clear beginning, the development of the plot, and a clear ending. This is usually referred to as linear narrative with the plot progressing from start to finish.

Other more complex styles of sequencing events in a narrative are often non-linear. These may start with a moment near the end/conclusion and then jump back to the beginning to show how events led to that moment. Flashbacks are also common, moments from the narrative that are inserted out of order to illuminate and further the plot. Similarly, parallel narrative structures involve more than one storyline happening simultaneously. The writer moves back and forth between them, often showing different perspectives.

The outcome of narratives can be clear or ambiguous. Ambiguous endings often lend themselves to speculative interpretation and frequently lead to 'sequels'. When the tension or conflict in a narrative builds towards a decisive moment, this moment is usually referred to as the climax. When the narrative continues after the climax, this is usually termed the denouement, the part of the narrative in which any unresolved elements are brought together.

Authors have great leeway in determining in structuring the sequence of events. What's most important is cohesion; this is often best achieved by planning.

Skill 5.4   Uses precise vocabulary, interesting details, and description to convey experiences, setting, characters, and events

See Skill 5.2

Skill 5.5   Provides a conclusion that is clearly connected to the experiences, observations, and events of the narrative

See Skill 5.2

Skill 5.6   Uses literary techniques such as allegory, stream of consciousness, irony, and ambiguity to affect meaning

See also Skill 4.9

Literary techniques such as allegory, stream of consciousness, irony, and ambiguity can all add to a narrative. A stream of consciousness narration can create, for example, a dream-like quality or even a sense of urgency in a story. Stream of consciousness writers like William Faulkner and James Joyce, used it to show the inner workings of the mind.

This can be an effective way to show reactions to events or the way in which the writer felt during an event. In a personal narrative, this can show how the writer was shaped by a formative experience. By revealing the thought processes of a character or narrator, the writer can show the jumble of memories, reactions, and thoughts that race through someone's head.

Ambiguity, as in real life, can help convey to the reader a sense of confusion about the meaning of an event or the intentions of a character. In many cases we do not know exactly what things mean. In a personal or fictional narrative, this sense of ambiguity captures the lack of certitude we may feel as life unfolds.

Skill 5.7   Adapts voice and language for different contexts and audiences

See also Skill 3.4

As with any written work, the voice, language, and style of narrative writing must be adapted to fit different contexts and audiences. A narrative work filled with references to early Mayan history may not be well received, despite being extremely well written if the audience is not familiar with the background references.

Some narrative work succeeds because it speaks to a specific audience. Other work succeeds because of its appeal to a wider audience. Particularly with personal narratives, some writers may find a connection to a niche audience as they tell about a specific personal experience.

Similarly, dialogue that relies heavily on slang and popular culture references may be popular with a younger audience but seem nonsensical to someone from a different country or age group. Writers must find their own voice, but if they have something to communicate, they must consider the audience they want to reach.

Point of view or voice is essentially the character through whose eyes the reader sees the action. There are at least thirteen possible choices for point of view (voice) in literature, as demonstrated and explained by Wallace Hildick in his 13 Types of Narrative. However, for purposes of helping students write essays about literature, three, or possibly four, are adequate. Students should think about how a writer's choice of voice impacts the overall effect of the work.

Skill 5.8   Improves narrative writing by planning, revising, editing, and rewriting

Like all other forms of writing, narratives benefit from the full writing process. Successful, engaging writers generally use the same steps because the first draft is never the best draft. Most writers plan before they write, make revisions along the way, edit their work and often do substantial rewriting to craft a narrative that captures the reader's imagination or tells a compelling story.

Planning

The planning stage may vary tremendously from writer to writer. Some writers sketch ideas, others use graphic organizers, and still others use outlines. In a strict sense, no one method is better than another; the best one is the one that suits the writer. The point of planning is to have a path forward, capture ideas/inspirations, and be able to view the 'whole' structure of the story before it is totally finished. This may change often along the way.

Below are some ways of making the planning process work to move a narrative forward.

Gather ideas before writing. Prewriting and planning may include clustering, listing, brainstorming, mapping, free writing, and charting. Providing many ways to develop ideas on a topic will increase the chances for success. Possible planning methods include:

- A writing journal or notebook
- Free writing to get ideas going
- Brainstorming
- Visual mapping
- Visualization

Revising and rewriting

Writers continually examine their work and make changes in sentences, wording, details and ideas. Revise comes from the Latin word "revidere", meaning, "to see again." This step is often overlooked, unfortunately. Sometimes writers confuse it with proofreading. Whereas proofreading involves looking for errors (in grammar, for example), revising involves the continual adjustments to phrasing, word choice, and organization that writers make as they create.

Elements of the narrative may be moved or deleted while others are added. At times, this is a collaborative process involving other writers who may see gaps, elements that need more development, or extraneous detail. Multiple drafts of a piece may be generated before the writer (or their editors) is satisfied.

Editing and proofreading

Near the final stages of the writing process, editing involves both the final stages of revision, looking at how a narrative and its different parts fit together. Additional writing may still take place. The last step is proofreading - finding errors in word choice, grammar, spelling, etc.

Very rarely are these steps 'finished' after one attempt. Plans are revisited and altered, proposed revisions are dropped while others are added, and the writer, friends, peers, or anyone else who may have constructive ideas does the editing. In short, the process is ongoing and recursive.

COMPETENCY 6   RESEARCHING TO BUILD AND PRESENT KNOWLEDGE

Skill 6.1   Generates a research question and knows how to narrow down or broaden inquiry

Choosing a research topic is a complex process for many writers. Sometimes writers are given a list of topics to choose from, which can help shorten this process as the list is limited and one topic may stand out above all others. At other times, choosing a topic can be a very challenging task.

It is important for writers to choose topics that interest them and if at first, even the brainstorming process is challenging. It might help to scan newspapers, journals or articles in the subject area for topic ideas.

The brainstorming process, which can be mindmapping or just writing ideas down in a list, is an important part of coming up with an initial inspired idea. The next stage is to narrow that topic down. Mind maps are good organizing structures for this activity because they allow you to graphically represent connections between topics and ideas. Narrowing a topic is a very important step in the process because if the topic is too broad, it will affect every step of the writing process. The research stage will take a long time, and the writing may not have a clear focus.

As noted in **Skill 4.1**, during the prewriting and planning stages, writers do initial research on a topic in order to formulate a thesis (or theses). It is during this stage that the writer must consider whether there is enough evidence to support the topic adequately. Similarly, the writer may determine that a topic needs to be narrowed down or broadened.

Referencing the previous example of proposals to combat climate change, a writer could start researching that solar energy as a method of reducing greenhouse gas emissions but soon discover that there are myriad proposals and technologies being considered. In that case, it would be appropriate to broaden the research question to investigate different approaches. For example, the question might shift from *'In what ways will current solar energy plans address climate change concerns?'* to *'What proposals to address climate change currently being considered are viable?'*

Similarly, if the issue were more local, the writer might find that in their particular state that only one or two technologies were being seriously considered. In that case, they would then need to jettison much of the previous line of inquiry and focus the research question more specifically.

The key in determining the research question is flexibility and ongoing review of the process. Research into a topic may reveal additional information or reveal that the context warrants greater focus. One way to assure this is through self-evaluation and also through review with peers. Feedback from another perspective may help in determining the best course of action.

Some guidelines for formulating a good question include:

- A good research question is not too broad or too narrow.
- A good research question can be answered relatively objectively, as in, does not involve the word 'should' or 'ought' which immediately involves a value judgment but not necessarily any research or evidence.
- A good research question can be answered using information that can be answered with data (either collected or read by the author)

These do not ensure a perfect research question, but they will help rule out weak ones.

Skill 6.2   Gathers relevant information from multiple sources (e.g., textual, digital, audio, visual, etc.)

Access to information on a topic has never been easier than it is today. Libraries continue to be invaluable resources for quality, credible information. Access to the internet, however, has changed the research process forever. On almost any topic, a writer can find news articles, encyclopedia entries, academic journals, documentary films, interviews with experts, and photographic evidence. In many cases, it is also possible to read primary source documents (historical documents, contracts, first person accounts, etc.).

For many people, the biggest difficulty in gathering information is wading through the overabundance of material. Determining whether information is credible and current can often be a tremendous challenge.

If library access is available, several tools are recommended for gathering relevant information. Check with library staff for the following:

- Subscriptions (digital or print) to discipline-specific journals and magazines
- Subscriptions to databases of articles
- Subscriptions to newspapers (digital or print)
- Digital/physical copies of books on the research topic
- Guidance about the credibility of websites

A focused research question (**Skill 6.1**) is essential in finding relevant information. Because of the sheer volume of information available, it is easy to be sidetracked and pursue tangents. Regularly referring to the research question is a key way to find relevant information. That said, it is possible that through the research process the writer may decide to change, broaden, or narrow the focus of research.

Primary sources are particularly valuable research sources because they are not interpretations of information. Instead, they are original sources of information. Primary sources are works or records that were created during the period being studied or the research being done. Primary sources are the basic materials that provide raw data and information. Some common ones include:

- Letters
- Original documents
- News reports
- Journals or diaries
- Government records
- Narrative accounts
- Research data
- Novels and poetry (if the writing is going to be about them)
- Quotations and interviews

Secondary sources contain explanations or examinations of events. Often they include a judgment or interpretation. These include:

- Editorials
- Speeches
- Sermons
- Literary criticism and analysis
- Historical fiction

After gathering sources for research and determining that they are appropriate and credible, it is important for writers to decide how they are going to organize their notes. Many writers use graphic organizers and/or index cards to list main ideas, evidence, and bibliographic information about the sources. This part of the process is extremely important.

Staying organized helps writers monitor if they have too much information in one argument and not enough in another. In that case, they may need to find new sources and/or may need to change an argument because they haven't found any information to support it.

Organizing the information they gather helps writers maintain focus in their writing and helps with the citation process. Using the outline of the composition from the planning phase, writers can organize their information so that when it is time for them to integrate it into the next, they know exactly where it's going to go. Part of this organizing stage includes taking notes on the main idea or argument in the text and, when required, noting or writing the part of the text that is going to be quoted in the composition.

Skill 6.3   Assesses the validity or suitability of a source in terms of task, purpose, and audience

Writers should be able to synthesize, analyze, and connect logically the main ideas and supporting details in several sources representing different viewpoints on the same topic and be able to point to the texts for support (**see Skill 6.2**). They must also be able to discern evidence given in support of an argument, and whether it is credible, relevant, and of high quality.

Determining credibility and relevance can be tricky. One strategy is the SQ3R method (Survey, Question, Read, Recite, and Review), which helps the reader determine the purpose different sources. After surveying or scanning a potential source as a whole to catch title, major headings, subheadings, and graphics, the writer then formulates questions, including the question of purpose, and analyzes the text to discern it. Reciting the answer, reviewing the main ideas and significant information, and further reflecting upon it will help in ascertaining the purpose of the text.

Several questions can help in determining the validity and point of view of different sources. These include:

- Who is the target audience for this worK?
- What is the point of view of the original author?
- What is 'left out' of the text? Is there a point of view deliberately omitted? Facts or ideas?
- Is there language that is exaggerated? Biased?

Similarly, as mentioned in 6.2, libraries and other information professionals can help in curating reliable sources of information. Examples might be:

- Newspapers and magazines
- Academic journals
- TED talks
- Interviews with known experts
- Google scholar searches instead of a simple Google search

To determine reliability, it should be possible to find the same information in more than one source. If this doesn't happen, they should continue their research until they have resolved any discrepancies. They should not use information that cannot be verified or test results that cannot be repeated.

Certain types of language should be red flags when doing research. Inflammatory language, hyperbole, and loaded terms are evidence of bias. It does not mean that there is nothing useful in the source, but it does mean that any information must be double verified. Generally however, it is best to avoid this type of source.

Skill 6.4   Integrates information into a text and maintains the flow of ideas

See also Skill 6.2

Incorporating quotes and information is partly governed by rules and part by a sense of flow in the writing. The latter takes practice and often revision to ensure that the results of hard work researching a topic 'fit' and do not interrupt the flow of ideas in the piece.

There are various stylistic guides (MLA, Harvard, Chicago, etc.) for doing this. The MLA rules (one of the most commonly used set of guidelines) for integrating quotes and examples are below.

Short quotes: Short quotes are considered to be those that are fewer than four lines of typed text (or three lines of typed verse). These are included within double quotation marks ("") and followed by the author's name and page number. If the author's name is referenced within the text, the page number is sufficient. The work mentioned should appear, properly cited, in the complete list of works referenced (bibliography) page.

Examples: We must consider whether "a right to catch a fish [is] the same thing as owning a piece of land" (Clover 237).

In his book, *The End of the Line*, Clover poses the question whether it "is a right to catch a fish the same thing as owning a piece of land" (237).

In the first example, in order to maintain the proper flow of the text, it was necessary to insert the word 'is'. Since this is not part of the actual quote, square brackets enclose it ([ ]).

Long quotes: When quotations are more than four lines long (or more than three of verse), they become a freestanding block of text separate from the rest of the writing. The quotation goes on a new line, is double space, and is indented ½ inch from the left margin. It does not get quotation marks. The citation should come at the end and be enclosed in parentheses. If the quote covers more than one paragraph, the new paragraph within the quote should be indented an additional ¼ inch. Again, a full citation of the work should be added to the bibliography page.

Example: Fish will remain an important food source for millions of people if we can find sustainable ways of producing it. Raising salmon on land offers a viable solution.

A new system of farming salmon on land, using pumped seawater, claims that it could slash production costs by a quarter. The production centers would be near markets, cutting transportation costs and food miles. The water would be recirculated and purified using bacteria, then sterilized, cutting the 20 percent mortality rate in sea cages, and the waste would become high-value products… (Clover 307)

Omitting words: At times it is necessary or preferable to omit words from a quotation. This may be because of length or in order to focus only on what is essential. In this case, the writer uses an ellipsis (…) where words are omitted.

Example: Clover suggest that the "water would be recirculated and purified...cutting the 20 percent mortality rate in sea cages... (307).

Summary and paraphrasing is also an important part of integrating information gleaned from research. Paraphrasing is the art of rewording text. The goal is to maintain the original purpose of the statement while translating it into your own words. Your newly generated sentence can be longer or shorter than the original. Concentrate on the meaning, not on the words. Do not change concept words, special terms, or proper names.

There are numerous ways to paraphrase effectively:

- Change the key words' form or part of speech.

Example: "American news coverage is frequently biased in favor of Western views" becomes "When American journalists cover events, they often display a Western bias."

- Use synonyms of "relationship words." Look for a relationship word, such as contrast, cause, or effect, and replace it with a word that conveys a similar meaning, thus creating a different structure for your sentence.

Example: "Unlike many cats, he can sit on command" becomes "Most cats are not able to be trained, but he can sit on command."

- Use synonyms of phrases and words

Example: "The Beatnik writers were relatively unknown at the start of the decade" becomes "Around the early 1950s, the Beatnik writers were still relatively unknown."

- Change passive voice to active voice or move phrases and modifiers.

Example: "Not to be outdone by the third graders, the fourth grade class added a musical medley to their Christmas performance" becomes "The fourth grade class added a musical medley to their Christmas performance to avoid being showed up by the third graders."

Again, it is essential to include a work that you have paraphrased or summarized in your Works Cited list.

Skill 6.5   Avoids plagiarism and cites sources using standard methodology and formatting

A key element in avoiding plagiarism is to cite every source used. Even if there is no quotation and you summarize an idea or fact that you encountered in your research, you need to cite it as a source. This gives credit to the original writer/researcher/thinker and shows clearly that you are not trying to pass off someone else's ideas as your own.

Documentation is an important skill in incorporating outside information into a piece of writing. Research is more than cut and paste from the Internet and plagiarism is a serious academic offense.

Tips for Documentation

Keep a record of all sources consulted during the research process. When taking notes, avoid unintentional plagiarism by summarizing and paraphrasing. If using a direct quote, copy it exactly as written and enclose in quotation marks.

Cite anything that is not common knowledge. This includes direct quotes as well as ideas or statistics.

A works cited page or bibliography should include any source from which the writer found information, quotes, or ideas. This includes text-based sources, websites, videos, interviews, etc. Formats for bibliographies vary (but for this guide we suggest MLA) and can be very tricky to get write if done 'by hand'.

Within the body of your document follow this blueprint for standard attribution following MLA style.

1. Begin the sentence with, "According to _____,"
2. Proceed with the material being cited, followed by the page number in parentheses.

In-Text Citation Example
According to Steve Mandel, "our average conversational rate of speech is about 125 words per minute" (78).

Once writers have mastered this basic approach, they can learn more sophisticated methods such as embedding information.

Each source used within the document will have a complete citation in a bibliography or works cited page.

Works Cited Entry
Mandel, Steve. Effective Presentation Skills. Menlo Park, California: Crisp Publications, 1993.

Luckily, there are many digital tools available today to make this process easier in general and as an ongoing process. Easybib, Bibme, and Refme are just three of them.

COMPETENCY 7   SPEAKING AND LISTENING

Skill 7.1   Communicates effectively with audiences from diverse backgrounds and perspectives

Different from the basic writing forms of discourse is the art of debating, discussion, and conversation. The ability to use language and logic to convince the audience to accept your reasoning and to side with you is an art. This form of writing/speaking is extremely confined or structured, and logically sequenced with supporting reasons and evidence. At its best, it is the highest form of propaganda. A position statement, evidence, reason, evaluation and refutation are integral parts of this writing schema.

Similar to written communication, determining the proper manner of communicating with one's audience is an essential part of discussion, debate, interviews, and speechmaking. The speaker must determine whether the situation calls for a formal approach, humor, or a friendly demeanor. In some cases, it is essential to appear authoritative about a topic and to demonstrate a command of factual information. At other times, it is better to come across as deferential and solicit opinions from an audience.

Informal and formal language is a distinction made on the basis of the occasion as well as the audience. At a formal occasion, for example, a meeting of executives or of government officials, even conversational exchanges are likely to be more formal. Parties or sports are examples where the language is likely to be informal. Formal language uses fewer or no contractions, less slang, longer sentences, and more organization in longer segments.

Speeches about educational policy are an example of those that are likely to be formal. Speeches made to fellow employees are likely to be informal. Sermons tend to be formal.

Jargon or technical language is a specialized vocabulary. It may be the vocabulary peculiar to a particular industry such as computers ("firewall") or of a field such as education ("ELL"). It may also be the vocabulary of a social group. The speaker must be knowledgeable about and sensitive to the jargon peculiar to the particular audience. That may require some research and some vocabulary development on the speaker's part.

Sensitivity to these shifting concerns will make communication more effective and powerful.

See also Skills 3.4, 4.10, and 5.7

Skill 7.2   Collaborates in groups in discussions, decision-making, and project tasks

Collaboration on project-based tasks is a common feature of almost any subject-area or professional discipline. Group decision-making, though not always easy, often results in solutions and ideas that are considered fairer (because more people had a voice) and more effective (because they incorporate and sift through a variety of ideas to arrive at a result). Nevertheless, effective collaboration is not always easy.

Ensuring that all members of a group feel that their contributions will make a difference is essential to collaboration. A key factor affecting this is group size. Groups that are too large often have members that are perceived as not contributing; conversely there are often members of the group who feel that their ideas are not 'heard'. The most effective group sizes are generally considered to be no more than 4 or 5.

Another factor to consider is developing effective timelines. Each task should have a clear date of completion so that each member knows when his or her task is due. This creates a sense of interdependence as all group members are focused on doing their part. Effective information sharing is also essential and should be part of the timeline.

Some guidelines for group discussion

- Ensure your discussion is inclusive – Not all participants will be at ease right away. Starting with introductions, asking for clarification about key points, and allowing wait time will bring more people into the discussion.
- Try to keep things positive – It's necessary to monitor your own contributions and those of others to make sure that a few people don't talk too much (at the expense of others). Avoid stereotyping by avoiding generalizations.
- Encourage others – Put comments where others can see them. Ask people to add on to or comment on others' contributions.
- Encourage active listening – Adopting group policies (like no screens open) will help all people feel like their ideas are valued.

Effective listening and speaking skills can be developed with practice and an understanding of the techniques.

Communication skills are crucial in a collaborative society. In particular, a person cannot be a successful communicator without being an active listener. Focus on what others say, rather than planning on what to say next. By listening to everything another person is saying, you may pick up on natural cues that lead to the next conversation move without so much added effort.

Starting a Discussion

It is quite acceptable to use standard opening lines to facilitate a conversation. Don't agonize trying to come up with witty "one-liners" as the main obstacle in initiating conversation is just getting the first statement over with. After that, the real substance begins. A useful technique may be to make a comment or ask a question about a shared situation. This may be anything from the weather to the food you are eating to a new policy at work. Use an opener you are comfortable with because your partner in conversation will be comfortable with it as well.

Stimulating Higher Level Critical Thinking Through Inquiry

Many people rely on questions to communicate with others. However, most fall back on simple clarifying questions rather than open-ended inquiries. For example, if you paraphrase a response by asking, "Did you mean this…" you may receive merely a "yes" or "no" answer. On open-ended inquiry would ask "What did you mean when you said…?"

Try to ask open-ended, deeper-level questions since those tend to have the greatest reward and lead to a greater understanding. With answers to those questions, you can make more complex connections and achieve more significant information.

The following strategies for educators, adapted from The Teaching Centre at Washingon University, St. Louis, can help all students be more effective participants in group discussions:

- Assign some students to encourage other students to speak
- Vary teaching methods so that shyer students get practice speaking with partners and/or in small groups before larger group discussions
- Include time for questions after each class/presentation with questions ready in case students don't have them
- Use verbal and nonverbal cues to encourage speakers and teach these cues to students
- Wait time can help students - teach this concept to students as well so that they will give each other that time in group discussions
- Encourage listening without interrupting so listeners can hear the whole thing before speaking or answering
- Teach students how to ask follow up questions and model those yourself
- Encourage constructive responses to disagreement including the use of "I statements"
- Redirect and teach how to do this to students so more students participate

Decision-making

For decision-making it is equally important to have guidelines that are inclusive. Below are some suggestions.

- Identify the decision you have to make clearly. This ensures that everyone knows what the group is working towards.
- Make the parameters for a decision clear (i.e., what kinds of options will not be considered viable).

- Once the goal is clear, make sure that you analyze the factors that go into the decision together. Questions to stay focused might be, "What is causing the problem?" or "Where can we find resources?"
- Brainstorm a variety of solutions if the decision is related to solving a problem.
- Evaluate all options and choose the best one.
- Make plans for implementing the solution.
- Give feedback on the implementation and share how it is progressing.

Group decision-making is often complicated. Having a clear process and guidelines that everyone understands will not only avoid conflict but also ensure a more successful implementation of the decision.

There are different approaches to decision-making. Brief summaries for each are below.

By authority
In this model, group members contribute ideas and give feedback in an open environment, but the final decision rests with pre-selected participants.

By majority
At the end of discussions, information sharing and feedback, the final decision is made by a vote with the majority determining next steps.

To eliminate
In this format, the majority votes to eliminate ideas that are considered unworkable or less promising.

By ranking
The group votes to rank proposals with a point value for each. The proposals that have the highest point total are selected.

By consensus
When consensus is reached, the group has worked to come up with an idea that is acceptable to all participants. This may take time and compromise, but the goal is that everyone is happy.

Project work

For project work to be successful, each member must have a clear understanding of his/her role. Establishing those guidelines and responsibilities helps to prevent conflict and to ensure that all members know that they have a valued contribution to make. This takes time at the beginning to define and clarify those roles, but it makes the project work go much more smoothly.

Skill 7.3 Moves conversations forward by asking and responding to questions

See also Skills 7.1 and 7.2

Moving conversations forward is a valuable skill when working collaboratively, in discussions, in interviews, and in debate. It involves a significant level of spontaneous thinking as the conversations shift and develop, but can also involve preparation and background knowledge. For interviews and discussions, for example, it is important to have prepared in advance. Questions, facts, and ideas prepared in advance can serve as fodder for discussion and provide ideas for new directions in the conversation. These can provide ideas for both responding to and asking additional questions, drawing others more deeply into the conversation.

In group work situations, one important goal should be to engage all participants in discussion and to encourage everyone to share ideas. Questioning is an essential part of this process. It elicits additional information, involves more people, and creates a more democratic environment. When it comes time for decision-making, this is particularly important as the decisions made will likely reflect more people' input.

Skill 7.4 Works to ensure that a range of perspectives is heard in group discussions

See Skills 7.1, 7.2 and 7.3

A risk in discussions and group work is that the conversation will come to be dominated by only a few voices. This can happen because some people have strong opinions or because other people take more time to formulate opinions before speaking. Many methods exist that can address this issue. These include:

- Providing/requiring wait time before anyone speaks
- Creating a time for reflection or note-taking before starting a group discussion
- Informal discussion in smaller groups or pairs before starting a full group discussion
- Sharing questions to be discussed beforehand

In addition, in some groups, someone is assigned to be the 'devil's advocate' and is responsible for questioning the group's ideas or proposals by expressing an alternative point of view. This is not meant to be confrontational, but instead broadens the discussion. In many instances, by expressing the alternative point of view, other people may feel more confident about expressing differing ideas as well.

Breaking a larger group into smaller groups is also an effective way to ensure that all opinions are heard. Small group discussion results can be shared with the larger group, often resulting in ideas that had not been heard previously.

Skill 7.5   Clarifies, verifies, and challenges ideas and conclusions

See Skill 7.4

Challenging ideas held by others, especially those held by a group, is often intimidating. Finding a way to do this effectively involves ensuring that challenging an idea or assumption is not seen as combative. The devil's advocate role can be an effective one in creating an atmosphere in which this is expected.

Furthermore, establishing processes for discussion can facilitate clarification and verification. For example, if there is an established protocol for sharing ideas first and then a protocol for questioning or examining an idea, no participant is likely to feel singled out. In addition, the protocol can require that all suggestions for further elaboration or clarification be done anonymously.

This can be followed by additional investigation or research before the next round of discussion. This way, participants can determine whether ideas are credible or workable.

Skill 7.6   Responds thoughtfully to diverse points of view; synthesizes claims and evidence on both sides of an issue; seeks to resolve contradictions; recognizes what additional information may be needed for research or to complete a task

See Skills 7.2, 7.3, 7.4 and 7.5

By employing methods such as those described in the previous skills, gaps in the information needed for a task or project will likely come to light. Developing effective ways to track these gaps is a valuable step in ensuring that a project runs smoothly. Many groups use graphic organizers or charts. Others take notes during meetings to record such gaps. Still others use collaboration software such as Trello or Asana to document tasks, needs, and responsibilities.

Listening is not a skill that is talked about much except when someone clearly does not listen. The truth is, though, that listening is a very specific skill for very specific circumstances. There are two aspects to listening that warrant attention. The first is comprehension or understanding what someone says, the purposes behind the message, and the contexts in which it is said. The second aspect is purpose. While someone may completely understand a message, what is the listener supposed to do with it—just nod and smile or go out and take action?

Often, when we understand the purpose of listening in various contexts, comprehension will be much easier. Furthermore, when we know the purpose of listening, we can better adjust our comprehension strategies.

Listening is often done for the purpose of enjoyment, and schools must teach students how to listen and enjoy such work. Teachers can accomplish this by making it fun and giving many possibilities and alternatives to capture the wide array of interests in each classroom.

Students like to listen to stories, poetry, and radio dramas and theater. Listening to literature can also be a great pleasure. In the classrooms of exceptional teachers, we will often find that students are captivated by the reading-aloud of good literature.

Strategies for Active Listening
Oral speech can be very difficult to follow. When complex or new information is provided to us orally, we must analyze and interpret that information. Often, making sense of this information can be tough when presented orally because students have no place to go back and review material already stated.

Students must have opportunities to listen in large and small group conversation. The difference here is that conversation requires more than just listening. It involves feedback and active involvement. This can be particularly challenging, as in our culture, we are trained to move conversations along, to discourage silence in a conversation, and to always get the last word in. This poses significant problems for the art of listening. In a discussion, for example, when we are instead preparing our next response—rather than listening to what others are saying—we do a large disservice to the entire discussion.

Students need to learn how listening carefully to others in discussions actually promotes better responses on the part of subsequent speakers. One way teachers can encourage this, in both large and small group discussions, is to expect students to respond directly to the previous student's comments before moving ahead with their new comments. This will encourage them to pose their new comments in light of the comments that came just before them.

Students must also be able to listen for transitions between ideas. Sometimes, in oral speech, this is pretty simple when voice tone or body language changes. Of course, we don't have the luxury of looking at paragraphs in oral language, but we do have the animation that comes along with live speech. Human beings would have to try very hard to be completely non-expressive in their speech. Listeners should take advantage of this and notice how the speaker changes character and voice in order to signal a transition of ideas. Also, simply looking to see expressions on the speaker's face can do more to signal irony, for example, than trying to extract irony from actual words.

One good way to follow oral speech is with taking notes and outlining major points. Because oral speech can be more circular (as opposed to linear) than written text, it can be of great assistance to keep track of an author's message. Other classroom methods can help students learn good listening skills. For example, teachers can have students practice following complex directions. They can also have students orally retell stories—or retell (in writing or in oral speech) oral presentations of stories or other materials. These activities give students direct practice in the very important skills of

English Language Arts 103

listening. They provide students with outlets in which they can slowly improve their abilities to comprehend oral language and take decisive action based on oral speech.

Challenges to effective listening can be grouped into three areas to the listener, the person speaking, or the environment in which the speaking and listening is taking place. Each of these areas contains a myriad of factors that can cause listening to be a challenge. It is essential that educators are aware of these challenges so that they can help students make maximum progress in developing effective listening skills.

Skill 7.7   Integrates multiple sources to make informed decisions and find solutions

See Skills 2.11, 4.3, 6.2, 7.1, 7.2, 7.3, 7.4, 7.5, and 7.6

Skill 7.8   Evaluates a speaker's point of view, basic premises and assesses the speaker's stance, tone, and word choice

In discussion or debate responding to a speaker effectively involves recognizing their basic premise(s), point of view and stance. Factors to consider include their tone and word choice.

The premises are the propositions that are necessary for the argument to continue. They are the evidence or reasons for accepting the argument and its conclusions. Premises (or assertions) are often indicated by phrases such as "because," "since," "obviously," and so on. (The phrase "obviously" is often viewed with suspicion, as it can be used to intimidate others into accepting suspicious premises. If something doesn't seem obvious to you, don't be afraid to question it. You can always say, "Oh, yes, you're right, it is obvious" when you've heard the explanation.)

Next, use the premise to derive further propositions by using inferencing. In inferencing, one proposition is arrived at on the basis of one or more other propositions already accepted. There are various forms of valid inferences. The propositions arrived at by the inference may then be used in further inferencing. Inferencing is often denoted by phrases such as "implies that" or "therefore."

Recognizing someone else's basic premise in discussion is essential in determining how to respond.

Tone and stance can often be deduced from word choice, tone of voice, and volume. Attention to these will help in deciding whether it is appropriate to ask additional questions, seek clarification, refute a point, or to concede a point.

Refutation and concession looks at opposing viewpoints to the writer's claims, anticipating objections from the audience, and allowing as much of the opposing viewpoints as possible without weakening the thesis.

English Language Arts   104

Skill 7.9   **Presents information to convey an organized, clear perspective; content, style, and language are appropriate to the audience and task**

The content to be presented orally plays a big role in how it is organized and delivered. For example, a literary analysis or a book report will be organized inductively, laying out the details and then presenting a conclusion, which will usually discuss the author's purpose, message, and intent. If the analysis is focusing on multiple layers in a story, then that will probably follow the preliminary conclusion. On the other hand, remember that the speaker will want to keep the audience's attention, if the content has to do with difficult-to-follow facts and statistics, images and/or infographics may be used as a guide to the presentation, and the speaker will intersperse interesting anecdotes, jokes, or humor from time to time to maintain listeners' interest.

Consider also the attitude of the audience when organizing a presentation. If the audience has a high level of knowledge about what is being presented, little would need to be done in the way of providing background information. However, if many in the audience are new to the subject, background information to support understanding is necessary. Carefully written introductions aimed specifically at this audience will go a long way to attract their interest in the topic.

No speaker should make a presentation if the purpose has not been carefully determined ahead of time. If the speaker is not focused on the purpose, the audience will quickly lose interest. Based on your particular purpose, decide the best way to present your strongest information. Should it appear in the beginning, middle, or end? Will displaying the purpose on a chart, PowerPoint, or banner enhance the presentation? The purpose might be the lead-in for a presentation if it can be counted on to grab the interest of the listeners, in which case the organization will be deductive. If it seems better to save the purpose until the end, the organization will be inductive.

The occasion, of course, plays an important role in the development and delivery of a presentation. A congratulatory or celebratory speech will be organized around recognizing those who were most responsible, the importance of the milestone, how it was achieved and what competition was faced. The presentation will be upbeat and not too long. On the other hand, if bad news is being presented, the bad-news announcement will come first followed with details about the news itself and probably end with a pep talk and encouragement to do better the next time.

Effective oral presentations are presented in a logically sequenced way and include supporting reasons and evidence. A position statement, evidence, reason, and evaluation and refutation are integral parts of this schema.

The art of rhetoric was first developed in Ancient Greece. Greece's pioneer was Socrates, who recognized the crucial role that rhetoric played in education, politics, and storytelling. Socrates argued that, presently effectively, speech could evoke any desired emotion or opinion. His method of dialectic syllogism, known today as the Socratic method, pursued truth through a series of questions. Socrates established three types of appeals used in persuasive speech:

Types of Appeal

Ethos: Refers to the credibility of the speaker. It establishes the speaker as a reliable and trustworthy authority by focusing on the speaker's credentials.

Pathos: Refers to the emotional appeal made by the speaker to the listeners. It emphasizes the fact that the audience responds to ideas with emotion. For example, when the government is trying to persuade citizens to go to war for the sake of "the fatherland," it is using the appeal to pathos to target their love of their country.

Logos: Refers to the logic of the speaker's argument. It uses the idea that facts, statistics, and other forms of evidence can convince an audience to accept a speaker's argument. Remember that information can be just as, if not more, persuasive than appeal tactics.

Today, rhetoric's evolution can be traced back to ancient Athens in many facets of our society. The structure of many governments and judicial systems reflect rhetorical tactics established by the Greeks so long ago. The media has taken rhetoric to a whole new level and has refined it to a very skilled art. Every word as well as the method of presentation is carefully planned. The audience is taken into account and speech tailored to their needs and motivations. Though the content has changed, this concept has been around since Socrates contemplated it thousands of years ago.

Posture
Maintain a straight but not stiff posture. Instead of shifting weight from hip to hip, point your feet directly at the audience and distribute your weight evenly. Keep shoulders toward the audience. If you have to turn your body to use a visual aid, turn 45 degrees and continue speaking toward the audience.

Movement
Instead of staying glued to one spot or pacing back and forth, stay within four to eight feet of the front row of your audience. Take a step or half-step to the side every once in a while. If you are using a lectern, feel free to move to the front or side of it to engage your audience more. Avoid distancing yourself from the audience; you want them to feel involved and connected.

Gestures
Gestures can help you maintain a natural atmosphere when speaking publicly. Use them just as you would when speaking to a friend. They shouldn't be exaggerated, but they should be used for added emphasis. Avoid keeping your hands in your pockets or locked behind your back, wringing your hands and fidgeting nervously, or keeping your arms crossed.

Eye contact
Many people are intimidated by using eye contact when speaking to large groups. Interestingly, eye contact usually helps the speaker overcome speech anxiety by

connecting with the attentive audience and easing feelings of isolation. Instead of looking at a spot on the back wall or at your notes, scan the room and make eye contact for one to three seconds per person.

Voice

Many people fall into one of two traps when speaking: using a monotone or talking too fast. These are both caused by anxiety. A monotone restricts your natural inflection but can be remedied by releasing tension in the upper and lower body muscles. Subtle movement will keep you loose and natural. Talking too fast, on the other hand, is not necessarily bad if you are exceptionally articulate. If you are not a strong speaker or if you are talking about very technical items, the audience will easily become lost. When you talk too fast and begin tripping over your words, consciously pause after every sentence you say. Don't be afraid of brief silences. The audience needs time to absorb what you are saying.

Volume

Problems with volume, whether too soft or too loud, can usually be overcome with practice. If you tend to speak too softly, have someone stand in the back of the room and signal you when your volume is strong enough. If possible, have someone stand in the front of the room as well to make sure you're not overcompensating with excessive volume. Conversely, if you have a problem with speaking too loudly, have the person in the front of the room signal you when your voice is soft enough and check with the person in the back to make sure it is still loud enough to be heard. In both cases, note your volume level for future reference. Don't be shy about asking your audience, "Can you hear me in the back?" Suitable volume is beneficial for both you and the audience.

Pitch

Pitch refers to the length, tension, and thickness of your vocal bands. As your voice gets higher, the pitch gets higher. In oral performance, pitch reflects emotional arousal level. More variation in pitch typically corresponds to more emotional arousal but can also be used to convey sarcasm or highlight specific words. By encouraging the development of proper techniques for oral presentations, you are enabling your students to develop self-confidence for higher levels of communication.

Skill 7.10   Uses digital media successfully in presentations to enhance understanding and interest

Digital media are an integral part of almost any presentation. Audiences today expect not just to hear a presentation but also to see images, video clips, audio clips, infographics, and elements of graphic design. For examples of compelling presentations that illustrate just how well media can add to a presentation, TED talks are readily available.

Thankfully, these elements are 'within reach' for any presentation. Platforms and applications make it easy to create slideshows (PowerPoint, Google docs, Prezi,

Slideshare, etc.) and to share them electronically to audiences. Incorporating different media in those slideshows is also incredibly easy.

Creating media and graphics is also incredibly easy and does not require a huge amount of technical skill. Finding media that is free to use in presentations is also easy. Creative Commons, Flickr, and Google image search (among others) all offer options for finding media that are licensed to be used by others, particularly for educational purposes. Creative Commons also offers audio files for songs and music clips.

More and more, presentations take the form of digital stories. Combining all types of media plus narration, platforms like YouTube, Vimeo, Adobe Spark, and Voicethread allow presentations that can be shared easily to reach a wide audience. Though the platforms and applications will likely change over time, the need to be able to include media in presentations is not going away.

With any media that is not created by the presenter/creator, proper attribution is expected. Just as citing quotations in an essay is required, it is also required to cite photographs, video clips, and audio clips. Again, citation tools like EasyBib make this process quite simple.

Students should be able to produce visual images, messages, and meaning to communicate with others using technology, to enhance an oral presentation, in place of a written assignment they could make or upload a video as an adjunct to an oral presentation, to illustrate a point or to add information and interest.

Add media (images, film/video clips and/or sound clips (voices, music or sound effects) **to a presentation:**

- To illustrate, explain, or represent an idea
- As evidence to support an idea
- To evoke emotions, to provide a subtext or commentary

An audiovisual message offers the easiest accessibility for learners. It has the advantages of each, the graphic and the audio, medium. Learners' eyes and ears are engaged. Non-readers get significant access to content. On the other hand, viewing an audiovisual presentation is an even more passive activity than listening to an audio message because information is coming to learners effortlessly through two senses. Activities to foster a critical perspective on an audiovisual presentation serve as valuable safeguards against any overall and unwelcome passivity.

COMPETENCY 8   LANGUAGE

Skill 8.1   Understands that conventions of English usage change over time and are sometimes contested

English is an Indo-European language that evolved through several periods. The origin of English dates to the settlement of the British Isles in the fifth and sixth centuries by Germanic tribes called the Angles, Saxons, and Jutes. The original Britons spoke a Celtic tongue while the Angles spoke a Germanic dialect. Modern English derives from the speech of the Anglo-Saxons who imposed not only their language but also their social customs and laws on their new land. From the fifth to the tenth century, Britain's language was the tongue we now refer to as Old English. During the next four centuries, the many French attempts at English conquest introduced many French words to English. However, the grammar and syntax of the language remained Germanic.

Middle English, most evident in the writings of Geoffrey Chaucer, dates loosely from 1066 to 1509. William Caxton brought the printing press to England in 1474 and increased literacy. Old English words required numerous inflections to indicate noun cases and plurals as well as verb conjugations. Middle English continued the use of many inflections and pronunciations that treated these inflections as separately pronounced syllables. English in 1300 would have been written "Olde Anglishe" with the e's at the ends of the words pronounced as our short a vowel. Even adjectives had plural inflections: "long dai" became "longe daies" pronounced "long-a day-as." Spelling was phonetic, thus every vowel had multiple pronunciations, a fact that continues to affect the language.

Modern English dates from the introduction of The Great Vowels Shift because it created guidelines for spelling and pronunciation. Before the printing press, books were copied laboriously by hand; the language was subject to the individual interpretation of the scribes. Printers and subsequently lexicographers like Samuel Johnson and America's Noah Webster influenced the guidelines. As reading matter was mass produced, the reading public was forced to adopt the speech and writing habits developed by those who wrote and printed books.

Teachers should stress to students that language, like customs, values, and other social factors, is constantly subject to change. Immigration, inventions, and cataclysmic events change language as much as any other facet of life is affected by these changes.

War and conflict can influence language tremendously. Beginning with the colonization of the Americas by England, France, Spain and Portugal, these European languages became firmly established, displacing many indigenous languages.

Though English in the United States originated in Britain, today there are clear differences between the way British and American people speak. The most obvious difference is accent, but there are also quite a few differences in vocabulary (even for common things) and even spelling. The two languages do have very few syntactical differences, however.

Modern inventions - particularly those that have allowed media to spread easily - have especially affected English pronunciation. Regional dialects, once a hindrance to clear understanding, have fewer distinct characteristics. The speakers from different parts of the United States of America can be identified by their accents, but as more and more educators and media personalities stress uniform pronunciations and proper grammar, the differences are diminishing.

Computers, and their spread, continue to change language. Tom Friedman called it "flattening" in his *The World is Flat: A Brief History of the Twenty-first Century*. New terms have been added ("blog"), old terms have changed meaning ("mouse"), and nouns have been verbalized ("prioritize").

The vocabulary of the English language is more extensive than any other language. Ours is a language of synonyms, words borrowed from other languages, and coined words - many of them introduced by the rapid expansion of technology.

Students should understand that language is in constant flux. They can demonstrate this when they use language for specific purposes and audiences. Negative criticism of a student's errors in word choice or sentence structures will inhibit creativity. Positive criticism suggesting ways to enhance communication skills will encourage exploration.

As language has changed, so have the conventions of spelling and punctuation. Attempts to standardize and even simplify English spelling have occurred periodically. Similarly, some rules of punctuation/proper syntax have also changed. As an example, starting a sentence with 'but' or 'because' used to be considered incorrect, but there is much more flexibility around this today.

Changes in language are sometimes the subject of debate with some defending tradition and others arguing that change is natural. 'Standard' English can be an elusive concept since there are so many variations in how we use the language. Demanding that only 'standard' English be used may not only be futile but also disrespectful of the way large groups of people speak.

Different schools of thought suggest that a study of dialect and idiom and recognition of various jargons is a vital part of language development. New words are entering English from other languages even as words and expressions that were common when we were children have become rare or obsolete. What may matter most is that we recognize when we need to adapt language to suit context and audience. Academic and professional languages, for example, have a clear place in education.

Skill 8.2   Has command of standard English conventions in spelling, capitalization, and punctuation

Spelling

Spelling rules are extremely complex, based as they are on rules of phonics and letter doubling, and replete with exceptions. Even adults who have a good command of written English benefit from using computer-based tools to aid in spelling or a dictionary.

Plurals

Adding "s" to most nouns that end in hard consonants or hard consonant sounds followed by a silent e plural. Some nouns ending in vowels only add s. For example, fingers, numerals, banks, bugs, riots, homes, gates, radios, bananas, etc.

Add an 'es' for:

- Nouns that end in the soft consonant sounds s, j, x, z, ch, and sh
- Some nouns ending in o

Examples: dresses, waxes, churches, brushes, tomatoes, potatoes, etc.

- Nouns ending in y preceded by a consonant change. First make sure to change the y to an i.

Examples: babies, corollaries, frugalities, poppies, etc.

Add an 's' for:

- Nouns ending in y preceded by a vowel

Examples: boys, alleys, etc.

- Letters, numbers, and abbreviations

Examples: fives and tens, IBMs, 1990s, ps and qs (Note that letters are italicized.)

Irregular Noun Plurals
Some noun plurals are formed irregularly or are the same as the singular.

Examples: sheep, deer, children, leaves, oxen, etc.

Derivations
Nouns derived from foreign words, especially Latin, may make their plurals in two different ways, one of them Anglicized. Sometimes, the meanings are the same; other times, the two plurals are used in slightly different contexts. It is always wise to consult the dictionary.

Examples: appendices/appendixes, criterion/criteria indexes/indices, crisis/crises

Compound Words
Make the plurals of closed (solid) compound words in the usual way except for words ending in -ful, which make their plurals on the root word.

Example: timelines, hairpins, cupsful, etc.

Make the plurals of open or hyphenated compounds by adding the change in inflection to the word that changes in number.

Examples: fathers-in-law, courts-martial, masters of art, doctors of medicine, etc.

Understand capitalization conventions when composing a text
Capitalize all proper names of persons (including specific organizations or agencies of government); places (countries, states, cities, parks, and specific geographical areas); things (political parties, structures, historical and cultural terms, and calendar and time designations); and religious terms (any deity, revered person or group, or sacred writing).

Examples: Percy Bysshe Shelley, Argentina, Mount Rainier National Park, Grand Canyon, League of Nations, the Sears Tower, Birmingham, Lyric Theater, Americans, Midwesterners, Democrats, Renaissance, Boy Scouts of America, Easter, God, Bible, Dead Sea Scrolls, Koran

Capitalize proper adjectives and titles used with proper names.

Examples: California Gold Rush, President John Adams, Senator Elizabeth Warren
Note: Some words that represent titles and offices are not capitalized unless used with a proper name.

Capitalized	Not Capitalized
Congressman Ellison Commander Alger Queen Elizabeth President George Washington	the congressman from Florida commander of the Pacific Fleet the queen of England the president

Punctuation can have a big impact on the overall message that you're trying to convey, and it's very likely that points will be deducted if punctuation is used incorrectly or omitted within your essay questions. Using improper punctuation in your writing will create incorrect grammar and will confuse the reader of your essay. It can also create inaccurate quotations and names of famous works of literature.

Using commas

Commas indicate a brief pause. They are used to set off dependent clauses and long introductory word groups and they can also separate words in a series.

Commas are used to:

- Set off unimportant material that interrupts the flow of the sentence
- Separate independent clauses joined by conjunctions.
- Separate two or more coordinate adjectives modifying the same word and three or more nouns, phrases, or clauses in a list
- Separate antithetical or complementary expressions from the rest of the sentence.

Using Apostrophes

Apostrophes are used to show either contractions or possession. Contractions show the omission of a letter (wouldn't = would + not. The apostrophe takes the place of the o.) and possession represents ownership (Sam's new car. The apostrophe lets the reader know the new car belongs to Sam).

Using terminal punctuation in relation to quotation marks

In a quoted statement that is either declarative or imperative, place the period inside the closing quotation marks:

"The airplane crashed on the runway during takeoff."

If the quotation is followed by other words in the sentence, place a comma inside the closing quotations marks and a period at the end of the sentence:

"The airplane crashed on the runway during takeoff," said the announcer.

In most instances in which a quoted title or expression occurs at the end of a sentence, the period is placed before either the single or double quotation marks.

"The middle school readers were unprepared to understand Bryant's poem 'Thanatopsis.'"

Early book-length adventure stories like Don Quixote and The Three Musketeers were known as "picaresque novels."

There is an instance in which the final quotation mark would precede the period: if the content of the sentence were about a speech or quote so that the understanding of the meaning would be confused by the placement of the period.

The first thing out of his mouth was, "Hi, I'm home."

but

The first line of his speech began, "I arrived home to an empty house".

In sentences that are interrogatory or exclamatory, the question mark or exclamation point should be positioned outside the closing quotation marks if the quote itself is a statement, a command, or a cited title.

Who decided to lead us in the recitation of the "Pledge of Allegiance"?

Why was Tillie shaking as she began her recitation, "Once upon a midnight dreary"?

In sentences that are declarative but in which the quotation is a question or an exclamation, place the question mark or exclamation point inside the quotation marks.

The hall monitor yelled, "Fire! Fire!"

The hall monitor asked, "Where's the fire?"

Using periods with parentheses or brackets
Place the period inside the parentheses or brackets if they enclose a complete sentence independent of the other sentences around it.

Stephen Crane was a confirmed alcohol and drug addict. (He admitted as much to other journalists in Cuba.)

If the parenthetical expression is a statement inserted within another statement, the period in the enclosure is omitted.

Mark Twain used the character Indian Joe (he also appeared in The Adventures of Tom Sawyer) as a foil for Jim in The Adventures of Huckleberry Finn.

When enclosed matter comes at the end of a sentence requiring quotation marks, place the period outside the parentheses or brackets.

"The secretary of state consulted with the ambassador [Albright]."

Using double quotation marks with other punctuation
Quotations—whether words, phrases, or clauses—should be punctuated according to the rules of the grammatical function they serve in the sentence.

The works of Shakespeare, "the bard of Avon," have been contested as originating with other authors.

"You'll get my money," the old man warned, "when hell freezes over."

Sheila cited the passage that began "Four score and seven years ago ...."
(Note the ellipsis followed by an enclosed period.)

Use quotation marks to enclose the titles of shorter works: songs, short poems, short stories, essays, and chapters of books. (For title of longer works, see "Using italics," below.)

"The Tell-Tale Heart"   *"Casey at the Bat"*   *"America the Beautiful"*

Using semicolons

Semicolons are needed to divide two or more closely related independent sentences. They are also needed to separate items in a series containing commas.

1. Use semicolons to separate independent clauses when the second clause is introduced by a transitional adverb. (These clauses may also be written as separate sentences, preferably by placing the adverb within the second sentence.)

Semicolon: The Elizabethans modified the rhyme scheme of the sonnet; thus, it was called the English sonnet.

Separate Clauses: The Elizabethans modified the rhyme scheme of the sonnet. It thus was called the English sonnet.

2. Use semicolons to separate items in a series that are long and complex or have internal punctuation.

The Italian Renaissance produced masters in the fine arts: Dante Alighieri, author of the Divine Comedy; Leonardo da Vinci, painter of The Last Supper; and Donatello, sculptor of the Quattro Santi Coronati, the Four Crowned Saints.

The leading scorers in the WNBA were Haizhou Zheng, averaging 23.9 points per game; Lisa Leslie, 22; and Cynthia Cooper, 19.5.

Using colons

Colons are used to introduce lists and to emphasize what follows. You place a colon at the beginning of a list of items. (Note its use in the sentence about Renaissance Italians under "Using semicolons," above.)

The teacher directed us to compare Faulkner's three symbolic novels: Absalom, Absalom!; As I Lay Dying; and Light in August.

Do not use a colon if the list is preceded by a verb.

Three of Faulkner's symbolic novels are Absalom, Absalom!, As I Lay Dying, and Light in August.

Using Dashes

Place "en" dashes (short dashes) to denote sudden breaks in thought.

Some periods in literature - the Romantic Age, for example - spanned different time periods in different countries.

Use "em" dashes (long dashes) instead of commas if commas are used elsewhere in the sentence for amplification or explanation.

The Fireside Poets included three Brahmans—James Russell Lowell, Henry Wadsworth Longfellow, Oliver Wendell Holmes—and John Greenleaf Whittier.

Using italics

Use italics to style the titles of long works of literature, names of periodical publications, musical scores, works of art, movies, and television and radio programs.

Idylls of the King	*Hiawatha*	*The Sound and the Fury*
Mary Poppins	*Newsweek*	*Nutcracker Suite*

<u>Note</u>: When unable to write in italics, you should underline where italics would be appropriate.

Skill 8.3	**Uses context clues to determine the meaning of unknown words and words with multiple meanings**

Context clues help readers determine the meaning of words they are not familiar with. The context of a word is the sentence or sentences that surround the word. Read the following sentences and attempt to determine the meanings of the words in bold print:

The brilliant luminosity of the room meant that there was no need for lights.

If there was no need for lights, then one must assume that the word "luminosity" has something to do with giving off light. The definition of "luminosity," therefore, is the emission of light.

Jamie could not understand Joe's feelings. His mood swings made understanding him something of an enigma.

The fact that he could not be understood made him somewhat of a puzzle. The definition of "enigma" is a mystery or puzzle.

Context can also provide clues when the reader is familiar with a word but encounters it in an unfamiliar usage. Consider the following example:

Despite the child's tears, David callously paid no attention and gave no solace.

A reader may know the word *callous* in the context of calloused skin (hard, thick skin that forms in areas where there is a lot friction such as hands and feet). Knowing that and examining the context of the word's use, it would not be difficult to determine that *callous* means unfeeling or insensitive in the example above.

More often than not, given sufficient context, a reader can successfully determine the meaning of new words.

Context clues in combination with the skills in word analysis described in **Skill 8.4** provide the reader with a substantial set of tools for determining the meaning of unfamiliar words.

Skill 8.4   Uses patterns of word changes indicating different meanings and parts of speech to determine the meaning of unknown words

Recognition of patterns in words is a valuable strategy both in building new vocabulary and in determining the meaning of unfamiliar words encountered in texts or orally. Key strategies in this approach include learning to recognize the building blocks of words such as morphemes, roots, prefixes and suffixes.

Morphemes are the smallest units of language that are considered to have meaning by themselves. Some morphemes are complete words in and of themselves (e.g., dog) while others are not (e.g., *-ing*). Dog cannot be broken up into any 'piece' that has linguistic meaning (only the sounds of the letters). *-ing*, though not a word, does have meaning; it is added to verbs to make them gerunds (e.g. *singing, dancing*).

By adding *-ing* we can now use *singing* in combination with a word like *am* to show an action that is currently taking place (e.g., *I am dancing*). Adding *-ing* also allows us to turn a verb into a noun (e.g. *Teaching is very rewarding*).

Identification of Common Morphemes, Prefixes, and Suffixes

The terms listed below are generally recognized as the key structural analysis components.

Root Words: A root word is a word from which another word is developed. The second word can be said to have its "root" in the first.   An example of a root word is "bene" which means "good" or "well." English words from this Latin root include "benefit," "beneficial," "beneficent," and "beneficiary."

Root words are perhaps the most useful part of word analysis in determining meanings of unfamiliar words. Common roots include:

- *Acu/acut* meaning sharp or pointed (acute, acumen, acupuncture)
- *Ambul* meaning walk (ambulatory, amble, ambulance)
- *Grav* meaning heavy (gravity, gravitas, gravitate, grief, aggravate)
- *Path* meaning feeling or disease (antipathy, pathogen, pathetic, sympathetic)

Readers can use knowledge of these as the basis for determining meanings of new words.

Base Words: A base word is a stand-alone linguistic unit that cannot be deconstructed or broken down into smaller words. For example, in the word "re-tell," the base word is "tell."

Prefixes: These are beginning units of meaning which can be added (the vocabulary word for this type of structural adding is "affixed") to a base word or root word. They cannot stand-alone. They are also sometimes known as "bound morphemes," meaning that they cannot stand alone as a base word. Some examples of prefixes are "pre," "ex," "trans," and "sub."

Suffixes: These are ending units of meaning that can be "affixed" or added on to the ends of root or base words. Suffixes transform the original meanings of base and root words. Like prefixes, they are also known as "bound morphemes," because they cannot stand alone as words. Some examples of suffixes are "ing," "ful," "ness," and "er."

Inflectional endings: These are types of suffixes that impart a new meaning to the base or root word. These endings in particular change the gender, number, tense, or form of the base or root words. Just like other suffixes, these are also termed "bound morphemes." Some examples are "ette," "es," and "ed."

Compound Words: These occur when two or more base words are connected to form a new word. The meaning of the new word is in some way connected with that of the base word. "Bookkeeper," besides being the only English word with three double letters in a row, is an example of a compound word.

Skill 8.5   Understands figurative language, word relationships, and subtle difference in word meanings by interpreting context and analyzing denotative meanings

See also Skill 1.6 for information on figurative language and Skill 8.3 on using context

Denotation is the literal meaning of a word, as opposed to its connotative meaning.

Connotation refers to the implications and associations of a given word, distinct from the denotative or literal meaning. Connotation is often used when a subtle tone is preferred. It may stir up a more effective emotional response than if the author had used direct, denotative language. For example, "Good night, sweet prince, and flights of angels sing thee to thy rest," a line from Shakespeare's Hamlet, refers to death; connotatively, it renders the harsh reality of death in gentle terms such as those used in putting a child to sleep.

Informative connotations are definitions agreed upon by the society in which the learner operates. A skunk is "a black and white mammal of the weasel family with a pair of pineal glands which secrete a pungent odor." The Merriam-Webster Collegiate Dictionary adds "… and offensive" odor. The color, species, and glandular characteristics are informative. The interpretation of the odor as offensive is subjective, but it is generally agreed upon that skunks do smell. This is often called an affective connotation.

Affective connotations are the personal feelings a word arouses. A child who has no personal experience with a skunk and its odor will feel differently about the word skunk than a child who has smelled the spray or been conditioned vicariously to associate offensiveness with skunks. The fact that our society views a skunk as an animal to be avoided will affect the child's interpretation of the word. In fact, it is not necessary for one to have actually seen a skunk (that is, have a denotative understanding) to use the word in either connotative expression. For example, one child might tell another child that they smell like a skunk, connoting an unpleasant reaction (affective use) or, seeing another small black and white animal, call it a skunk based on the definition (informative use).

Figurative language often requires us to use context to determine meaning. This is most frequently true with poetry and literary fiction, but it is present in all language use. When we encounter idiomatic expressions (old or new) we are often able to determine the intended meaning through context. Even the shorthand used online or in social media direct messaging is easy to figure out given the right context. Someone new to social media, could likely figure out that *ttyl* means *talk to you later* if they saw it at the end of a conversation.

Skill 8.6   Understand the usage of verbs in the passive and active voices, imperative, interrogative, conditional, and subjunctive mood; uses verbs in different moods to create different effects

We rarely teach these skill or terms in isolation anymore, but knowledge of them is still important for many reasons. One simple one is that in helping students to become better writers or to analyze writing, it is essential to understand how to talk about elements of grammar, syntax, punctuation, and word usage. This short guide can serve as a refresher.

Parts of Speech

There are eight parts of speech: nouns, verbs, adjectives, adverbs, pronouns, conjunctions, prepositions, and interjections.

Noun	A person, place or thing. (*student, school, textbook*)
Verb	An action word. (*study, read, run*)
Adjective	Describes a verb or noun. (*smart, beautiful, colorful*)
Adverb	Describes a verb. (*quickly, fast, intelligently*)
Pronoun	Substitution for a noun. (he, she, it)
Conjunction	Joins two phrases. (*because, but, so*)
Preposition	Used before nouns to provide additional details. (*before, after, on*)
Interjection	Express emotion. (*Ha!, Hello!, Stop!*)

Syntax

Although widely different in many aspects, written and spoken English share a common basic structure or syntax (subject, verb, and object) and the common purpose of fulfilling the need to communicate—but there, the similarities end.

Spoken English follows the basic word order mentioned above (subject, verb object) as does written English. We would write as we would speak: "I sang a song." It is usually only in poetry or music that that word order or syntax is altered: "Sang I a song."

Types of Sentences

Declarative	Makes a statement. *I bought a new textbook.*
Interrogative	Asks a question. *Where did you buy the textbook?*
Exclamatory	Expresses strong emotion. *I can't believe it's your birthday today!*
Imperative	Gives a command. *Put the birthday cake on the table.*

Passive	Suggests something was done **to** someone or something. Suggests an external cause. *He was sent away.*
Conditional	Speculates about what could happen, what might have happened, or what we wish would happen. Often uses the word 'if'. *If it snows, you will be cold.* Often uses 'would'. *If I won the lottery, I would go on a big trip.* *If you had been nicer, you would have gotten the job.*
Subjunctive	Not very commonly used in English (though several hundred years ago it was). *If I were a bird, I would fly away.* Using 'were' shows that the speaker is NOT a bird. *I recommend that he study more frequently.* Normally we would say 'he studies', but in this sentence, the recommendation is an implied command causing the verb change.

Types of Clauses

Clauses are connected word groups that are composed of at least one subject and one verb. (A subject is the doer of an action or the element that is being joined. A verb conveys either the action or the link.)

> *Students are waiting for the start of the assembly.*
> subject verb

> *At the end of the play, students waited for the curtain to come down.*
> subject verb

Clauses can be independent or dependent. **Independent clauses** can stand alone or can be joined to other clauses, either independent or dependent. Words that can be used to join clauses include the following:

- for
- and
- nor
- but
- or
- yet
- so

Dependent clauses, by definition, contain at least one subject and one verb. However, they cannot stand alone as a complete sentence. They are structurally dependent on an independent clause (the main clause of the sentence). There are two types of dependent clauses: (1) those with a subordinating conjunction and (2) those with a relative pronoun. Coordinating conjunctions include the following:

- although
- when
- if
- unless
- because

Example: *Unless a cure is discovered, many more people will die of the disease.*
(dependent clause with coordinating conjunction [unless] + independent clause)

Relative pronouns include the following:

- who
- whom
- which
- that

Example: *The White House has an official website, which contains press releases, news updates, and biographies of the president and vice president.*
(independent clause + relative pronoun [which] + relative dependent clause)

Sentence Structure

Recognize simple, compound, complex, and compound-complex sentences. Use dependent (subordinate) and independent clauses correctly to create these sentence structures.

Simple	Joyce wrote a letter.
Compound	Joyce wrote a letter and Dot drew a picture.
Complex	While Joyce wrote a letter, Dot drew a picture.
Compound/complex	When Mother asked the girls to demonstrate their newfound skills, Joyce wrote a letter and Dot drew a picture.

Note: Do not confuse compound sentence elements with compound sentences.

Simple sentence with compound subject:
Rosie and Marissa wrote letters.
The girl in row three and the boy next to her were passing notes across the aisle.

Simple sentence with compound predicate:
Sumiyo wrote letters and drew pictures.
The captain of the high school debate team graduated with honors and studied broadcast journalism in college.

Simple sentence with compound object of preposition:
Claudia graded the students' essays for style and mechanical accuracy.

Parallelism
Recognize parallel structures using phrases (prepositional, gerund, participial, and infinitive) and omissions from sentences that create the lack of parallelism.

Prepositional phrase/single modifier:
Incorrect: Francesca ate the ice cream with enthusiasm and hurriedly.
Correct: Francesca ate the ice cream with enthusiasm and in a hurry.
Correct: Francesca ate the ice cream enthusiastically and hurriedly.

Participial phrase/infinitive phrase:
Incorrect: After hiking for hours and to sweat profusely, Mateo sat down to rest and drinking water.
Correct: After hiking for hours and sweating profusely, Mateo sat down to rest and drink water.

Recognition of Misplaced and Dangling Phrases
Dangling phrases are attached to sentence parts in such a way that they create ambiguity and incorrectness of meaning.

Participial phrase:
Incorrect: Hanging from her skirt, Akiko tugged at a loose thread.
Correct: Akiko tugged at a loose thread hanging from her skirt.

Infinitive phrase:
Incorrect: To improve his behavior, the dean warned Anders.
Correct: The dean warned Anders to improve his behavior.

Prepositional phrase:
Incorrect: On the floor, Suada saw the dog eating table scraps.
Correct: Suada saw the dog eating table scraps on the floor.

Recognition of Syntactic Omission
These errors occur when superfluous words have been added to a sentence or keywords have been omitted from a sentence.

Incorrect: He was a **mere** skeleton of his former self.
Correct: He was a skeleton of his former self.

Omission

Incorrect: Ryan opened his book, recited her textbook, and answered the teacher's subsequent question.

Correct: Ryan opened his book, recited **from the** textbook, and answered the teacher's subsequent question.

Avoidance of Double Negatives

This error occurs from positioning two negatives that cancel each other out (create a positive statement).

Incorrect: Madeleine didn't have no double negatives in her paper.
Correct: Madeleine didn't have **any** double negatives in her paper.

Skill 8.7	Is familiar with and uses domain-specific vocabulary at the college and career readiness level

There are elements of academic language that are both generic and domain-specific. Many disciplines, for example, use terminology such as *analyze, estimate,* and *demonstrate*. What these words mean to a chemist and to teacher of language arts may differ, but the expectation and outcome would likely recognizable to both. Academic language is, after all, "the language that is used by teachers and students for the purpose of acquiring new knowledge and skills . . . imparting new information, describing abstract ideas, and developing students' conceptual understandings" (Chamot & O'Malley, 1994, p. 40).

English Language Arts, like other disciplines, has its own domain-specific language as well. Terms like *symbolism, characterization, alliteration, denouement,* and *idiom* all describe something very specific relating the academic activities and expectations that are part of Language Arts. Similarly *ablation, accelerant,* and *polymer* all have specific meanings and uses in chemistry.

We can often 'talk around' (or use circumlocution) domain-specific terms with students by explaining them using examples, detailed description, or substituting other words, but we should. We should teach and then regularly use the academic language of our subject for several reasons:

- These are the words that form the basis for academic discussion and analysis in English Language Arts;
- In doing research in Language Arts, students will encounter the words themselves without an intermediary explaining what the terms mean;
- In order to participate in and add to the discipline, students will need to use the language themselves; and
- Inevitably, either professionally or in later education, students will be in situations in which they are expected to know the terminology.

The academic language of English Language Arts can be viewed in three different categories.

Content words: These include words related to literature and expository writing such as conflict, setting, and characters. Words related to writing analysis include imagery and sentence structure. Grammar-related terms include clause, fragment, and homonym.

Process words: These words and phrases describe the things we are expected to do in language arts such as:

- Analyze the author's message
- Explain the use of perspective
- Describe the narrative structure

Words (and parts of words) that teach the structure of English: These are things that allow students to learn new vocabulary and language. Many of them are morphemes and include roots, suffixes, and prefixes.

The Common Core includes a number of skill-related terms. They include:

analyze	articulate	cite	compare
contrast	delineate	describe	demonstrate
determine	develop	distinguish	draw
evaluate	explain	identify	infer
integrate	interpret	locate	organize
paraphrase	refer	retell	suggest
support	summarize	synthesize	trace
alliteration	analogy	argument	central idea
conclusions	connections	connotative language	details
evidence	figurative language	metaphor	mood
point of view	rhetoric	simile	stanza
structure	theme	tone	meter

These words make up a part of the language inherent in the study and analysis of language and writing.

Skill 8.8   Demonstrates ability to gather vocabulary knowledge

See Skills 8.3 and 8.4

Despite the strategies for determining the meanings of words noted in the above skills, there will still be times in which it is impossible to determine the meaning of a word. Fortunately, there are many effective ways to find meanings, many of them assisted by technology.

- Browser-based dictionaries are available in most web browsers.
- Dictionaries, both the traditional printed varieties and dictionary apps, make looking up a word easy anytime, anywhere.
- High frequency word lists

COMPETENCY 9   PEDAGOGICAL CONTENT KNOWLEDGE

Skill 9.1   Is able to assess whether a student is ready for a new learning goal related to analyzing informational or narrative texts

To determine whether a student is ready for a new learning goal related to analysis of informational and narrative texts, teachers must have knowledge of the learning standards and engage in regular assessment of student progress. One way to ensure this is to use formative assessment (**see Skill 9.6**) regularly. This will provide information and insight into students' ability to interact with delve into the meaning of class texts.

A key element in this regard is to ensure that students have opportunities to read different texts in many different situations. Whole class readings (novels, articles, etc.) provide a structured way of guiding students in developing analytical skills. Some students may not be particularly interested in the readings selected for whole class use, so elements of choice should be a part of any reading program.

Literature circles in which students select books based on interest can often engage readers in different ways than whole class texts. Similarly, independent reading programs should allow students great leeway in what they read to build interest.

With any reading, however, analytical skills are developed (and monitored) through frequent reflection. Class discussions, teacher-student meetings, peer discussions, reading journals, and book talks are opportunities to build analytical skills and for teachers to monitor student readiness for additional challenge.

Skill 9.2   Designs effective instructional experiences that connect students' prior knowledge to new learning

Schema
Schemata need to be activated to draw upon the previous knowledge and learning of the English Language Learner. The use of graphics to encourage pre-reading thought about a topic (e.g., brainstorming, web maps, and organizational charts) activates this knowledge and shows how information is organized in the students' minds. Schumm (2006) states that research has shown:

- More prior knowledge permits a reader to understand and remember more (Brown, Bransford, Ferrara, & Campione, 1983).
- Prior knowledge must be activated to improve comprehension (Bransford & Johnson, 1972).
- Failure to activate prior knowledge is one cause of poor readers (Paris & Lindauer, 1976).
- Good readers may reject ideas that conflict with their prior knowledge (Pressley, 2000).

The research on schema has important implications for instruction. Not only is connection to prior knowledge a powerful tool in building comprehension, it is also effective in helping students to more deeply explore a topic or question (**see Skill 9.3**). When students can connect prior knowledge to new learning, they are more likely to approach challenges with confidence. They may read more challenging texts, pursue a new line of thinking in analyzing literature, or attempt more complex writing styles.

One element of this is ensuring that the lesson objectives and teacher expectations are clear from the start of the lesson. Having a clear picture of the overall learning goals helps students to integrate knowledge and make connections to what they already know. In addition, they will be more likely to retain information.

Moll (1988) discusses the value of the funds of knowledge that students bring to the classroom. This knowledge regarding students' lives can be incorporated into lessons and content for course work. It helps choose topics that would be of interest to the students and in engages them in the learning process.

Pre-reading activities can be designed to motivate student interest, activate prior knowledge, or pre-teach potentially difficult concepts and vocabulary. This is also a great opportunity to introduce comprehension components such as cause and effect, compare and contrast, personification, main idea, sequencing, and others. Pre-reading activities can involve related readings, background knowledge explorations, presentations, discussions, use of media (e.g., films), or research.

Though not always practical because of scheduling or curricular demands, integrated units of study are excellent ways to connect students' prior learning to new learning. Fiction from a particular time period can be linked to history, art, and music. This also increases the likelihood that students will have experiences or learning that connect to the new topic.

Another advantage of designing activities like these to connect students' prior knowledge to new units is that there is little 'risk' for students. As they begin to explore a topic, they can do so without worrying about grades or evaluation. Teachers can also use this as formative assessment to inform instruction.

Skill 9.3   Employs knowledge of instructional strategies to help students develop effective questions to further their learning about a topic in an informational or a literary text

See Skill 6.1

In addition to the skills for developing good questions described in Skill 6.1, an important part of developing successful questions is metacognitive. Evaluating one's own level of knowledge and understanding of a text is a key part of delving deeper into a topic. As students recognize what they know, don't know, need clarification about, or want to know about a subject, they are better able to develop questions for a topic with informational and literary texts. This self-monitoring is a valuable skill not only as a reader and researcher in English but in any discipline.

Encouraging students to be reflective about their strengths, challenges and strategies for success involves asking questions. When students take responsibility for their own learning, they will be able to do what teachers do: set goals, assess their progress, analyze their needs and make action plans to improve their learning and proficiency. In order for students to do this, they need to feel comfortable asking questions, and admitting when they don't understand or need input to be repeated. A respectful, safe, cooperative classroom environment is crucial in helping students improve academic, communicative, and metacognitive skills.

The metacognitive aspect of asking questions to deepen understanding overlaps with several very practical classroom strategies. As students work with informational and literary texts, it is useful for them to have an established method for tracking what they have learned/gleaned from a text and what they may still need to find out. This involves close reading.

Close reading is active with the reader examining multiple elements of a text including:

- Ideas, concepts and themes
- Important details
- Craft and structure
- How the content of the text connects to prior knowledge

To facilitate close reading, teachers should teach students methods of self-monitoring their reading. Annotation, either in the text itself or in a notebook, is essential. Students look for key information, underline important passages, and write down questions about the reading. In many cases, teachers can help get this process started by providing graphic organizers.

While building these habits, teachers should also engage in frequent discussions of student reading. This can be done in small groups, large groups, or even in one on one conferencing. Teachers can model how they respond to texts, showing the questions the texts provoke and how they can then follow up to investigate them. Some activities to build questioning skills and habits include:

- Shared readings
- Literature circles
- 'Questioning the author' (pondering author's intent or underlying ideas)
- Connecting to original questions and curricular standards
- Annotations and post it notes

Finally, teachers must work with students to help them see reading and research as recursive processes in which the student returns to his/her original premise or research question repeatedly. This allows the reader to determine whether they are 'on track', need to do additional investigation, or whether new questions have arisen.

Skill 9.4   Designs instructional approaches that help students to analyze multiple interpretations of literary texts; helps students understand how each interprets the text differently

In some ways there is no 'wrong' interpretation of a literary text. There are, instead, interpretations that lack evidence and support. Literary analysis and interpretation are subjective and have a great deal to do with factors like the reader's personal experience, educational background, and even political beliefs. The key, then, to successful literary interpretation is supporting that interpretation with evidence, often drawn from the text itself, to make a convincing case for one's analysis.

Teachers must design learning experiences that require students to look at different interpretations. This not only helps them to see that different interpretations exist but also the ways that readers/writers support their views with evidence.

Teachers can begin this learning process with different types of activities.

Film

Introducing students to interpretation through film is easy and engaging. By selecting a series of film clips that are somewhat ambiguous, the teacher can facilitate discussions of meaning, pushing students to support their interpretations with evidence.

Start short

Poetry and short stories are excellent ways to introduce students to multiple interpretations of a work. The figurative language of poetry and the length of both can allow for analyses of multiple works within a short time frame. This gives students practice and exposure to the process and use of evidence.

Open-ended questioning

Perhaps the most important aspect, however, is open-ended questioning. Engaging students in writing and discussion about questions with no definitive answer will prompt disagreement, debate, and analysis of literary work. Each work engenders its own set of specific questions, but questions of the type below will provoke different answers from different students.

- What is the significance of...?
- Why did the character...?
- What experiences motivated the character to...?
- What was the author trying to show by...?

- Why is this considered an important work?

The next step of course in helping students to understand that there are different interpretations of literary texts is to introduce them the literary analyses of others. Literary criticism (either excerpted or not) can reveal new perspectives to students. Selecting contrasting interpretations of the same work or author is particularly useful.

One way of doing this is to introduce students to some of the different schools of literary criticism. Though none of them is necessarily defined by a set of fixed rules, each has a distinct perspective. A few of these schools are:

- Feminist criticism
- Structuralism and Semiotics
- Post-Colonial criticism
- Cultural Studies
- Gender Studies

Each one can be viewed like a lens through which writing can be interpreted, demonstrating to students the multiplicity of ways writing can be viewed and interpreted.

Skill 9.5 **Assists students in creating interpretive and responsive texts that demonstrate knowledge and understanding of connections between life and literary work**

There is no magical way of turning students into good writers overnight, but there are proven methods of helping all students develop writing skills. It is essential to have frequent exposure to quality writing, analysis of the characteristics of good writing, frequent practice, and regular participation in drafting, revising, and editing work.

Exposure: Mentor texts

When teachers plan different writing units (narratives, essays, poetry, persuasive, etc.) they should seek out examples of each text type (**mentor texts**) that are accessible and engaging for students. Teachers should plan activities where students analyze each mentor text to ascertain the qualities that make the writing stand out. As a class, these traits should be documented. Examples of traits that might come up include:

- Phrasing of introductory sentences in essays that engage readers right away
- Descriptive phrasing in narratives or poetry
- Strong opening lines/paragraphs in fiction
- Smooth integration of quotes and evidence in essays
- Conclusions that tie ideas together
- Artful punctuation
- Gathering of evidence to support analysis and interpretation of writing
- Transitional phrases that connect ideas well

- Natural sounding dialogue

Writing

As students begin exploring these text types, frequent writing practice is essential. Referring to the characteristics identified in the mentor texts, teachers can ask students to begin trying to emulate stylistic choices and practicing techniques from the mentor texts. Peer reviews, one on one student-teacher meetings, and even analysis of student writing can all be used to further encourage students to bring the characteristics from the mentor texts into their own writing.

As the writing unit progresses and it is time to move towards a final assignment (literary essay, magazine article, etc.), students can set goals of elements of good writing that they want to incorporate into their own pieces. In conferences with peers or with the teacher, they can discuss how to accomplish that [[[;p';goal and ask for ideas for editing.

Revision and editing

All major writing assignments (the final essay in an essay writing unit, for example) should go through several drafts. Again, with peer and teacher input, students should work towards refining their pieces to incorporate traits from the mentor texts and reach their writing goals.

Skill 9.6   Employs effective assessment methods that measure and promote student learning

Teachers should employ both formative and summative (formal) assessment techniques in order to monitor progress, promote growth, and promote student learning.

Formal Assessments

Formal assessment is summative in nature. It refers to tests or projects given to students at the end of a unit, term, or course of study. The results of formal assessment usually translate into a mark or grade that the students receive to determine progress towards meeting a learning standard. The teacher controls the testing environment for formal assessment. Another formal assessment is a diagnostic assessment. It's given at the end of a grade level and the results are compared to that of a control group.

For assessing growth, formal assessment can take the form of:

- Presentations that students have to prepare for and deliver to a group
- Debates
- Scheduled interviews between the teacher and student in which the student has to prepare answers to questions
- Knowledge checks

- Quizzes
- Homework
- Journal responses

Informal Assessments

Informal or formative assessments pave the way for formal assessment. These assessments take place throughout the course of study and help prepare the student to succeed. The teacher uses informal assessments to determine where the student needs help or where the instruction needs to change to meet the needs of the student. For formative assessments to be effective, they must involve extensive feedback to students. Feedback can take the form of notes, conferencing, comments on work, etc.

Some methods or opportunities for informal assessment include:

- Student discussion in Literature Circles
- Overall conversation in the class
- Interviews between student and teacher, such as in discussing the books students are reading and questioning on comprehension
- Anecdotal records of student performance, needs, and improvement
- Skills checklists
- Small group instruction
- Running records of students' reading
- Student questions and answers in class discussion

Ways in which teachers can use informal assessment include:

- To assist student learning
- To identify students' strengths and weaknesses
- To assess the effectiveness of a particular instructional strategy
- To assess and improve the effectiveness of curriculum programs
- To assess and improve teaching effectiveness
- To provide data that assists in decision making
- To communicate with and involve parents
- To adapt instruction to meet student needs

Some skills to evaluate during informal assessments include:

- Writing skill development (punctuation, grammar, language usage)
- Vocabulary development and use
- Knowledge/mastery of content
- Ability to summarize
- Reading comprehension

Teachers can take the objectives for each grade and plan experiences that allow for formative assessment of progress **before** summative assessment takes place. By making notes about specific observations, teachers can tailor instruction in subsequent classes to reteach, challenge, conference, or simply monitor. These can take the form of mini-lessons for the whole class or small groups of students that need this instruction.

The purpose of informal assessment is to help our learners learn better. This form of assessment helps the teacher to understand how well the learners are learning and progressing. Informal assessment can be applied to homework assignments, field journals, and daily class work – all good indicators of student progress and comprehension.

Formal assessment, on the other hand, is highly structured, keeping the learner in mind. It must be done at regular intervals, and if the progress is not satisfactory, parent involvement is absolutely essential. A test or exam is a good example of formal assessment.

The types of assessment discussed below represent many of the more common types of assessment, but the list is not comprehensive.

Anecdotal Records

These are notes recorded by the teacher concerning an area of interest or concern with a particular student. These records can be used to note milestones, areas in which a student might need extra support, or to record successful teaching strategies or student groupings. Reviewing these records periodically can help a teacher refine instruction to meet the needs of students.

Comprehension

Independent reading inventories can assist a teacher in determining reading fluency as well as strengths and weaknesses in the progress of reading comprehension. The inventory provides graded word lists and graded passages that assess oral reading, silent reading, and listening comprehension. Some IRIs provide narrative and expository passages with longer passage options. After reading a passage, the student answers questions or retells the passage. IRIs record students' errors while they are reading to the teacher, as well as provide information about a student's word recognition, oral reading fluency, and listening comprehension. Analyzing a student's reading abilities includes: phonological awareness, letter identification, sound-letter correspondence knowledge, and recognizing sight-words.

Using inventories this way can help in identifying areas in which students need support or reteaching.

Rubrics

Rubrics offer several advantages in grading multi-faceted work like projects. First they allow teachers to clearly delineate success criteria to students. Students who know what they are expected to learn or what skills they are supposed to demonstrate are more likely to do well. They also allow students to see a description of what the differences between exceptional work and acceptable work are. For students who aspire to excel, this can be a helpful way of guiding them to the next level.

Similarly, rubrics allow teachers to give feedback that is more instructive. A student who demonstrates knowledge of a topic in their project but who has difficulty with writing can see that reflected in the rubric. The knowledge component may receive a high mark while the writing component could highlight the need for further work and revision. This also prevents a situation in which a student's overall grade is not 'penalized' because skills in one are still developing. Separating out different skill/knowledge components helps the student better understand his/her strengths and weaknesses.

Portfolio Assessment

The use of student portfolios for some aspects of assessment has become quite common. The purpose, nature, and policies of portfolio assessment vary greatly from one setting to another. In general, though, a student's portfolio contains samples of work collected over an extended period. The nature of the subject, age of the student, and scope of the portfolio all contribute to the specific mechanics of analyzing, synthesizing and, otherwise, evaluating the portfolio contents.

In most cases, the student and teacher make joint decisions as to which work samples go into the student's portfolios. A collection of work compiled over an extended time period allows teachers, students, and parents to view progress from a unique perspective. Qualitative changes over time can be readily apparent from work samples. Such changes are difficult to establish with strictly quantitative records typical of the scores recorded in the teacher's grade book.

Questioning

One of the most frequently occurring forms of assessment in the classroom is oral questioning by the teacher. As the teacher questions the students, a great deal of information can be collected about the degree of student learning and potential sources of confusion for the students. While questioning is often viewed as a component of instructional methodology, it is also a powerful assessment tool.

Tests

Tests and similar direct-assessment methods represent the most easily identified types of assessment. Thorndike (1997) identifies three types of assessment instruments:

1. Standardized achievement tests
2. Assessment material packaged with curricular materials
3. Teacher-made assessment instruments
   o Pencil and paper tests

- o Oral tests
- o Product evaluations
- o Performance tests
- o Effective measures

REFERENCES

Stangor, Dr. Charles. "Principles of Social Psychology – 1st International Edition." *Improving Group Performance and Decision Making | Principles of Social Psychology – 1st International Edition.* 26 Sept. 2014. Web. 21 Feb. 2017.

"Welcome to the Purdue OWL." *The Purdue OWL: Research and Citation.* Web. 21 Feb. 2017.

"Welcome to the Purdue OWL." *Purdue OWL: MLA Formatting and Style Guide.* Web. 21 Feb. 2017.

Zygouris-Coe, Vassiliki I., and Vassiliko I. Zygouris Coe. *Teaching Discipline-specific Literacies in Grades 6-12: Preparing Students for College, Career, and Workforce Demands.* New York, NY: Routledge, 2015. Print.

SAMPLE TEST

1. In Poe's poem, *The Bells*, words such as *twanging*, and *tintinnabulation* are examples of: *(Skill 1.6)*

    A. Consonance
    B. Figurative language
    C. Alliteration
    D. Free verse

2. Expressions in the English language that are casual, slang, or jargons in relation to cultural associations are considered to be: *(Skill 8.1)*

    A. Allusions
    B. Idioms
    C. Aphorisms
    D. Euphemisms

3. "My daughter was told that there would be no homework, but when she got to school she got in trouble for not turning in an assignment," said Allan. *(Skill 8.6)*

    By using the passive voice, what effect does the speaker intend?

    A. To imply that it was not his daughter's fault
    B. To express anger
    C. To calmly explain the situation
    D. To defuse tension

4. For a presentation on actions the school board should take to reduce energy use, which strategy would students most likely find successful? *(Competency 7)*

    A. Link reduced energy use to reduced costs and greater environmental responsibility
    B. Explain in detail the different uses of energy at schools
    C. Complain about the board's lack of environmental responsibility
    D. Read letters from other students

5. In this paragraph from a student essay, identify the sentence that provides a detail. *(Skill 4.3)*

    (1) The poem concerns two different personality types and the human relation between them. (2) Their approach to life is totally different. (3) The neighbor is a very conservative person who follows routines. (4) He follows the traditional wisdom of his father and his father's father. (5) The purpose in fixing the wall and keeping their relationship separate is only because it is all he knows.

    A. Sentence 1
    B. Sentence 3
    C. Sentence 4
    D. Sentence 5

6. The substitution of *went to his rest* for *died* is an example of a/an *(Skill 4.1)*

    A. Bowdlerism.
    B. Jargon.
    C. Euphemism.
    D. Malapropism.

7. Select the correct version of the sentence below. *(Skill 8.2)*

    A. I climbed to the top of the mountain, it took me three hours.
    B. I climbed to the top of the mountain it took me three hours.
    C. I climbed to the top of the mountain: it took me three hours.
    D. I climbed to the top of the mountain; it took me three hours.

8. Which of the following techniques is an effective tool of characterization? *(Skill 5.1)*

    A. Dialogue
    B. Denouement
    C. Sensory language
    D. First person narration

9. Which of the following descriptions most relies on sensory language? *(Competency 5)*

    A. As a child their frequent arguments tore him apart.
    B. As a child their frequent arguments were like wounds that never healed.
    C. As a child he had to put up with the sound of their frequent arguments.
    D. As a child their frequent arguments echoed through the house.

10. **The literary device of personification is used in which example below?** *(Skill 1.6)*

    A. "Beg me no beggary by soul or parents, whining dog!"
    B. "Happiness sped through the halls cajoling as it went."
    C. "O wind thy horn, thou proud fellow."
    D. "And that one talent which is death to hide."

11. **Arthur Miller wrote *The Crucible* as a parallel to what twentieth century event?** *(Competency 1)*

    A. Sen. McCarthy's House un-American Activities Committee Hearing
    B. The Cold War
    C. The fall of the Berlin Wall
    D. The Persian Gulf War

12. **Which of the following is the best definition of existentialism?** *(Skill 1.11)*

    A. The philosophical doctrine that matter is the only reality and that everything in the world, including thought, will and feeling, can be explained only in terms of matter.
    B. Philosophy that views things as they should be or as one would wish them to be.
    C. A philosophical and literary movement, variously religious and atheistic, stemming from Kierkegaard and represented by Sartre.
    D. The belief that all events are determined by fate and are hence inevitable.

13. **How does Henry David Thoreau seek to persuade readers in this excerpt from "Civil Disobedience"?** *(Competencies 2 and 3)*

    Unjust laws exist; shall we be content to obey them, or shall we endeavor to amend them, and obey them until we have succeeded, or shall we transgress them at once? Men generally, under such a government as this, think that they ought to wait until they have persuaded the majority to alter them. They think that, if they should resist, the remedy would be worse than the evil. But it is the fault of the government itself that the remedy *is* worse than the evil. … Why does it always crucify Christ, and excommunicate Copernicus and Luther, and pronounce Washington and Franklin rebels?
    --"Civil Disobedience" by Henry David Thoreau

    A. Through appeals to emotion
    B. By using parallelism to tie two themes together
    C. Through reason
    D. By using symbolism

14. **In presenting a report to peers about the effects of Hurricane Katrina on New Orleans, the students wanted to use various media in their argument to persuade their peers that more needed to be done. Which of these would be the most effective?** *(Competency 3)*

   A. A presentation showing the blueprints of the levees before the flood and redesigned now for current construction.
   B. A collection of music clips made by the street performers in the French Quarter before and after the flood.
   C. A recent video showing the areas devastated by the floods and the current state of rebuilding.
   D. A collection of recordings of interviews made by the various government officials and local citizens affected by the flooding.

15. **Which of the following should *not* be included in the opening paragraph of an informative essay?** *(Skill 4.1)*

   A. Thesis sentence
   B. Details and examples supporting the main idea
   C. Broad general introduction to the topic
   D. A style and tone that grabs the reader's attention

16. **In the paragraph below, which sentence does *not* contribute to the overall task of supporting the main idea?** *(Skill 4.2)*

   The Springfield City Council met Friday to discuss new zoning restrictions for the land to be developed south of the city. 2) Residents who opposed the new restrictions were granted 15 minutes to present their case. 3) Their argument focused on the dangers that increased traffic would bring to the area. 4) It seemed to me that the Mayor Simpson listened intently. 5) The council agreed to table the new zoning until studies would be performed.

   A. Sentence 2
   B. Sentence 3
   C. Sentence 4
   D. Sentence 5

17. **In preparing your class to write a research paper about a social problem, what requirements can you put in place so they take steps to determine the credibility of their information?** *(Competency 6)*

   A. Only go to major news sites
   B. Find one solid, reputable source and use that exclusively
   C. Use only primary sources
   D. Ensure that information they find is also available elsewhere

18. **Which of the following are secondary research materials?**
(Competency 6)

A. The conclusions and inferences of other historians.
B. Literature and nonverbal materials, novels, stories, poetry and essays from the period, as well as coins, archaeological artifacts, and art produced during the period.
C. Interviews and surveys conducted by the researcher.
D. Statistics gathered as the result of the research's experiments.

19. **Which of the following situations is *not* an ethical violation of intellectual property?** *(Competency 6)*

A. A student visits ten different websites and writes a report to compare the costs of downloading music. He uses the names of the websites without their permission.
B. A student copies and pastes a chart verbatim from the Internet but does not document it because it is available on a public site.
C. From an online article found in a subscription database, a student paraphrases a section on the problems of music piracy. She includes the source in her Works Cited but does not provide an in-text citation.
D. A student includes a YouTube from a popular fan site in a project without including an entry in Works Cited.

20. **Students have been asked to write a research paper on automobiles and have brainstormed a number of questions they will answer based on their research findings. Which of the following is *not* an interpretive question to guide research?** *(Competency 6)*

A. What were the first ten automotive manufacturers in the United States?
B. What types of vehicles will be used fifty years from now?
C. How do automobiles manufactured in the United States compare and contrast with each other?
D. What do you think is the best solution for the fuel shortage?

21. Which transition word would show contrast between these two ideas? *(Competency 4)*

We are confident in our skills to teach English. We welcome new ideas on this subject.

A. We are confident in our skills to teach English, and we welcome new ideas on this subject.
B. Because we are confident in our skills to teach English, we welcome new ideas on the subject.
C. When we are confident in our skills to teach English, we welcome new ideas on the subject.
D. We are confident in our skills to teach English; however, we welcome new ideas on the subject.

22. Which part of a classical argument is illustrated in this excerpt from the essay "What Should Be Done About Rock Lyrics?" *(Competency 3)*

But violence against women is greeted by silence. It shouldn't be.

This does not mean censorship, or book (or record) burning. In a society that protects free expression, we understand a lot of stuff will float up out of the sewer. Usually, we recognize the ugly stuff that advocates violence against any group as the garbage it is, and we consider its purveyors as moral lepers. We hold our nose and tolerate it, but we speak out against the values it proffers.

--"What Should Be Done About Rock Lyrics?" Caryl Rivers

A. Narration
B. Confirmation
C. Refutation and concession
D. Summation

23. What was likely the biggest responsible for the standardizing of dialects across America in the 20th century? *(Competency 8)*

A. With the immigrant influx, American became a melting pot of languages and cultures.
B. Trains enabled people to meet other people of different languages and cultures.
C. The spread of different media featured actors and announcers who spoke without pronounced dialects.
D. Newspapers and libraries developed programs to teach people to speak English with an agreed-upon common dialect.

24. **Two of the first distinctly American writers include:** *(Competency 1)*

    A. Nathaniel Hawthorne and Herman Melville
    B. Arthur Miller and Zora Neale Hurston
    C. Samuel Beckett and Victor Hugo
    D. Richard Wright and F. Scott Fitzgerald

25. **In the following quotation, addressing the dead body of Caesar as though he were still a living being is to employ an:** *(Competency 1)*

    O, pardon me, though
    Bleeding piece of earth
    That I am meek and gentle with
    These butchers.
        -Marc Antony from *Julius Caesar*

    A. Apostrophe
    B. Allusion
    C. Antithesis
    D. Anachronism

26. **A student wrote the following passage for a short response item about a novel. What is the biggest potential issue in the writing?** *(Competency 3)*

    So the theme of the novel is clearly like the struggle of the individual to be good. In the book, the main character guy really wants to be good, you know, but there are all these things stopping. The author, he's trying to show how all of us are like living our lives but these obstacles come up.

    A. Correct grammar
    B. Adapting to audience
    C. Using evidence to support a claim
    D. Organizational strategies

27. **Which of the following Common Morphemes are NOT considered 'bound' Morphemes?** *(Competency 8)*

    A. Prefix
    B. Suffix
    C. Root
    D. Inflectional endings

28. **Which of the following sentences contains a capitalization error?** *(Competency 8)*

   A. The commander of the English navy was Admiral Nelson.
   B. Napoleon was the president of the French First Republic.
   C. Queen Elizabeth II is the Monarch of the British Empire.
   D. William the Conqueror led the Normans to victory over the British.

29. **Which of the following would likely be the best conclusion for an essay analyzing potential projects to combat climate change.** *(Competencies 2 and 3)*

   A. A variety of projects and technologies exist that may help the country find a way to deal with climate change. The challenge is to decide which projects are viable and which are not. The best path forward may in fact be to provide seed funding to a variety of projects and see which ones thrive. Betting the farm on one proposal is too risky; we must look at all our options.
   B. Given the budget considerations facing the government, there is no clear path forward. Climate change may be a major issue facing different parts of the country, without substantial increases in revenue, it will be difficult for the current government to move forward.
   C. Climate change is not the threat people make it out to be. Our planet has gone through swings in climate before and will do so again. As a species, we will do what we have always done - adapt.
   D. Climate change is the biggest threat facing our species and many others. We must act now or we will risk losing countless species. The mounting costs will affect all of us to some extent.

30. **Which of the following sentences would likely be the best transitional sentence to follow this paragraph.** *(Competency 4)*

   The main character wrestles with her own moral code. Though she feels a tremendous sense of obligation towards her community, she cannot turn her back on what she feels is right. This internal conflict drives the novel forward.

   A. But the conflict is too much for her and she cannot cope.
   B. While she is torn between two seemingly impossible choices, the world seems to move forward without her.
   C. Impossible choices are everywhere in the novel.
   D. The world seems to move forward, and she is torn between impossible choices.

31. **Identify the correctly punctuated sentence.** *(Competency 8)*

    Wally said with a <u>groan, "Why</u> do I have to do an oral interpretation <u>of "The Raven."</u>

    A. groan, "Why... of 'The Raven'?"
    B. groan "Why... of "The Raven"?
    C. groan ", Why... of "The Raven?"
    D. groan, "Why... of "The Raven."

32. **Which of the following is NOT an effective research question?** *(Competency 6)*

    A. How was Arthur Miller influenced by the politics of his time?
    B. In what ways does social media influence adolescents?
    C. What causes some children to become bullies?
    D. What were the major battles of World War II?

33. **Considered one of the first feminist plays, this Ibsen drama ends with a door slamming symbolizing the lead character's emancipation from traditional societal norms.** *(Competency 1)*

    A. *The Wild Duck*
    B. *Hedda Gabler*
    C. *Ghosts*
    D. *The Doll's House*

34. **An extended metaphor comparing two very dissimilar things (one lofty one lowly) is a definition of a/an** *(Competency 1)*

    A. Antithesis.
    B. Aphorism.
    C. Apostrophe.
    D. Conceit.

35. **Which of the following literary elements and devices, is the word that describes the human practice of associating emotional effects stemming from the implications of a word, beyond its literal meaning?** *(Competency 2)*

    A. Denotation
    B. Connotation
    C. Caesura
    D. Conceit

36. Which of the following strategies will likely increase participation by shy students in class discussion? *(Competency 7)*

    A. Increasing wait time
    B. Requiring each participant to join in at least twice
    C. Giving participants something to read before the discussion
    D. Not allowing participants who talk a lot to join in

37. In which context might it not be a good idea to use jargon or technical language to discuss curriculum? *(Competency 7)*

    A. At back to school night
    B. A staff meeting
    C. A discussion of teaching materials
    D. A professional development conference

38. Which of the following is an example of an informational text suitable for use in the classroom? *(Competency 2)*

    A. A sonnet
    B. The results of a chemistry experiment
    C. A magazine article on habitat loss
    D. A speech

39. In this excerpt from *The Merchant of Venice*, what example of figurative language is evident? *(Competency 1)*

    Why, if two gods should play some heavenly match
    And on the wager lay two earthly women,
    And Portia one, there must be something else
    Pawned with the other, for the poor rude world
    Hath not her fellow.

    A. Pathos
    B. Hyperbole
    C. Alliteration
    D. Personification

40. The following passage is written from which point of view?
    (Competency 1)

As she mused the pitiful vision of her mother's life laid its spell on the very quick of her being –that life of commonplace sacrifices closing in final craziness. She trembled as she heard again her mother's voice saying constantly with foolish insistence: *Derevaun Seraun! Derevaun Seraun!**
    * "The end of pleasure is pain!" (Gaelic)

A. First person, narrator
B. Second person, direct address
C. Third person, omniscient
D. First person, omniscient

41. Based on the excerpt below from Kate Chopin's short story "The Story of an Hour," what can students infer about the main character?
    (Competency 1)

She did not stop to ask if it were or were not a monstrous joy that held her. A clear and exalted perception enabled her to dismiss the suggestion as trivial. She knew that she would weep again when she saw the kind, tender hands folded in death; the face that had never looked save with love upon her, fixed and gray and dead. But she saw beyond that bitter moment a long procession of years to come that would belong to her absolutely. And she opened and spread her arms out to them in welcome.

A. She dreaded her life as a widow.
B. Although she loved her husband, she was glad that he was dead for he had never loved her.
C. She worried that she was too indifferent to her husband's death.
D. Although they had both loved each other, she was beginning to appreciate that opportunities had opened because of his death.

Read the passage below to answer the following questions:

Most people who bother with the matter at all would admit that the English language is in a bad way, but it is generally assumed that we cannot by conscious action do anything about it. Our civilization is decadent and our language — so the argument runs — must inevitably share in the general collapse. It follows that any struggle against the abuse of language is a sentimental archaism, like preferring candles to electric light or hansom cabs to aeroplanes. Underneath this lies the half-conscious belief that language is a natural growth and not an instrument which we shape for our own purposes.

Now, it is clear that the decline of a language must ultimately have political and economic causes: it is not due simply to the bad influence of this or that individual writer. But an effect can become a cause, reinforcing the original cause and producing the same effect in an intensified form, and so on indefinitely. A man may take to drink because he feels himself to be a failure, and then fail all the more completely because he drinks. It is rather the same thing that is happening to the English language. It becomes ugly and inaccurate because our thoughts are foolish, but the slovenliness of our language makes it easier for us to have foolish thoughts. The point is that the process is reversible. Modern English, especially written English, is full of bad habits which spread by imitation and which can be avoided if one is willing to take the necessary trouble. If one gets rid of these habits one can think more clearly, and to think clearly is a necessary first step toward political regeneration: so that the fight against bad English is not frivolous and is not the exclusive concern of professional writers. I will come back to this presently, and I hope that by that time the meaning of what I have said here will have become clearer. Meanwhile, here are five specimens of the English language as it is now habitually written.

42. What does the author mean by "archaism"? *(Competency 8)*

    A. Mystery
    B. Misidentification
    C. Anachronism
    D. Ignorance

43. "A man may take to drink because he feels himself to be a failure, and then fail all the more completely because he drinks." In context, this sentence is best described as a: *(Competency 8)*

    A. Analogy
    B. Metaphor
    C. Simile
    D. Allusion

44. What does this author think of the English language? *(Competency 3)*

    A. It is in unavoidable decline
    B. It should not be altered
    C. Its rules are subject to the whims of speakers
    D. It can be improved through good habits

45. What can we assume will follow this passage? *(Competency 3)*

    A. A screed on the decline of English
    B. Further evidence that English is being destroyed
    C. Names of authors who have contributed to the decline of English
    D. Specific examples of bad English in use

46. What is the subject of the verb "lies" in the last sentence of the first paragraph? *(Competency 8)*

    A. Language
    B. Growth
    C. This
    D. Underneath

47. The author believes the decline of English is due to: *(Competencies 3 and 4)*

    A. The imitation of bad habits
    B. Societal decadence
    C. People preferring what is simple
    D. Political quibbling

48. By characterizing language as a "natural growth", the author emphasizes its: *(Competency 3)*

    A. Personified qualities
    B. Duplicitous nature
    C. Inconsistency
    D. Changeability

49. What tone is the author striving for in this piece? *(Competency 5)*

    A. Humorous
    B. Academic
    C. Angry
    D. Disappointed

Read the following passage carefully to answer the questions below.

On the domestic front, life was not easy. England was not a wealthy country and its people endured relatively poor living standards. The landed classes — many of them enriched by the confiscated wealth of former monasteries — were determined in the interests of profile to convert their arable land into pasture for sheep, so as to produce the wool that supported the country's chief economic asset, the woolen cloth trade. But the enclosing of the land only added to the misery of the poor, many of whom, evicted and displaced, left their decaying villages and gravitated to the towns where they joined the growing army of beggars and vagabonds that would become such a feature of Elizabethan life. Once, the religious houses would have dispensed charity to the destitute, but Henry VIII had dissolved them all in the 1530s, and many former monks and nuns were now themselves beggars. Nor did the civic authorities help: they passed laws in an attempt to ban the poor from towns and cities, but to little avail. It was a common sight to see men and women lying in the dusty streets, often dying in the dirt like dogs or beasts, without human compassion being shown to them. 'Certainly, wrote a Spanish observer in 1558, 'the state of England lay now most afflicted.' And although people looked to the new Queen Elizabeth to put matters right, there were so many who doubted if she could overcome the seemingly insurmountable problems she faced, or even remain queen long enough to begin tacking them. Some, both at home and abroad, were the opinion that her title to the throne rested on very precarious foundations. Many regarded the daughter of Henry VII and Anne Boleyn as a bastard from the time of her birth on 7 September 1533, although, ignoring such slurs on the validity of his second marriage, Henry had declared Elizabeth his heir.

50. **Why was land confiscated from the poor?** *(Competency 2)*

   A. The town wanted to build a new monastery.
   B. To create pastures for sheep, ultimately increasing the export of wool.
   C. The town wanted to create housing for monks and nuns.
   D. Queen Elizabeth wanted to expand her property.

51. **A vagabond is a _____.** *(Competency 8)*

   A. Wanderer
   B. Prisoner
   C. Poor person
   D. Rich person

52. **Why didn't the poor have shelter with the churches?** *(Competency 2)*

    A. They were already filled with beggars.
    B. Religious houses have never offered shelter to the poor.
    C. They were also being used to raise sheep.
    D. Henry VIII had dissolved them all in the 1530s.

53. **How were civic authorities unsuccessful?** *(Competency 2)*

    A. Poor people remained within city limits
    B. Public service funds ran out
    C. Public housing plans extended deadlines
    D. Churches did not open their doors to the poor

54. **What is a synonym for precarious?** *(Competency 8)*

    A. Strong
    B. Illegitimate
    C. Risky
    D. Determined

55. **What is the author's view towards Queen Elizabeth?** *(Competency 7)*

    A. Doubtful
    B. Vengeful
    C. Resentful
    D. Supportive

56. **How is the English culture portrayed in this passage?** *(Competency 2)*

    A. Religious
    B. Elitist
    C. Racist
    D. Diverse

57. **What is Elizabeth's relationship to Henry?** *(Competency 2)*

    A. Wife
    B. Cousin
    C. Lover
    D. Daughter

Read the following passage to answer the questions that follow.

The brazen, vicious attack occurred in broad daylight. The cowardly action took the lives of 32 innocent victims. So far no single group has claimed responsibility though several have issued statements noting its importance...

58. In doing research, a student has second thoughts about using this new story as a source. What is evidence of a flaw with the story? *(Competency 6)*

    A. It is not corroborated by other sources.
    B. The language is inflammatory and biased.
    C. There is no image to accompany the story.
    D. No other point of view is included.

59. Which of the following sentences best incorporates a quote from the passage above? *(Competency 6)*

    A. The writer's description of this as a "vicious attack" reveals bias.
    B. Saying, "The brazen, vicious attack occurred in broad daylight. The cowardly action took the lives of 32 innocent victims" reveals bias.
    C. The characterization of the incident as a "brazen, vicious attack" and a "cowardly action" reveals bias.
    D. When the writer says the brazen, vicious attack it shows bias.

Read the passage and answer the following questions carefully.

I have often thought of it as one of the most barbarous customs in the world, considering us as a civilized and a Christian country, that we deny the advantages of learning to women. We reproach the sex every day with folly and impertinence; while I am confident, had they the advantages of education equal to us, they would be guilty of less than ourselves.

One would wonder, indeed, how it should happen that women are conversible at all; since they are only beholden to natural parts, for all their knowledge. Their youth is spent to teach them to stitch and sew or make baubles. They are taught to read, indeed, and perhaps to write their names, or so; and that is the height of a woman's education. And I would but ask any who slight the sex for their understanding, what is a man (a gentleman, I mean) good for, that is taught no more? I need not give instances, or examine the character of a gentleman, with a good estate, or a good family, and with tolerable parts; and examine what figure he makes for want of education.

The soul is placed in the body like a rough diamond; and must be polished, or the luster of it will never appear. And 'tis manifest, that as the rational soul distinguishes us from brutes; so education carries on the distinction, and makes some less brutish than others. This is too evident to need any demonstration. But why then should women be denied the benefit of instruction? If knowledge and understanding had been useless additions to the sex, GOD Almighty would never have given them capacities; for he made nothing needless. Besides, I would ask such, What they can see in ignorance, that they should think it a necessary ornament to a woman?

60. **What is the author saying with the second sentence of the first paragraph?** *(Competency 7)*

   A. Education for women is a necessity, and the fact that we deny it to them is a national disgrace
   B. If women possessed education, they would be able to give men a taste of their own medicine
   C. Men often oppress women, and if women were educated, they likely would not do the same
   D. Education is a privilege, one that women must earn for themselves

61. **"The soul is placed in the body like a rough diamond". This is an example of a:** *(Competency 3)*

   A. Simile
   B. Metaphor
   C. Analogy
   D. Juxtaposition

62. **With the last sentence of paragraph two, the author is implying that:** *(Competency 2)*

   A. A man with no education is hardly impressive, even if he has other advantages
   B. Certain qualities of upbringing handily offset the downsides of no education
   C. Upper class men have little need for education
   D. Men of good stature do not appreciate education as they should

63. **The author primarily supports his argument with:** *(Competency 3)*

   A. Citations
   B. Direct observation
   C. Common sense
   D. Examples

64. **Throughout the piece, the author makes frequent use of:** *(Competency 7)*

   A. Rhetorical questions
   B. Hyperbole
   C. Direct quotation
   D. Appeals to authority

Read the passage and answer the following questions carefully.

When it was first perceived, in early times, that no middle course for America remained between unlimited submission to a foreign legislature and a total independence of its claims, men of reflection were less apprehensive of danger from the formidable power of fleets and armies they must determine to resist than from those contests and dissensions which would certainly arise concerning the forms of government to be instituted over the whole and over the parts of this extensive country. Relying, however, on the purity of their intentions, the justice of their cause, and the integrity and intelligence of the people, under an overruling Providence which had so signally protected this country from the first, the representatives of this nation, then consisting of little more than half its present number, not only broke to pieces the chains which were forging and the rod of iron that was lifted up, but frankly cut asunder the ties which had bound them, and launched into an ocean of uncertainty.

The zeal and ardor of the people during the Revolutionary war, supplying the place of government, commanded a degree of order sufficient at least for the temporary preservation of society. The Confederation which was early felt to be necessary was prepared from the models of the Batavian and Helvetic confederacies, the only examples which remain with any detail and precision in history, and certainly the only ones which the people at large had ever considered. But reflecting on the striking difference in so many particulars between this country and those where a courier may go from the seat of government to the frontier in a single day, it was then certainly foreseen by some who assisted in Congress at the formation of it that it could not be durable.

Negligence of its regulations, inattention to its recommendations, if not disobedience to its authority, not only in individuals but in States, soon appeared with their melancholy consequences—universal languor, jealousies and rivalries of States, decline of navigation and commerce, discouragement of necessary manufactures, universal fall in the value of lands and their produce, contempt of public and private faith, loss of consideration and credit with foreign nations, and at length in discontents, animosities, combinations, partial conventions, and insurrection, threatening some great national calamity

65. **What best summarizes the first sentence of this piece?** *(Competency 2)*

  A. When we first realize there was no middle ground between subservience and independence, intelligent men were less afraid of war than they were of deciding how to govern our new nation
  B. When our ancestors first realized they must be free instead of obedient, they realized that combat was far less challenging than the bureaucracy that would follow
  C. When men realized, in the past, that freedom would be hard to win, they decided to craft a new form of government to aid in this process
  D. When our new nation first achieved independence, the true struggle was not the war that followed, but the arguments between learned me who could not agree on anything

66. **What does the author identify as a problem in the second paragraph?** *(Competency 2)*

  A. The similarities between his new nation and the Batavian and Helvetic confederacies
  B. The ignorance of the common people
  C. The unrestrained zeal of common citizens
  D. The vast size of this new country

67. **The author identifies all of these as problems in the third paragraph EXCEPT:** *(Competency 4)*

  A. Laziness
  B. Increased dependence on foreign powers
  C. Poor trade
  D. Religious intolerance

68. **In the first paragraph, what does the author NOT credit with aiding the representatives?** *(Competency 2)*

  A. Providence
  B. Intelligence
  C. Integrity
  D. The Nation

69. For which of the following research questions would this passage likely be best suited? *(Competency 6)*

   A. How did economic issues influence the causes of the Revolutionary War?
   B. What philosophical schools of thought influenced leaders of the Revolution?
   C. What were some of the post-Revolutionary challenges facing the country?
   D. How did Britain try to influence the economy of the United States after the Revolution?

Read the following excerpt to answer the questions that follow.

Excerpt from Speech to the Council on Foreign Relations, Tony Blair, December 3, 2008

The past 40 years are littered with initiatives, signposts to various potential breakthroughs, unsatisfactory compromises, new dawns that swiftly turned to dusk and failed negotiations. Along the way, there have been immense gains that sometimes are obscured by the central impasse. Egypt and Jordan are at peace with Israel. The Arab Peace Initiative of the then Crown Prince Abdullah in 2002 signalled a new pan-Arab approach. The contours of the final status issues, if not their outcomes, have been clarified.

The Annapolis process and the limited but, nonetheless, real change on the West Bank during the past year - for which the President and Secretary Rice deserve much credit - have yielded a genuine platform for the future.

But the central impasse does indeed remain. My view - formed since I came to Jerusalem and refining much of what I thought when I tussled intermittently with the issue for 10 years as British Prime Minister - is that it remains because the reality on the ground does not, as yet, sufficiently support the compromises necessary to secure a final, negotiated settlement. In other words, we have tended to proceed on the basis that if we could only agree the terms of the two state solution - territory, refugees, Jerusalem - i.e. the theory, we would then be able to change the reality of what was happening on the ground i.e. the practice. In my view, it is as much the other way around. The political process and changing the reality have to march in lock-step. Until recently, they haven't.

The reason this is critical to resolving this dispute is as follows. The problem is not that reasonable people do not agree, roughly, what the two states look like. I don't minimize the negotiation challenge. But listen to sensible Palestinians and sensible Israelis and you will quickly find the gaps are not that big; certainly are not unbridgeable.

70. **In what way(s) does Tony Blair demonstrate that he acknowledges the different perspectives of Palestinians and Israelis?** *(Competency 7)*

    A. He addresses the importance of peace for both sides.
    B. He talks about past failed negotiations.
    C. He does not blame either side for the lack of results.
    D. He makes an emotional appeal to both sides.

71. **In this speech, how did Blair organize his ideas?** *(Competency 7)*

    A. He linked past events to the present state of negotiations.
    B. He described past peace proposals and gave evidence of why they make sense.
    C. He thanked people for their past work and showed why it was important to continue what they had started.
    D. He analyzed the issue point by point.

Read the following passage carefully before you decide on your answers to the questions.

International baggage claim in the Brussels airport was large and airy, with multiple carousels circling endlessly. I scurried from one to another, desperately trying to find my black suitcase. Because it was stuffed with drug money, I was more concerned than one might normally be about lost luggage.

I was twenty-four in 1993 and probably looked like just another anxious young professional woman. My Doc Martens had been jettisoned in favor of my beautiful handmade black suede heels. I wore black silk pants and a beige jacket, a typical jeune fille, not a big counterculture, unless you spotted the tattoo on my neck. I had done exactly as I had been instructed, checking my bag Chicago through Paris, where I had to switch planes to take a short flight to Brussels.

When I arrived in Belgium, I looked for my black rollie at the baggage claim. It was nowhere to be seen. Fighting a rushing tide of panic, I asked in my mangled high school French what had become of my suitcase. "Bags don't make it onto the right flight sometimes," said the big lug working in baggage handling. "Wait for the next shuttle from Paris— It's probably on that plane."

Had my bag been detected? I knew that carrying more than $10,000 undeclared was illegal, let alone carrying it for a West African drug lord. Were the authorities closing in on me? Maybe I should try to get through customs and run? Or perhaps the bag really was just delayed, and I would be abandoning a large sum of money that belonged to someone who could probably have killed me with a simple phone call. I decided that the later choice was slightly more terrifying. So I waited.

The next flight from Paris finally arrived. I sidled over to my new "friend" in baggage handling, who was sorting things out. It is hard to flirt when you're frightened. I spotted the suitcase. "Mon bag!" I exclaimed in ecstasy, seizing the Tumi. I thanked him effusively, waving with giddy affection as I sailed through one of the unmanned doors into the terminal, where I spotted my friend Billy waiting for me. I had inadvertently skipped customs.

"I was worried. What happened?" Billy asked.
"Get me into a cab!" I hissed.
I didn't breathe until we had pulled away from the airport and were halfway across Brussels.

—*Orange is the New Black*. Piper Kerman

72. **Why did the author explain her attire?** *(Competency 1)*

    A. She wanted the audience to know how much she stood out in Europe
    B. She used her clothing to try to fit in with the culture she was immersed in
    C. She wanted to explain that she was a young, hip woman
    D. She explained how difficult it was to wait around for her bag in heels

73. **Why didn't she breathe until pulling away from the airport?**
    (Competency 1)

    A. Tension
    B. Sadness
    C. Health issues
    D. She was talking to Billy

74. **What is the overall message of this passage?** *(Competency 1)*

    A. Young professional women can get away with crimes
    B. Security guards are not always watching every door in the airport
    C. It's important to blend in when doing something suspicious
    D. When you have done something illegal, even small mishaps can seem scary

75. **How did she avoid going through customs?** *(Competency 1)*

    A. She flirted with the luggage man
    B. Her friend Billy came to get her
    C. She slipped through an unmanned door
    D. She went through customs in Paris and Chicago, so it wasn't required

76. **What part of the plot does "Mon bag!" represent?** *(Competency 1)*

    A. Climax
    B. Rising action
    C. Exposition
    D. Falling action

Use the following passage to answer the questions that follow.

When rays of light pass through a prism, they undergo a change of direction: they are always deflected away from the refractive edge. It is possible to conceive an assembly of prisms whose refractive surfaces progressively become more nearly parallel to each other towards the middle: light rays passing through the outer prisms will undergo the greatest amount of refraction, with consequent deflection of their path towards the center, whereas the middle prism with its two parallel surfaces causes no deflection at all. When a beam of parallel rays passes through these prisms, the rays are all deflected towards the axis and converge at one point. Rays emerging from a point are also deflected by the prisms that they converge. A lens can be conceived as consisting of a large number of such prisms placed close up against one another, so that their surfaces merge into a continuous spherical surface. A lens of this kind, which collects the rays and concentrates them at one point, is called a convergent lens. Since it is thicker in the middle than at the edge, it is known as a convex lens.

In the case of a concave lens, which is thinner in the middle than at the edge, similar considerations show that all rays diverge from the center. Hence such a lens is called a divergent lens. After undergoing refraction, parallel rays appear to come from one point, while rays reemerging from a point will, after passing through the lens, appear to emerge from another point. Lenses have surfaces in the same direction but having a different radii of curvature, these are known as meniscus lenses and are used more particularly in spectacles.

77. Which of the following is NOT true of convergent lenses? *(Competency 2)*

    A. They are concave
    B. They are made of prisms
    C. They can refract light
    D. They have different radii

78. Parallel surfaces in prisms cause: *(Competency 2)*

    A. Very little refraction
    B. Divergence of light rays
    C. No refraction
    D. Radii to vary

79. **Which of the following would be the best choice of a conclusion for this piece?** *(Competency 4)*

A. Prisms were used by many ancient civilizations. They must have seemed like a form of magic to the first people who saw them, and they continue to amaze people today. Though perhaps an accidental discovery, they changed the world.

B. Prisms were an integral part of the study of the different properties of light. The use of prisms allowed people to see the different component colors of the light around them. The discovery of these different properties opened up new fields of research.

C. There are dispersive prisms, reflective prisms, deflecting prisms, and polarizing prisms. Each type is very important and has different qualities.

D. We wake up every morning and there is light. We may not know it, but people have always been fascinated by light for many years. Prisms explained how light works.

80. **Spectacles use meniscus lenses, which are:** *(Competency 2)*

A. Flat
B. Varying radii of concave lenses
C. Varying radii of convex lenses
D. Round on both sides of the lens, meaning they have double refraction.

Read the following passage to answer the questions below.

Ana woke suddenly and peered into the darkness. Something had moved or made some kind of sound; she was sure of it. She reached across the bed to the lamp on the nightstand, but there was nothing there. She fumbled in the dark until her hand came to rest on something solid, something cold, something wet.

"Looking for something?" came a voice out of the darkness.

Without hesitation, Ana replied, "Yes, actually. My glasses."

"You know why I'm here. No need for games," replied the voice.

"No, I suppose you're right," Ana sighed.

81. **For what effect does the author repeat 'something..., something...'** *(Competency 5)*

    A. To show how frustrating it was not to be able to see
    B. To build tension
    C. To show that the character was helpless
    D. To lighten the mood.

82. **Ana's reply creates what effect?** *(Competency 5)*

    A. The reader sees her as confident and calm.
    B. The reader sees her as confused and fearful.
    C. The reader knows that this is not a serious story.
    D. The reader knows that this is the source of conflict.

83. **In this short passage, what two techniques is the writer using to add to the story?** *(Competency 5)*

    A. Alliteration and descriptive details
    B. Irony and reflection
    C. Pacing and figurative language
    D. Dialogue and setting

84. **What does the conversation between the two characters imply?** *(Competency 5)*

    A. The two characters are enemies.
    B. Ana is bored.
    C. Ana is afraid of the other character.
    D. There is something the reader doesn't know.

85. **The deliberate lack of clarity about what is happening is called...?** *(Competency 5)*

    A. Connotation
    B. Ambiguity
    C. Allusion
    D. Denouement

86. **How can ambiguity move a plot forward?** *(Competency 5)*

    A. It doesn't. It simply creates confusion.
    B. It is like a symbol and represents something important.
    C. It makes the reader want to know more.
    D. It clarifies important parts of the plot.

87. **In which type of fiction does setting tend to be most important?** *(Competency 5)*

    A. Historical fiction
    B. Contemporary fiction
    C. Young adult fiction
    D. Multicultural fiction

88. **What is the correct way to include a quotation from** *Orange is the New Black*? *(Competency 6)*

    A. Kerman was terrified but continued with the plan anyway. "Were the authorities closing in on me? Maybe I should try to get through customs and run? Or perhaps the bag really was just delayed, and I would be abandoning a large sum of money that belonged to someone who could probably have killed me with a simple phone call. I decided that the later choice was slightly more terrifying."

    B. Kerman was terrified but continued with the plan anyway. "Were the authorities closing in on me? Maybe I should try to get through customs and run? Or perhaps the bag really was just delayed, and I would be abandoning a large sum of money that belonged to someone who could probably have killed me with a simple phone call. I decided that the later choice was slightly more terrifying" (Kerman 1).

    C. Kerman was terrified but continued with the plan anyway.

    "Were the authorities closing in on me? Maybe I should try to get through customs and run? Or perhaps the bag really was just delayed, and I would be abandoning a large sum of money that belonged to someone who could probably have killed me with a simple phone call. I decided that the later choice was slightly more terrifying." (Kerman 1)

    D. Kerman was terrified but continued with the plan anyway.

    Were the authorities closing in on me? Maybe I should try to get through customs and run? Or perhaps the bag really was just delayed, and I would be abandoning a large sum of money that belonged to someone who could probably have killed me with a simple phone call. I decided that the later choice was slightly more terrifying. (Kerman 1)

Read the following passage carefully before you decide on your answers to the questions.

She was forty-two, in poor health. She had recently been diagnosed with diabetes, and her doctor had urged her to get out and walk more. But her son has been shot to death a few blocks away, and Pritchett was too frightened to venture out. She spent days lying in the dark, unable to will herself to move or speak. That morning, as always, she was wearing a big loose T-shirt with Bovon's picture on it. All around her, in the tiny living room, were mementos of her murdered son. Sports trophies, photos, sympathy cards, certificates, stuffed animals.

With great care, Pritchett perched the shoebox on the arm of a vinyl armchair by the door and solely lifted one shoe. It was worn, black, dusted with red Watts dirt. It was not quite big enough to be a man's shoe, not small enough to be a child's. She leaned against the wall, pressed the open top of the shoe against her mouth and nose, and inhaled its scent with a long, deep breath. Then she closed her eyes and wept.

Skaggs stood back. Pritchett's knees gave out. Skaggs watched her side down the wall in slow motion, her face still pressed into the shoe. She landed with a thump on the green carpet. One of her orange slippers came off. On the TV across the room, the FOX 11 morning anchored pattered brightly over the sound of her sobs.

Skaggs had been a homicide detective for twenty years. In that time, he had been in a thousand living rooms like this one- each with its large TV, Afrocentric knickknacks, and imponderable grief. —*Ghettoside* by Jill Leovy

89. **What is the intended audience for this text?** *(Competency 5)*

    A. All classes and races
    B. White police officers
    C. Students
    D. Affluent communities

90. **How does the author appeal to the emotions of the audience?** *(Competency 5)*

    A. Including a detailed scene, including memorabilia and Pritchett's physical and emotional response to the situation
    B. Opening the scene with a description of Pritchett's poor health
    C. Implying that this is a very common scene to this detective
    D. Mentioning things the audience can relate to, such as watching the morning news

CONSTRUCTED RESPONSE

You plan to teach a lesson relating to George Washington's Farewell Address using the excerpts below.

[This relates to New York standard: Analyze seventeenth-, eighteenth-, and nineteenth-century foundational U.S. documents of historical and literary significance (including The Declaration of Independence, the Preamble to the Constitution, the Bill of Rights, and Lincoln's Second Inaugural Address) for their themes, purposes, and rhetorical features.

so frequently afflict neighbouring countries, not tied together by the same government; which their own rivalships alone would be sufficient to produce, but which opposite foreign alliances, attachments & intriegues would stimulate & imbitter. Hence likewise they will avoid the necessity of those overgrown Military establishments, which under any form of Government are inauspicious to liberty, and which are to be regarded as particularly hostile to Republican Liberty: In this sense it is, that your union ought to be considered as a main prop of your liberty, and that the love of the one ought to endear to you the preservation of the other.

These considerations speak a persuasive language to every reflecting & virtuous mind, and exhibit the continuance of the Union as a primary object of Patriotic desire. Is there a doubt, whether a common government can embrace so large a sphere? Let experience solve it. To listen to mere speculation in such a case were criminal. We are authorized to hope that a proper organization of the whole, with the auxiliary agency of governments for the respective Subdivisions, will afford a happy issue to the experiment. 'Tis well worth a fair and full experiment.

Using your knowledge of English language arts instructional methodology and content, write a response of between 400-600 words that addresses the following:

- A specific learning goal related to the excerpt of the speech;
- Your students' readiness for this learning goal;
- An effective instructional strategy that builds on students' prior knowledge while connecting to new learning;
- Your rationale for your approach;
- At least one potential challenge related to this learning goal and strategies for addressing it;
- Any modifications in instruction you might make to meet the needs of all students; and
- Assessment of student learning.

[On the exam, it is estimated that you will take approximately 60 minutes for this portion of the test.]

ANSWER KEY

1. B	2. B	3. A	4. A	5. C	6. C	7. D	8. A	9. D
10. B	11. A	12. C	13. C	14. C	15. B	16. C	17. D	18. A
19. A	20. A	21. D	22. C	23. C	24. A	25. A	26. B	27. C
28. C	29. A	30. B	31. A	32. D	33. D	34. D	35. B	36. A
37. A	38. C	39. B	40. C	41. D	42. C	43. A	44. D	45. D
46. C	47. A	48. D	49. B	50. B	51. A	52. D	53. A	54. C
55. A	56. B	57. D	58. B	59. C	60. C	61. A	62. A	63. C
64. A	65. A	66. D	67. B	68. D	69. C	70. C	71. A	72. B
73. A	74. D	75. C	76. A	77. A	78. C	79. B	80. B	81. B
82. A	83. D	84. D	85. B	86. C	87. A	88. D	89. A	90. A

RATIONALES

1. In Poe's poem, *The Bells*, words such as *twanging*, and *tintinnabulation* are examples of: *(Skill 1.6)*

    A. Consonance
    B. Figurative language
    C. Alliteration
    D. Free verse

The correct answer is B. Figurative language
The use of *twanging* and *tintinnabulation* are actually used by the poet to convey the feeling of movement and sound of the bells.

2. Expressions in the English language that are casual, slang, or jargons in relation to cultural associations are considered to be: *(Skill 8.1)*

    A. Allusions
    B. Idioms
    C. Aphorisms
    D. Euphemisms

The correct answer is B. Idioms
The answer is B, as an idiom is a word, or expression, that conveys an expression that is not easily translated, such as an expression (ex. Chip off the old block).

3. "My daughter was told that there would be no homework, but when she got to school she got in trouble for not turning in an assignment," said Allan.

    By using the passive voice, what effect does the speaker intend? *(Skill 8.6)*

    A. To imply that it was not his daughter's fault
    B. To express anger
    C. To calmly explain the situation
    D. To defuse tension

The correct answer is A. To imply that it was not his daughter's fault
By saying that his "daughter was told" the speaker implies that it was not her fault that she did not have her assignment.

4. **For a presentation on actions the school board should take to reduce energy use, which strategy would students most likely find successful?** *(Competency 7)*

    A. Link reduced energy use to reduced costs and greater environmental responsibility
    B. Explain in detail the different uses of energy at schools
    C. Complain about the board's lack of environmental responsibility
    D. Read letters from other students

The correct answer is A. Link reduced energy use to reduced costs and greater environmental responsibility
Strategy provides concrete strategies and gives the board reasons for their adoption.

5. **In this paragraph from a student essay, identify the sentence that provides a detail.** *(Skill 4.3)*

    (1) The poem concerns two different personality types and the human relation between them. (2) Their approach to life is totally different. (3) The neighbor is a very conservative person who follows routines. (4) He follows the traditional wisdom of his father and his father's father. (5) The purpose in fixing the wall and keeping their relationship separate is only because it is all he knows.

    A. Sentence 1
    B. Sentence 3
    C. Sentence 4
    D. Sentence 5

The correct answer is C. Sentence 4
Sentence 4 provides a detail to sentence 3 by explaining how the neighbor follows routine. Sentence 1 is the thesis sentence, which is the main idea of the paragraph. Sentence 3 provides an example to develop that thesis. Sentence 4 is a reason that explains why.

6. **The substitution of *went to his rest* for *died* is an example of a/an: *(Competency 1)***

   A. Bowdlerism
   B. Jargon
   C. Euphemism
   D. Malapropism

The correct answer is C. Euphemism
A euphemism replaces an unpleasant or offensive word or expression by a more agreeable one. It also alludes to distasteful things in a pleasant manner, and it can even paraphrase offensive texts. Bowdlerism is named after Thomas Bowdler who excised from Shakespeare what he considered vulgar and offensive. Jargon is a specialized language used by a particular group. What was "groovy" to one generation has become "awesome" to another. Named after Mrs. Malaprop, a character in a play by Richard Sheridan, a malapropism is a misuse of words, often to comical effect. Mrs. Malaprop once said "...she's as headstrong as an allegory on the banks of Nile" misusing allegory for alligator.

7. **Select the correct version of the sentence below. *(Skill 8.2)***

   A. I climbed to the top of the mountain, it took me three hours.
   B. I climbed to the top of the mountain it took me three hours.
   C. I climbed to the top of the mountain: it took me three hours.
   D. I climbed to the top of the mountain; it took me three hours.

The correct answer is D. I climbed to the top of the mountain; it took me three hours.
A comma alone cannot separate two independent clauses. Instead a semicolon is needed to separate two related sentences.

8. **Which of the following techniques is an effective tool of characterization? *(Skill 5.1)***

   A. Dialogue
   B. Denouement
   C. Sensory language
   D. First person narration

The correct answer is A. Dialogue
Dialogue reveals a great deal about a character. The way in which characters speak and interact with others shows what a character is like.

9. **Which of the following descriptions most relies on sensory language?** *(Competency 5)*

    A. As a child their frequent arguments tore him apart.
    B. As a child their frequent arguments were like wounds that never healed.
    C. As a child he had to put up with the sound of their frequent arguments.
    D. As a child their frequent arguments echoed through the house.

The correct answer is D. As a child their frequent arguments echoed through the house.
Answers A and B include figurative language, but Answer D uses sensory language (the way the arguments sounded) to describe the situation.

10. **The literary device of personification is used in which example below?** *(Skill 1.6)*

    A. "Beg me no beggary by soul or parents, whining dog!"
    B. "Happiness sped through the halls cajoling as it went."
    C. "O wind thy horn, thou proud fellow."
    D. "And that one talent which is death to hide."

The correct answer is B. "Happiness sped through the halls cajoling as it went."
"Happiness," an abstract concept, is described as if it were a person with the words "sped" and "cajoling."

11. **Arthur Miller wrote *The Crucible* as a parallel to what twentieth century event?** *(Competency 1)*

    A. Sen. McCarthy's House un-American Activities Committee Hearing
    B. The Cold War
    C. The fall of the Berlin Wall
    D. The Persian Gulf War

The correct answer is A. Sen. McCarthy's House un-American Activities Committee Hearing
The episode of the seventeenth century witch-hunt in Salem, Mass., gave Miller a storyline that was very comparable to what was happening to persons suspected of communist beliefs in the 1950s.

12. **Which of the following is the best definition of existentialism?** *(Skill 1.11)*

   A. The philosophical doctrine that matter is the only reality and that everything in the world, including thought, will and feeling, can be explained only in terms of matter.
   B. Philosophy that views things as they should be or as one would wish them to be.
   C. A philosophical and literary movement, that held that the individual gives meaning to life, stemming from Kierkegaard and represented by Sartre.
   D. The belief that all events are determined by fate and are hence inevitable.

The correct answer is C. A philosophical and literary movement, that held that the individual gives meaning to life, stemming from Kierkegaard and represented by Sartre.
Even though there are other very important thinkers in the movement known as Existentialism, such as Camus and Merleau-Ponty, Sartre remains the main figure in this movement.

13. **How does Henry David Thoreau seek to persuade readers in this excerpt from "Civil Disobedience"?** *(Competencies 2 and 3)*

   Unjust laws exist; shall we be content to obey them, or shall we endeavor to amend them, and obey them until we have succeeded, or shall we transgress them at once? Men generally, under such a government as this, think that they ought to wait until they have persuaded the majority to alter them. They think that, if they should resist, the remedy would be worse than the evil. But it is the fault of the government itself that the remedy *is* worse than the evil. … Why does it always crucify Christ, and excommunicate Copernicus and Luther, and pronounce Washington and Franklin rebels?
   --"Civil Disobedience" by Henry David Thoreau

   A. Through appeals to emotion
   B. By using parallelism to tie two themes together
   C. Through reason
   D. By using symbolism

The correct answer is C. Through reason
Thoreau starts with an opening premise (that unjust laws exist) and then proceeds to examine reasons (especially the government's role in suppressing dissent).

14. **In presenting a report to peers about the effects of Hurricane Katrina on New Orleans, the students wanted to use various media in their argument to persuade their peers that more needed to be done. Which of these would be the most effective?** *(Competency 3)*

A. A presentation showing the blueprints of the levees before the flood and redesigned now for current construction.
B. A collection of music clips made by the street performers in the French Quarter before and after the flood.
C. A recent video showing the areas devastated by the floods and the current state of rebuilding.
D. A collection of recordings of interviews made by the various government officials and local citizens affected by the flooding.

The correct answer is C. A recent video showing the areas devastated by the floods and the current state of rebuilding.
For maximum impact, a video would offer dramatic scenes of the devastated areas. A video by its very nature is more dynamic than a static PowerPoint presentation. Further, the condition of the levees would not provide as much impetus for change as seeing the devastated areas. Oral messages such as music clips and interviews provide another way of supplementing the message but, again, they are not as dynamic as video.

15. **Which of the following should *not* be included in the opening paragraph of an informative essay?** *(Skill 4.1)*

A. Thesis sentence
B. Details and examples supporting the main idea
C. Broad general introduction to the topic
D. A style and tone that grabs the reader's attention

The correct answer is B. Details and examples supporting the main idea
The introductory paragraph should introduce the topic, capture the reader's interest, state the thesis and prepare the reader for the main points in the essay. Details and examples, however, should be given in the second part of the essay to help develop the thesis presented at the end of the introductory paragraph. This is followed by the inverted triangle method consisting of a broad general statement followed by some information, and then the thesis at the end of the paragraph.

16. In the paragraph below, which sentence does *not* contribute to the overall task of supporting the main idea? *(Skill 4.2)*

The Springfield City Council met Friday to discuss new zoning restrictions for the land to be developed south of the city. 2) Residents who opposed the new restrictions were granted 15 minutes to present their case. 3) Their argument focused on the dangers that increased traffic would bring to the area. 4) It seemed to me that the Mayor Simpson listened intently. 5) The council agreed to table the new zoning until studies would be performed.

   A. Sentence 2
   B. Sentence 3
   C. Sentence 4
   D. Sentence 5

The correct answer is C. Sentence 4
The other sentences provide detail to the main idea of the new zoning restrictions. Because sentence 4 provides no example or relevant detail, it should be omitted.

17. In preparing your class to write a research paper about a social problem, what requirements can you put in place so they take steps to determine the credibility of their information? *(Competency 6)*

   A. Only go to major news sites
   B. Find one solid, reputable source and use that exclusively
   C. Use only primary sources
   D. Ensure that information they find is also available elsewhere

The correct answer is D. Ensure that information they find is also available elsewhere
When researchers find the same information in multiple reputable sources, the information is considered credible. Using the Internet for research requires strong critical evaluation of the source. To rely on only one source is dangerous and shortsighted. Most high school students would have limited skills to conduct primary research for a paper about a social problem.

18. **Which of the following are secondary research materials?** *(Competency 6)*

    A. The conclusions and inferences of other historians.
    B. Literature and nonverbal materials, novels, stories, poetry and essays from the period, as well as coins, archaeological artifacts, and art produced during the period.
    C. Interviews and surveys conducted by the researcher.
    D. Statistics gathered as the result of the research's experiments.

The correct answer is A. The conclusions and inferences of other historians.
Secondary sources are works written significantly after the period being studied and based upon primary sources. In this case, historians have studied artifacts of the time and drawn their conclusion and inferences. Primary sources are the basic materials that provide raw data and information. Students or researchers may use literature and other data they have collected to draw their own conclusions or inferences.

19. **Which of the following situations is *not* an ethical violation of intellectual property?** *(Competency 6)*

    A. A student visits ten different websites and writes a report to compare the costs of downloading music. He uses the names of the websites without their permission.
    B. A student copies and pastes a chart verbatim from the Internet but does not document it because it is available on a public site.
    C. From an online article found in a subscription database, a student paraphrases a section on the problems of music piracy. She includes the source in her Works Cited but does not provide an in-text citation.
    D. A student includes a YouTube from a popular fan site in a project without including an entry in Works Cited.

The correct answer is A. A student visits ten different websites and writes a report to compare the costs of downloading music. He uses the names of the websites without their permission.
In this scenario, the student is conducting primary research by gathering the data and using it for his own purposes. He is not violating any principle by using the names of the websites. In Choice B, students who copy and paste from the Internet without documenting the sources of their information are committing plagiarism, a serious violation of intellectual property. Even when a student puts information in her own words by paraphrasing or summarizing as in Choice C, the information is still secondary and must be documented. Even though the video in the project is directly accessible on the original site (D), it needs to be added to Works Cited.

20. **Students have been asked to write a research paper on automobiles and have brainstormed a number of questions they will answer based on their research findings. Which of the following is *not* an interpretive question to guide research?** *(Competency 6)*

   A. What were the first ten automotive manufacturers in the United States?
   B. What types of vehicles will be used fifty years from now?
   C. How do automobiles manufactured in the United States compare and contrast with each other?
   D. What do you think is the best solution for the fuel shortage?

The correct answer is A. What were the first ten automotive manufacturers in the United States?
The question asks for objective facts. Choice B is a prediction that asks how something will look or be in the future, based on the way it is now. Choice C asks for similarities and differences, which is a higher-level research activity that requires analysis. Choice D is a judgment question that requires informed opinion.

21. **Which transition word would show contrast between these two ideas?** *(Competency 6)*

   We are confident in our skills to teach English. We welcome new ideas on this subject.

   A. We are confident in our skills to teach English, and we welcome new ideas on this subject.
   B. Because we are confident in our skills to teach English, we welcome new ideas on the subject.
   C. When we are confident in our skills to teach English, we welcome new ideas on the subject.
   D. We are confident in our skills to teach English; however, we welcome new ideas on the subject.

The correct answer is D. We are confident in our skills to teach English; however, we welcome new ideas on the subject.
Transitional words, phrases and sentences help clarify meanings. In Choice A, the transition word "and" introduces another equal idea. In Choice B, the transition word "because" indicates cause and effect. In Choice C, the transition word "when" indicates order or chronology. In Choice D, "however," shows that these two ideas contrast with each other.

22. **Which part of a classical argument is illustrated in this excerpt from the essay "What Should Be Done About Rock Lyrics?"** *(Competency 3)*

> But violence against women is greeted by silence. It shouldn't be. This does not mean censorship, or book (or record) burning. In a society that protects free expression, we understand a lot of stuff will float up out of the sewer. Usually, we recognize the ugly stuff that advocates violence against any group as the garbage it is, and we consider its purveyors as moral lepers. We hold our nose and tolerate it, but we speak out against the values it proffers.
>
> --"What Should Be Done About Rock Lyrics?" Caryl Rivers

A. Narration
B. Confirmation
C. Refutation and concession
D. Summation

The correct answer is C. Refutation and concession
The author acknowledges refutes the idea of censorship and concedes that society tolerates offensive lyrics as part of our freedom of speech. Narration provides background material to produce an argument. In confirmation, the author details the argument with claims that support the thesis. In summation, the author concludes the argument by offering the strongest solution.

23. **What was likely the biggest responsible for the standardizing of dialects across America in the 20th century?** *(Competency 8)*

A. With the immigrant influx, American became a melting pot of languages and cultures.
B. Trains enabled people to meet other people of different languages and cultures.
C. The spread of different media featured actors and announcers who spoke without pronounced dialects.
D. Newspapers and libraries developed programs to teach people to speak English with an agreed-upon common dialect.

The correct answer is C. The spread of different media featured actors and announcers who spoke without pronounced dialects.
The growth of immigration in the early part of the 20th century created pockets of language throughout the country. Coupled with regional differences already in place, this could have caused the number of regional differences to grow. Transportation did have an effect as it enabled people to move to different regions where languages and dialects continued to merge. With the growth of radio and television, however, people were introduced to a standardized dialect through actors and announcers who spoke so that anyone across American could understand them. What people saw and heard as media became national shaped the way people spoke. Newspapers and libraries never developed programs to standardize spoken English.

24. **Two of the first distinctly American writers include:** *(Competency 1)*

   A. Nathaniel Hawthorne and Herman Melville
   B. Arthur Miller and Zora Neale Hurston
   C. Samuel Beckett and Victor Hugo
   D. Richard Wright and F. Scott Fitzgerald

The correct answer is A. Nathaniel Hawthorne and Herman Melville
Hawthorne and Melville were two of the first distinctly American novelists, writing in a uniquely American voice.

25. **In the following quotation, addressing the dead body of Caesar as though he were still a living being is to employ an:** *(Competency 1)*

   O, pardon me, though
   Bleeding piece of earth
   That I am meek and gentle with
   These butchers.
      -Marc Antony from *Julius Caesar*

   A. Apostrophe
   B. Allusion
   C. Antithesis
   D. Anachronism

The correct answer is A. Apostrophe
This rhetorical figure addresses personified things, absent people or gods. An allusion, on the other hand, is a quick reference to a character or event known to the public. An antithesis is a contrast between two opposing viewpoints, ideas, or presentation of characters. An anachronism is the placing of an object or person out of its time with the time of the text. The best-known example is the clock in Shakespeare's *Julius Caesar*.

26. A student wrote the following passage for a short response item about a novel. What is the biggest potential issue in the writing? *(Competency 3)*

So the theme of the novel is clearly like the struggle of the individual to be good. In the book, the main character guy really wants to be good, you know, but there are all these things stopping. The author, he's trying to show how all of us are like living our lives but these obstacles come up.

A. Correct grammar
B. Adapting to audience
C. Using evidence to support a claim
D. Organizational strategies

The correct answer is B. Adapting to audience
Since this appears to be an introduction, it wouldn't likely have many examples to support an argument. The grammar is not good, but the student's biggest issue seems to be a lack of understanding of audience. This is written in a very casual style that undermines the main point of the writing.

27. Which of the following Common Morphemes are NOT considered 'bound' Morphemes? *(Competency 8)*

A. Prefix
B. Suffix
C. Root
D. Inflectional endings

The correct answer is C. Root
The answer is C because a bound morpheme is a unit that cannot stand alone as actual words. Root words, by definition can do so.

28. Which of the following sentences contains a capitalization error? *(Competency 8)*

A. The commander of the English navy was Admiral Nelson.
B. Napoleon was the president of the French First Republic.
C. Queen Elizabeth II is the Monarch of the British Empire.
D. William the Conqueror led the Normans to victory over the British.

The correct answer is C. Queen Elizabeth II is the Monarch of the British Empire
Words that represent titles and offices are not capitalized unless used with a proper name. This is not the case here.

29. **Which of the following would likely be the best conclusion for an essay analyzing potential projects to combat climate change?**
   (Competencies 2 and 3)

   A. A variety of projects and technologies exist that may help the country find a way to deal with climate change. The challenge is to decide which projects are viable and which are not. The best path forward may in fact be to provide seed funding to a variety of projects and see which ones thrive. Betting the farm on one proposal is too risky; we must look at all our options.

   B. Given the budget considerations facing the government, there is no clear path forward. Climate change may be a major issue facing different parts of the country, without substantial increases in revenue, it will be difficult for the current government to move forward.

   C. Climate change is not the threat people make it out to be. Our planet has gone through swings in climate before and will do so again. As a species, we will do what we have always done - adapt.

   D. Climate change is the biggest threat facing our species and many others. We must act now or we will risk losing countless species. The mounting costs will affect all of us to some extent.

The correct answer is A. A variety of projects and technologies exist that may help the country find a way to deal with climate change. The challenge is to decide which projects are viable and which are not. The best path forward may in fact be to provide seed funding to a variety of projects and see which ones thrive. Betting the farm on one proposal is too risky; we must look at all our options. Since the essay in question is supposed to be analyzing projects, this one is the one that addresses the idea of the quality of the proposals. B addresses budgets instead of the projects. C and D are opinions about climate change.

30. **Which of the following sentences would likely be the best transitional sentence to follow this paragraph?** *(Competency 4)*

The main character wrestles with her own moral code. Though she feels a tremendous sense of obligation towards her community, she cannot turn her back on what she feels is right. This internal conflict drives the novel forward.

   A. But the conflict is too much for her and she cannot cope.
   B. While she is torn between two seemingly impossible choices, the world seems to move forward without her.
   C. Impossible choices are everywhere in the novel.
   D. The world seems to move forward, and she is torn between impossible choices.

The correct answer is B. While she is torn between two seemingly impossible choices, the world seems to move forward without her.
This sentence best illustrates the dilemma faced by the main character and emphasizes it with the word *while*. A is awkward but does try to address the conflict. D includes the same idea but does not transition as well. C does not flow well.

31. **Identify the correctly punctuated sentence:** *(Competency 8)*

Wally said with a <u>groan, "Why</u> do I have to do an oral interpretation <u>of "The Raven."</u>

   A. groan, "Why... of 'The Raven'?"
   B. groan "Why... of "The Raven"?
   C. groan ", Why... of "The Raven?"
   D. groan, "Why... of "The Raven."

The correct answer is A. groan, "Why... of 'The Raven'?"
The question mark in a quotation that is an interrogation should be within the quotation marks. Also, when quoting a work of literature within another quotation, one should use single quotation marks ('...') for the title of this work, and they should close before the final quotation mark.

32. **Which of the following is NOT an effective research question?** *(Competency 6)*

    A. How was Arthur Miller influenced by the politics of his time?
    B. In what ways does social media influence adolescents?
    C. What causes some children to become bullies?
    D. What were the major battles of World War II?

The correct answer is D. What were the major battles of World War II?
All the other questions generate answers that are multi-faceted and complex. There are multiple answers and perspectives that must be supported by evidence. D results in a list that could likely be found with a quick Internet search.

33. **Considered one of the first feminist plays, this Ibsen drama ends with a door slamming symbolizing the lead character's emancipation from traditional societal norms. (*Competency 1*)**

    A. *The Wild Duck*
    B. *Hedda Gabler*
    C. *Ghosts*
    D. *The Doll's House*

The correct answer is D. *The Doll's House*
Nora in *The Doll's House* leaves her husband and her children when she realizes her husband is not the man she thought he was. Hedda Gabler, another feminist icon, shoots herself. *The Wild Duck* deals with the conflict between idealism and family secrets. *Ghosts,* considered one of Ibsen's most controversial plays, deals with many social ills, some of which include alcoholism, incest, and religious hypocrisy.

34. **An extended metaphor comparing two very dissimilar things (one lofty one lowly) is a definition of a/an *(Competency 1)***

    A. Antithesis.
    B. Aphorism.
    C. Apostrophe.
    D. Conceit.

The correct answer is D. Conceit
A conceit is an unusually far-fetched metaphor in which an object, person or situation is presented in a parallel and simpler analogue between two apparently very different things or feelings, one very sophisticated and one very ordinary, usually taken either from nature or a well-known everyday concept, familiar to both reader and author alike. The conceit was first developed by Petrarch and spread to England in the sixteenth century.

35. Which of the following literary elements and devices, is the word that describes the human practice of associating emotional effects stemming from the implications of a word, beyond its literal meaning? *(Competency 2)*

   A. Denotation
   B. Connotation
   C. Caesura
   D. Conceit

The correct answer is B. Connotation
The answer is B, because 'connotation' is the attached personal meaning of a word as opposed to its literal definition.

36. Which of the following strategies will likely increase participation by shy students in class discussion? *(Competency 7)*

   A. Increasing wait time
   B. Requiring each participant to join in at least twice
   C. Giving participants something to read before the discussion
   D. Not allowing participants who talk a lot to join in

The correct answer is A. Increasing wait time
Increasing the amount of time between the time a question is asked and the time you start taking answers will give more participants time to formulate a response.

37. In which context might it not be a good idea to use jargon or technical language to discuss curriculum? *(Competency 7)*

   A. At back to school night
   B. A staff meeting
   C. A discussion of teaching materials
   D. A professional development conference

The correct answer is A. At back to school night
Back to school night is generally an opportunity to meet parents and talk about general curricular plans. Using technical language may overcomplicate the topic and actually cause parents to lose interest.

38. **Which of the following is an example of an informational text suitable for use in the classroom?** *(Competency 2)*

    A. A sonnet
    B. The results of a chemistry experiment
    C. A magazine article on habitat loss
    D. A speech

The correct answer is C. A magazine article on habitat loss
The answer is A, because expository content is informative in nature. The results of a chemistry experiment are highly technical. A sonnet is a form of poetry, and a speech may not be informative in nature.

39. **In this excerpt from *The Merchant of Venice*, what example of figurative language is evident?** *(Competency 1)*

    Why, if two gods should play some heavenly match
    And on the wager lay two earthly women,
    And Portia one, there must be something else
    Pawned with the other, for the poor rude world
    Hath not her fellow.

    A. Pathos
    B. Hyperbole
    C. Alliteration
    D. Personification

The correct answer is B. Hyperbole
Hyperbole is deliberate exaggeration for comparison or comic effect.

40. **The following passage is written from which point of view?**
    (Competency 1)

    As she mused the pitiful vision of her mother's life laid its spell on the very quick of her being –that life of commonplace sacrifices closing in final craziness. She trembled as she heard again her mother's voice saying constantly with foolish insistence: *Derevaun Seraun! Derevaun Seraun!**
    * "The end of pleasure is pain!" (Gaelic)

    A. First person, narrator
    B. Second person, direct address
    C. Third person, omniscient
    D. First person, omniscient

The correct answer is C Third person, omniscient
The passage is clearly in the third person (the subject is "she"), and it is omniscient since it gives the characters' inner thoughts.

41. **Based on the excerpt below from Kate Chopin's short story "The Story of an Hour," what can students infer about the main character?** *(Competency 1)*

    She did not stop to ask if it were or were not a monstrous joy that held her. A clear and exalted perception enabled her to dismiss the suggestion as trivial. She knew that she would weep again when she saw the kind, tender hands folded in death; the face that had never looked save with love upon her, fixed and gray and dead. But she saw beyond that bitter moment a long procession of years to come that would belong to her absolutely. And she opened and spread her arms out to them in welcome.

    A. She dreaded her life as a widow.
    B. Although she loved her husband, she was glad that he was dead for he had never loved her.
    C. She worried that she was too indifferent to her husband's death.
    D. Although they had both loved each other, she was beginning to appreciate that opportunities had opened because of his death.

The correct answer is D. Although they had both loved each other, she was beginning to appreciate that opportunities had opened because of his death
Dismissing her feeling of "monstrous joy" as insignificant, the young woman realizes that she will mourn her husband who had been good to her and had loved her. But that "long procession of years" does not frighten her; instead she recognizes that this new life belongs to her alone and she welcomes it with open arms.

Read the passage below to answer the following questions.

Most people who bother with the matter at all would admit that the English language is in a bad way, but it is generally assumed that we cannot by conscious action do anything about it. Our civilization is decadent and our language — so the argument runs — must inevitably share in the general collapse. It follows that any struggle against the abuse of language is a sentimental archaism, like preferring candles to electric light or hansom cabs to aeroplanes. Underneath this lies the half-conscious belief that language is a natural growth and not an instrument which we shape for our own purposes.

Now, it is clear that the decline of a language must ultimately have political and economic causes: it is not due simply to the bad influence of this or that individual writer. But an effect can become a cause, reinforcing the original cause and producing the same effect in an intensified form, and so on indefinitely. A man may take to drink because he feels himself to be a failure, and then fail all the more completely because he drinks. It is rather the same thing that is happening to the English language. It becomes ugly and inaccurate because our thoughts are foolish, but the slovenliness of our language makes it easier for us to have foolish thoughts. The point is that the process is reversible. Modern English, especially written English, is full of bad habits which spread by imitation and which can be avoided if one is willing to take the necessary trouble. If one gets rid of these habits one can think more clearly, and to think clearly is a necessary first step toward political regeneration: so that the fight against bad English is not frivolous and is not the exclusive concern of professional writers. I will come back to this presently, and I hope that by that time the meaning of what I have said here will have become clearer. Meanwhile, here are five specimens of the English language as it is now habitually written.

42. What does the author mean by "archaism"? *(Competency 8)*

    A. Mystery
    B. Misidentification
    C. Anachronism
    D. Ignorance

The correct answer is C. Anachronism
An archaism is a synonym for anachronism.

43. "A man may take to drink because he feels himself to be a failure, and then fail all the more completely because he drinks." In context, this sentence is best described as a: *(Competency 8)*

   A. Analogy
   B. Metaphor
   C. Simile
   D. Allusion

The correct answer is A. Analogy
The idiom is used by the author to describe the degradation of the English language. He goes onto explain this more explicitly in the next sentence.

44. **What does this author think of the English language?** *(Competency 3)*

   A. It is in unavoidable decline
   B. It should not be altered
   C. Its rules are subject to the whims of speakers
   D. It can be improved through good habits

The correct answer is D. It can be improved through good habits
The author states that English can be improved through positive action. He states the direct opposite of the other answers in the selection.

45. **What can we assume will follow this passage?** *(Competency 3)*

   A. A screed on the decline of English
   B. Further evidence that English is being destroyed
   C. Names of authors who have contributed to the decline of English
   D. Specific examples of bad English in use

The correct answer is D. Specific examples of bad English in use
The last sentence states the author's intention to illustrate some examples of misused English.

46. **What is the subject of the verb "lies" in the last sentence of the first paragraph?** *(Competency 8)*

   A. Language
   B. Growth
   C. This
   D. Underneath

The correct answer is C. This
"This" is the subject of "lies" and "belief " is the object.

47. **The author believes the decline of English is due to:**
(Competencies 3 and 4)

    A. The imitation of bad habits
    B. Societal decadence
    C. People preferring what is simple
    D. Political quibbling

The correct answer is A. The imitation of bad habits
The author takes great pains to explain that bad English is the result of bad habits that have been allowed to grow and spread without care.

48. **By characterizing language as a "natural growth", the author emphasizes its:**
(Competency 3)

    A. Personified qualities
    B. Duplicitous nature
    C. Inconsistency
    D. Changeability

The correct answer is D. Changeability
The author believes language grows naturally, and thus can be corrupted or corrected. This is the central understanding of this piece.

49. **What tone is the author striving for in this piece?** *(Competency 5)*

    A. Humorous
    B. Academic
    C. Angry
    D. Disappointed

The correct answer is B. Academic
The author is discussing English, specifically its defects and methods to improve them. This is a topic of academic interest, and the author explores it with a professional, scholarly tone.

Read the following passage carefully to answer the questions below.

On the domestic front, life was not easy. England was not a wealthy country and its people endured relatively poor living standards. The landed classes — many of them enriched by the confiscated wealth of former monasteries — were determined in the interests of profile to convert their arable land into pasture for sheep, so as to produce the wool that supported the country's chief economic asset, the woolen cloth trade. But the enclosing of the land only added to the misery of the poor, many of whom, evicted and displaced, left their decaying villages and gravitated to the towns where they joined the growing army of beggars and vagabonds that would become such a feature of Elizabethan life. Once, the religious houses would have dispensed charity to the destitute, but Henry VIII had dissolved them all in the 1530s, and many former monks and nuns were now themselves beggars. Nor did the civic authorities help: they passed laws in an attempt to ban the poor from towns and cities, but to little avail. It was a common sight to see men and women lying in the dusty streets, often dying in the dirt like dogs or beasts, without human compassion being shown to them. 'Certainly, wrote a Spanish observer in 1558, 'the state of England lay now most afflicted.' And although people looked to the new Queen Elizabeth to put matters right, there were so many who doubted if she could overcome the seemingly insurmountable problems she faced, or even remain queen long enough to begin tacking them. Some, both at home and abroad, were the opinion that her title to the throne rested on very precarious foundations. Many regarded the daughter of Henry VII and Anne Boleyn as a bastard from the time of her birth on 7 September 1533, although, ignoring such slurs on the validity of his second marriage, Henry had declared Elizabeth his heir.

50. Why was land confiscated from the poor? *(Competency 2)*

   A. The town wanted to build a new monastery.
   B. To create pastures for sheep, ultimately increasing the export of wool.
   C. The town wanted to create housing for monks and nuns.
   D. Queen Elizabeth wanted to expand her property.

The correct answer is B. To create pastures for sheep, ultimately increasing the export of wool

The landed classes are stated to have confiscated the lands of the poor, and sometimes abandoned monasteries, in order to convert their "arable land" into grazing fields for sheep.

51. A vagabond is a _____. *(Competency 8)*

A. Wanderer
B. Prisoner
C. Poor person
D. Rich person

The correct answer is A. Wanderer
The root "vagari" of the word "vagabond" might remind you of "vague" and "vagaries" and suggest the root meaning of "wandering." You can also look at the word in context and see that only (A) and (C) are likely answers, and that (C) would ultimately be redundant.

52. Why didn't the poor have shelter with the churches? *(Competency 2)*

A. They were already filled with beggars.
B. Religious houses have never offered shelter to the poor.
C. They were also being used to raise sheep.
D. Henry VIII had dissolved them all in the 1530s.

The correct answer is D. Henry VIII had dissolved them all in the 1530s
The text states that Henry dissolved houses of worship that could have housed peasants, thus turning many of the clergy into beggars.

53. How were civic authorities unsuccessful? *(Competency 2)*

A. Poor people remained within city limits
B. Public service funds ran out
C. Public housing plans extended deadlines
D. Churches did not open their doors to the poor

The correct answer is A. Poor people remained within city limits
The text states that civic authorities attempted to ban the poor, but it did little to stem the tide of beggars.

54. What is a synonym for precarious? *(Competency 8)*

    A. Strong
    B. Illegitimate
    C. Risky
    D. Determined

The correct answer is C. Risky
While "illegitimate" might remind you of the questions of legitimacy hovering around Elizabeth's birth, and so seem to fit the context, originally the word "precarious" meant "depending on another person's favor" and in the 20th century its meaning shifted to suggest physical instability. "Risky" is not a perfect synonym but is the best answer out of the group.

55. What is the author's view towards Queen Elizabeth? *(Competency 7)*

    A. Doubtful
    B. Vengeful
    C. Resentful
    D. Supportive

The correct answer is A. Doubtful
The author states that it was widely understood that the throne's position was precarious, and Elizabeth was considered unlikely to retain it.

56. How is the English culture portrayed in this passage? *(Competency 2)*

    A. Religious
    B. Elitist
    C. Racist
    D. Diverse

The correct answer is B. Elitist
The primary characteristic of English culture in this passage is its elitism and hierarchy. The poor are described as a nuisance with few rights, having their lands stripped from them and then being barred from entering villages or receiving charity.

57. What is Elizabeth's relationship to Henry? *(Competency 2)*

A. Wife
B. Cousin
C. Lover
D. Daughter

The correct answer is D. Daughter
The text states "many regarded the daughter of Henry and Anne Boleyn to be a bastard", indicating that Elizabeth is Henry's daughter.

Read the following passage to answer the questions that follow.

The brazen, vicious attack occurred in broad daylight. The cowardly action took the lives of 32 innocent victims. So far no single group has claimed responsibility though several have issued statements noting its importance...

58. In doing research, a student has second thoughts about using this new story as a source. What is evidence of a flaw with the story? *(Competency 6)*

A. It is not corroborated by other sources.
B. The language is inflammatory and biased.
C. There is no image to accompany the story.
D. No other point of view is included.

The correct answer is B. The language is inflammatory and biased
The language used in this excerpt shows the bias of the writer. Words like *brazen, vicious,* and *cowardly* reveal that this may be a problematic source.

59. Which of the following sentences best incorporates a quote from the passage above? *(Competency 6)*

A. The writer's description of this as a "vicious attack" reveals bias.
B. Saying, "The brazen, vicious attack occurred in broad daylight. The cowardly action took the lives of 32 innocent victims" reveals bias.
C. The characterization of the incident as a "brazen, vicious attack" and a "cowardly action" reveals bias.
D. When the writer says the brazen, vicious attack it shows bias.

The correct answer is C. The characterization of the incident as a "brazen, vicious attack" and "cowardly action" reveals bias
B is awkward, and D does not use quotation marks. A leaves out two potentially valid pieces of evidence.

60. What is the author saying with the second sentence of the first paragraph? *(Competency 7)*

    A. Education for women is a necessity, and the fact that we deny it to them is a national disgrace

    B. If women possessed education, they would be able to give men a taste of their own medicine

    C. Men often oppress women, and if women were educated, they likely would not do the same

    D. Education is a privilege, one that women must earn for themselves

The correct answer is C. Men often oppress women, and if women were educated, they likely would not do the same
The author is espousing the virtues of women with that sentence, claiming that educated women likely would not be as petty as men are.

61. "The soul is placed in the body like a rough diamond". This is an example of a: *(Competency 3)*

    A. Simile

    B. Metaphor

    C. Analogy

    D. Juxtaposition

The correct answer is A. Simile
"The soul is placed in the body like a rough diamond" is a simile, using the word "like" to draw a comparison between the soul and a rough diamond.

62. With the last sentence of paragraph two, the author is implying that: *(Competency 2)*

    A. A man with no education is hardly impressive, even if he has other advantages

    B. Certain qualities of upbringing handily offset the downsides of no education

    C. Upper class men have little need for education

    D. Men of good stature do not appreciate education as they should

The correct answer is A. A man with no education is hardly impressive, even if he has other advantage
"Examine what figure he makes for want of education" suggests that a man who lacks education still has very little to offer, even if he is rich and well-raised.

63. The author primarily supports his argument with: *(Competency 3)*

    A. Citations
    B. Direct observation
    C. Common sense
    D. Examples

The correct answer is C. Common sense
The author primarily supports his argument with assertions that he insists should be obvious. It is "manifest" that education is a necessity, and it is likewise obvious that a woman being denied it is a travesty. He also insists, based on his own common sense, that if women were educated as men are, they likely would not be as oppressive.

64. Throughout the piece, the author makes frequent use of: *(Competency 7)*

    A. Rhetorical questions
    B. Hyperbole
    C. Direct quotation
    D. Appeals to authority

The correct answer is A. Rhetorical questions
The piece contains many rhetorical questions throughout, and makes less use of hyperbole, and no uses of satire or appeal to authority.

Read the passage and answer the following questions carefully.

When it was first perceived, in early times, that no middle course for America remained between unlimited submission to a foreign legislature and a total independence of its claims, men of reflection were less apprehensive of danger from the formidable power of fleets and armies they must determine to resist than from those contests and dissensions which would certainly arise concerning the forms of government to be instituted over the whole and over the parts of this extensive country. Relying, however, on the purity of their intentions, the justice of their cause, and the integrity and intelligence of the people, under an overruling Providence which had so signally protected this country from the first, the representatives of this nation, then consisting of little more than half its present number, not only broke to pieces the chains which were forging and the rod of iron that was lifted up, but frankly cut asunder the ties which had bound them, and launched into an ocean of uncertainty.

The zeal and ardor of the people during the Revolutionary war, supplying the place of government, commanded a degree of order sufficient at least for the temporary preservation of society. The Confederation which was early felt to be necessary was prepared from the models of the Batavian and Helvetic confederacies, the only examples which remain with any detail and precision in history, and certainly the only ones which the people at large had ever considered. But reflecting on the striking difference in so many particulars between this country and those where a courier may go from the seat of government to the frontier in a single day, it was then certainly foreseen by some who assisted in Congress at the formation of it that it could not be durable.

Negligence of its regulations, inattention to its recommendations, if not disobedience to its authority, not only in individuals but in States, soon appeared with their melancholy consequences—universal languor, jealousies and rivalries of States, decline of navigation and commerce, discouragement of necessary manufactures, universal fall in the value of lands and their produce, contempt of public and private faith, loss of consideration and credit with foreign nations, and at length in discontents, animosities, combinations, partial conventions, and insurrection, threatening some great national calamity

65. **What best summarizes the first sentence of this piece?** *(Competency 2)*

    A. When we first realize there was no middle ground between subservience and independence, intelligent men were less afraid of war than they were of deciding how to govern our new nation

    B. When our ancestors first realized they must be free instead of obedient, they realized that combat was far less challenging than the bureaucracy that would follow

    C. When men realized, in the past, that freedom would be hard to win, they decided to craft a new form of government to aid in this process

    D. When our new nation first achieved independence, the true struggle was not the war that followed, but the arguments between learned me who could not agree on anything

The correct answer is A. When we first realize there was no middle ground between subservience and independence, intelligent men were less afraid of war than they were of deciding how to govern our new nation
The first sentence illustrates the author's belief that the true obstacle for early Americans was not the war itself, but the idea of how to govern such a massive and unruly nation after the war was won.

66. **What does the author identify as a problem in the second paragraph?** *(Competency 2)*

    A. The similarities between his new nation and the Batavian and Helvetic confederacies

    B. The ignorance of the common people

    C. The unrestrained zeal of common citizens

    D. The vast size of this new country

The correct answer is D. The vast size of this new country
In the second paragraph, the author states the massive size of the new nation is a major obstacle, explaining that it would be difficult to govern a nation that couriers could not easily cross.

67. **The author identifies all of these as problems in the third paragraph EXCEPT:** *(Competency 4)*

    A. Laziness

    B. Increased dependence on foreign powers

    C. Poor trade

    D. Religious intolerance

The correct answer is B. Increased dependence on foreign powers
The author describes all of the stated obstacles except E, dependence on foreign powers.

68. **In the first paragraph, what does the author NOT credit with aiding the representatives?** *(Competency 2)*

    A. Providence
    B. Intelligence
    C. Integrity
    D. The Nation

The correct answer is D. The Nation
Since the author is referring to the founding of the nation, citing "the nation" as an aid in this process makes no sense. All of the other questions are mentioned in some form in the first paragraph.

69. **For which of the following research questions would this passage likely be best suited?** *(Competency 6)*

    A. How did economic issues influence the causes of the Revolutionary War?
    B. What philosophical schools of thought influenced leaders of the Revolution?
    C. What were some of the post-Revolutionary challenges facing the country?
    D. How did Britain try to influence the economy of the United States after the Revolution?

The correct answer is C. What were some of the post-Revolutionary challenges facing the country?
In the passage the writer addresses economic, political, and policy challenges facing the country after the Revolutionary War.

Read the following excerpt to answer the questions that follow.

Excerpt from Speech to the Council on Foreign Relations, Tony Blair, December 3, 2008

The past 40 years are littered with initiatives, signposts to various potential breakthroughs, unsatisfactory compromises, new dawns that swiftly turned to dusk and failed negotiations. Along the way, there have been immense gains that sometimes are obscured by the central impasse. Egypt and Jordan are at peace with Israel. The Arab Peace Initiative of the then Crown Prince Abdullah in 2002 signaled a new pan-Arab approach. The contours of the final status issues, if not their outcomes, have been clarified.

The Annapolis process and the limited but, nonetheless, real change on the West Bank during the past year - for which the President and Secretary Rice deserve much credit - have yielded a genuine platform for the future.

But the central impasse does indeed remain. My view - formed since I came to Jerusalem and refining much of what I thought when I tussled intermittently with the issue for 10 years as British Prime Minister - is that it remains because the reality on the ground does not, as yet, sufficiently support the compromises necessary to secure a final, negotiated settlement. In other words, we have tended to proceed on the basis that if we could only agree the terms of the two state solution - territory, refugees, Jerusalem - i.e. the theory, we would then be able to change the reality of what was happening on the ground i.e. the practice. In my view, it is as much the other way around. The political process and changing the reality have to march in lock-step. Until recently, they haven't.

The reason this is critical to resolving this dispute is as follows. The problem is not that reasonable people do not agree, roughly, what the two states look like. I don't minimize the negotiation challenge. But listen to sensible Palestinians and sensible Israelis and you will quickly find the gaps are not that big; certainly are not unbridgeable.

70. **In what way(s) does Tony Blair demonstrate that he acknowledges the different perspectives of Palestinians and Israelis?** *(Competency 7)*

    A. He addresses the importance of peace for both sides.
    B. He talks about past failed negotiations.
    C. He does not blame either side for the lack of results.
    D. He makes an emotional appeal to both sides.

The correct answer is C. He does not blame either side for the lack of results.
Though Blair does talk about past failed negotiations, he does not blame either side for the lack of a peace agreement. He instead talks about the things many people from both sides agree on. The speech was not an emotional appeal and did not focus on the importance of peace. Instead he made peace seem like a logical step.

71. **In this speech, how did Blair organize his ideas?** *(Competency 7)*

    A. He linked past events to the present state of negotiations.
    B. He described past peace proposals and gave evidence of why they make sense.
    C. He thanked people for their past work and showed why it was important to continue what they had started.
    D. He analyzed the issue point by point.

The correct answer is A. He linked past events to the present state of negotiations
Blair outlined some of the past negotiations and the agreements they reached and then connected those to the current state of negotiations.

Read the following passage carefully before you decide on your answers to the questions.

International baggage claim in the Brussels airport was large and airy, with multiple carousels circling endlessly. I scurried from one to another, desperately trying to find my black suitcase. Because it was stuffed with drug money, I was more concerned than one might normally be about lost luggage.

I was twenty-four in 1993 and probably looked like just another anxious young professional woman. My Doc Martens had been jettisoned in favor of my beautiful handmade black suede heels. I wore black silk pants and a beige jacket, a typical jeune fille, not a big counterculture, unless you spotted the tattoo on my neck. I had done exactly as I had been instructed, checking my bag Chicago through Paris, where I had to switch planes to take a short flight to Brussels.

When I arrived in Belgium, I looked for my black rollie at the baggage claim. It was nowhere to be seen. Fighting a rushing tide of panic, I asked in my mangled high school French what had become of my suitcase. "Bags don't make it onto the right flight sometimes," said the big lug working in baggage handling. "Wait for the next shuttle from Paris— It's probably on that plane."

Had my bag been detected? I knew that carrying more than $10,000 undeclared was illegal, let alone carrying it for a West African drug lord. Were the authorities closing in on me? Maybe I should try to get through customs and run? Or perhaps the bag really was just delayed, and I would be abandoning a large sum of money that belonged to someone who could probably have killed me with a simple phone call. I decided that the later choice was slightly more terrifying. So I waited.

The next flight from Paris finally arrived. I sidled over to my new "friend" in baggage handling, who was sorting things out. It is hard to flirt when you're frightened. I spotted the suitcase. "Mon bag!" I exclaimed in ecstasy, seizing the Tumi. I thanked him effusively, waving with giddy affection as I sailed through one of the unmanned doors into the terminal, where I spotted my friend Billy waiting for me. I had inadvertently skipped customs.

"I was worried. What happened?" Billy asked.
"Get me into a cab!" I hissed.
I didn't breathe until we had pulled away from the airport and were halfway across Brussels.

—*Orange is the New Black*. Piper Kerman

72. **Why did the author explain her attire?** *(Competency 1)*

   A. She wanted the audience to know how much she stood out in Europe
   B. She used her clothing to try to fit in with the culture she was immersed in
   C. She wanted to explain that she was a young, hip woman
   D. She explained how difficult it was to wait around for her bag in heels

The correct answer is B. She used her clothing to try to fit in with the culture she was immersed in
The author used her attire to make herself mesh with the setting that she was immersed in. She was out of the country and trying her best to fit in, particularly because she was involved in illegal activity. Because she was trying to use her clothing to fit in, (B) is the best answer.

73. **Why didn't she breathe until pulling away from the airport?** *(Competency 1)*

   A. Tension
   B. Sadness
   C. Health issues
   D. She was talking to Billy

The correct answer is A. Tension
She had just gotten away with illegal activity, making her adrenaline at an all-time high. It's clear that she was not sad, and there's no mention of health issues in this passage. A is the best answer.

74. **What is the overall message of this passage?** *(Competency 1)*

   A. Young professional women can get away with crimes
   B. Security guards are not always watching every door in the airport
   C. It's important to blend in when doing something suspicious
   D. When you have done something illegal, even small mishaps can seem scary

The correct answer is D. When you have done something illegal, even small mishaps can seem scary
The author left plenty of room in the passage for the reader to think she might get caught. Because she portrays the emotions involved in doing something illegal in the airport, and her thoughts of how she might get caught, (D) is the best answer.

75. **How did she avoid going through customs?** *(Competency 1)*

    A. She flirted with the luggage man
    B. Her friend Billy came to get her
    C. She slipped through an unmanned door
    D. She went through customs in Paris and Chicago, so it wasn't required

The correct answer is C. She slipped through an unmanned door
Using the details in the passage, it's easy to zero in on (C) as the correct answer.

76. **What part of the plot does "Mon bag!" represent?** *(Competency 1)*

    A. Climax
    B. Rising action
    C. Exposition
    D. Falling action

The correct answer is A. Climax
This statement represents the main character getting away with the crime that she was committing, making it the climax.

Use the following passage to answer the questions that follow.

When rays of light pass through a prism, they undergo a change of direction: they are always deflected away from the refractive edge. It is possible to conceive an assembly of prisms whose refractive surfaces progressively become more nearly parallel to each other towards the middle: light rays passing through the outer prisms will undergo the greatest amount of refraction, with consequent deflection of their path towards the center, whereas the middle prism with its two parallel surfaces causes no deflection at all. When a beam of parallel rays passes through these prisms, the rays are all deflected towards the axis and converge at one point. Rays emerging from a point are also deflected by the prisms that they converge. A lens can be conceived as consisting of a large number of such prisms placed close up against one another, so that their surfaces merge into a continuous spherical surface. A lens of this kind, which collects the rays and concentrates them at one point, is called a convergent lens. Since it is thicker in the middle than at the edge, it is known as a convex lens.

In the case of a concave lens, which is thinner in the middle than at the edge, similar considerations show that all rays diverge from the center. Hence such a lens is called a divergent lens. After undergoing refraction, parallel rays appear to come from one point, while rays reemerging from a point will, after passing through the lens, appear to emerge from another point. Lenses have surfaces in the same direction but having a different radii of curvature, these are known as meniscus lenses and are used more particularly in spectacles.

77. **Which of the following is NOT true of convergent lenses?** *(Competency 2)*

    A. They are concave
    B. They are made of prisms
    C. They can refract light
    D. They have different radii

The correct answer is A. They are concave
Convergent lenses are stated to be convex, not concave.

78. **Parallel surfaces in prisms cause:** *(Competency 2)*

    A. Very little refraction
    B. Divergence of light rays
    C. No refraction
    D. Radii to vary

The correct answer is C. No refraction
The answer is in the first paragraph: "whereas parallel surfaces cause no deflection at all".

79. **Which of the following would be the best choice of a conclusion for this piece?** *(Competency 4)*

    A. Prisms were used by many ancient civilizations. They must have seemed like a form of magic to the first people who saw them, and they continue to amaze people today. Though perhaps an accidental discovery, they changed the world.
    B. Prisms were an integral part of the study of the different properties of light. The use of prisms allowed people to see the different component colors of the light around them. The discovery of these different properties opened up new fields of research.
    C. There are dispersive prisms, reflective prisms, deflecting prisms, and polarizing prisms. Each type is very important and has different qualities.
    D. We wake up every morning and there is light. We may not know it, but people have always been fascinated by light for many years. Prisms explained how light works.

The correct answer is B. Prisms were an integral part of the study of the different properties of light. The use of prisms allowed people ot see the different component colors of the light around them. The discovery of these different properties opened up new fields of research.
Option B links together what prisms do with what they might be used for. A talks primarily about the history of prisms, C only addresses the types of prisms, and D does not link prisms to how we might explain and understand light.

80. **Spectacles use meniscus lenses, which are:** *(Competency 2)*

    A. flat
    B. varying radii of concave lenses
    C. varying radii of convex lenses
    D. round on both sides of the lens, meaning they have double refraction.

The correct answer is B. varying radii of concave lenses
This is indicated in the last sentence of the selection.

Read the following passage to answer the questions below.

Ana woke suddenly and peered into the darkness. Something had moved or made some kind of sound; she was sure of it. She reached across the bed to the lamp on the nightstand, but there was nothing there. She fumbled in the dark until her hand came to rest on something solid, something cold, something wet.

"Looking for something?" came a voice out of the darkness.

Without hesitation, Ana replied, "Yes, actually. My glasses."

"You know why I'm here. No need for games," replied the voice.

"No, I suppose you're right," Ana sighed.

81. **For what effect does the author repeat 'something…, something…'** *(Competency 5)*

    A. To show how frustrating it was not to be able to see
    B. To build tension
    C. To show that the character was helpless
    D. To lighten the mood.

The correct answer is B. To build tension
The author wants to build tension to keep the reader interested in what is about to happen. By repeating herself, she can make the character seem anxious but also make the plot move more slowly.

82. **Ana's reply creates what effect?** *(Competency 5)*

    A. The reader sees her as confident and calm.
    B. The reader sees her as confused and fearful.
    C. The reader knows that this is not a serious story.
    D. The reader knows that this is the source of conflict.

The correct answer is A. The reader sees her as confident and calm.
After creating tension, Ana's response is very casual. Though we cannot be sure what will happen next, she seems confident and calm.

83. **In this short passage, what two techniques is the writer using to add to the story?** *(Competency 5)*

    A. Alliteration and descriptive details
    B. Irony and reflection
    C. Pacing and figurative language
    D. Dialogue and setting

The correct answer is D. Dialogue and setting
The dialogue is used to give the reader a sense of Ana's character. The setting is used to create a sense of tension and build up to something.

84. **What does the conversation between the two characters imply?** *(Competency 5)*

    A. The two characters are enemies.
    B. Ana is bored.
    C. Ana is afraid of the other character.
    D. There is something the reader doesn't know.

The correct answer is D. There is something the reader doesn't know
Though the characters might be enemies, we really can't tell. Similarly, Ana's feelings are unclear at this point. When she woke up, she seemed scared, but when she spoke, she seemed confident.

85. **The deliberate lack of clarity about what is happening is called...?** *(Competency 5)*

    A. Connotation
    B. Ambiguity
    C. Allusion
    D. Denouement

The correct answer is B. Ambiguity
Ambiguity is the lack of clarity or the deliberate creation of doubt.

86. **How can ambiguity move a plot forward?** *(Competency 5)*

   A. It doesn't. It simply creates confusion.
   B. It is like a symbol and represents something important.
   C. It makes the reader want to know more.
   D. It clarifies important parts of the plot.

The correct answer is C. It makes the reader want to know more
Ambiguity creates a sense of mystery and makes the reader want to know more.

87. **In which type of fiction does setting tend to be most important?** *(Competency 5)*

   A. Historical fiction
   B. Contemporary fiction
   C. Young adult fiction
   D. Multicultural fiction

The correct answer is A. Historical fiction
In historical fiction, details about the places, the clothing of the period, and even the way characters speak is very important. Other genres in which this is true include science fiction and utopian/dystopian fiction.

88. **What is the correct way to include a quotation from *Orange is the New Black*? *(Competency 6)***

   A. Kerman was terrified but continued with the plan anyway. "Were the authorities closing in on me? Maybe I should try to get through customs and run? Or perhaps the bag really was just delayed, and I would be abandoning a large sum of money that belonged to someone who could probably have killed me with a simple phone call. I decided that the later choice was slightly more terrifying."

   B. Kerman was terrified but continued with the plan anyway. "Were the authorities closing in on me? Maybe I should try to get through customs and run? Or perhaps the bag really was just delayed, and I would be abandoning a large sum of money that belonged to someone who could probably have killed me with a simple phone call. I decided that the later choice was slightly more terrifying" (Kerman 1).

   C. Kerman was terrified but continued with the plan anyway.

   "Were the authorities closing in on me? Maybe I should try to get through customs and run? Or perhaps the bag really was just delayed, and I would be abandoning a large sum of money that belonged to someone who could probably have killed me with a simple phone call. I decided that the later choice was slightly more terrifying." (Kerman 1)

   D. Kerman was terrified but continued with the plan anyway.

   Were the authorities closing in on me? Maybe I should try to get through customs and run? Or perhaps the bag really was just delayed, and I would be abandoning a large sum of money that belonged to someone who could probably have killed me with a simple phone call. I decided that the later choice was slightly more terrifying. (Kerman 1)

The correct answer is D.
In A and B, the quote should be included as a block quote because it is more than four lines long. In C it does not need quotation marks because it is a block quote.

Read the following passage carefully before you decide on your answers to the questions.

She was forty-two, in poor health. She had recently been diagnosed with diabetes, and her doctor had urged her to get out and walk more. But her son has been shot to death a few blocks away, and Pritchett was too frightened to venture out. She spent days lying in the dark, unable to will herself to move or speak. That morning, as always, she was wearing a big loose T-shirt with Bovon's picture on it. All around her, in the tiny living room, were mementos of her murdered son. Sports trophies, photos, sympathy cards, certificates, stuffed animals.

With great care, Pritchett perched the shoebox on the arm of a vinyl armchair by the door and solely lifted one shoe. It was worn, black, dusted with red Watts dirt. It was not quite big enough to be a man's shoe, not small enough to be a child's. She leaned against the wall, pressed the open top of the shoe against her mouth and nose, and inhaled its scent with a long, deep breath. Then she closed her eyes and wept.

Skaggs stood back. Pritchett's knees gave out. Skaggs watched her side down the wall in slow motion, her face still pressed into the shoe. She landed with a thump on the green carpet. One of her orange slippers came off. On the TV across the room, the FOX 11 morning anchored pattered brightly over the sound of her sobs.

Skaggs had been a homicide detective for twenty years. In that time, he had been in a thousand living rooms like this one- each with its large TV, Afrocentric knickknacks, and imponderable grief. —*Ghettoside* by Jill Leovy

89. What is the intended audience for this text? *(Competency 5)*

    A. All classes and races
    B. White police officers
    C. Students
    D. Affluent communities

The correct answer is A. All classes and races
This passage gives the perspective of a white police officer and an African American mother who is grieving over the loss of a child. The message intends to give insight on a variety of classes and races; everyone that reads it can learn from it, regardless of their background. Therefore, A is the best answer.

90. **How does the author appeal to the emotions of the audience?**
    (Competency 5)

    A. Including a detailed scene, including memorabilia and Pritchett's physical and emotional response to the situation
    B. Opening the scene with a description of Pritchett's poor health
    C. Implying that this is a very common scene to this detective
    D. Mentioning things the audience can relate to, such as watching the morning news

The correct answer is A. Including a detailed scene, including memorabilia and Pritchett's physical and emotional response to the situation
The author appeals to the emotions of the audience by including things that elicit an emotional response. While options B, C, and D may have some truth, the best answer is (A).